The jewell house of art and nature conteining diuers rare and profitable inuentions, together with sundry new experimentes in the art of husbandry, distillation, and moulding (1594)

Hugh Plat

The jewell house of art and nature conteining diuers rare and profitable inuentions, together with sundry new experimentes in the art of husbandry, distillation, and moulding
Plat, Hugh, Sir, 1552-1611?
"Diuerse new sorts of soyle not yet brought into any publique vse" and "Diuers chimicall conclusions concerning the art of distillation" each has special t.p. and separate pagination.
Signatures: A4(-A1) C-O4, 2A-G4 2H2, 3A-I4 3K2.
Title within ornamental border.
[6], 96, 60, 76 p. :
London : Printed by Peter Short, dwelling on Breadstreat-hill, at the signe of the star, and are to be solde in Paules Church-yard, by William Ponsonby, 1594.
STC (2nd ed.) / 19991.5
English
Reproduction of the original in the Cambridge University Library

Early English Books Online (EEBO) Editions

Imagine holding history in your hands.

Now you can. Digitally preserved and previously accessible only through libraries as Early English Books Online, this rare material is now available in single print editions. Thousands of books written between 1475 and 1700 and ranging from religion to astronomy, medicine to music, can be delivered to your doorstep in individual volumes of high-quality historical reproductions.

We have been compiling these historic treasures for more than 70 years. Long before such a thing as "digital" even existed, ProQuest founder Eugene Power began the noble task of preserving the British Museum's collection on microfilm. He then sought out other rare and endangered titles, providing unparalleled access to these works and collaborating with the world's top academic institutions to make them widely available for the first time. This project furthers that original vision.

These texts have now made the full journey -- from their original printing-press versions available only in rare-book rooms to online library access to new single volumes made possible by the partnership between artifact preservation and modern printing technology. A portion of the proceeds from every book sold supports the libraries and institutions that made this collection possible, and that still work to preserve these invaluable treasures passed down through time.

This is history, traveling through time since the dawn of printing to your own personal library.

Initial Proquest EEBO Print Editions collections include:

Early Literature

This comprehensive collection begins with the famous Elizabethan Era that saw such literary giants as Chaucer, Shakespeare and Marlowe, as well as the introduction of the sonnet. Traveling through Jacobean and Restoration literature, the highlight of this series is the Pollard and Redgrave 1475-1640 selection of the rarest works from the English Renaissance.

Early Documents of World History

This collection combines early English perspectives on world history with documentation of Parliament records, royal decrees and military documents that reveal the delicate balance of Church and State in early English government. For social historians, almanacs and calendars offer insight into daily life of common citizens. This exhaustively complete series presents a thorough picture of history through the English Civil War.

Historical Almanacs

Historically, almanacs served a variety of purposes from the more practical, such as planting and harvesting crops and plotting nautical routes, to predicting the future through the movements of the stars. This collection provides a wide range of consecutive years of "almanacks" and calendars that depict a vast array of everyday life as it was several hundred years ago.

Early History of Astronomy & Space

Humankind has studied the skies for centuries, seeking to find our place in the universe. Some of the most important discoveries in the field of astronomy were made in these texts recorded by ancient stargazers, but almost as impactful were the perspectives of those who considered their discoveries to be heresy. Any independent astronomer will find this an invaluable collection of titles arguing the truth of the cosmic system.

Early History of Industry & Science

Acting as a kind of historical Wall Street, this collection of industry manuals and records explores the thriving industries of construction; textile, especially wool and linen; salt; livestock; and many more.

Early English Wit, Poetry & Satire

The power of literary device was never more in its prime than during this period of history, where a wide array of political and religious satire mocked the status quo and poetry called humankind to transcend the rigors of daily life through love, God or principle. This series comments on historical patterns of the human condition that are still visible today.

Early English Drama & Theatre

This collection needs no introduction, combining the works of some of the greatest canonical writers of all time, including many plays composed for royalty such as Queen Elizabeth I and King Edward VI. In addition, this series includes history and criticism of drama, as well as examinations of technique.

Early History of Travel & Geography

Offering a fascinating view into the perception of the world during the sixteenth and seventeenth centuries, this collection includes accounts of Columbus's discovery of the Americas and encompasses most of the Age of Discovery, during which Europeans and their descendants intensively explored and mapped the world. This series is a wealth of information from some the most groundbreaking explorers.

Early Fables & Fairy Tales

This series includes many translations, some illustrated, of some of the most well-known mythologies of today, including Aesop's Fables and English fairy tales, as well as many Greek, Latin and even Oriental parables and criticism and interpretation on the subject.

Early Documents of Language & Linguistics

The evolution of English and foreign languages is documented in these original texts studying and recording early philology from the study of a variety of languages including Greek, Latin and Chinese, as well as multilingual volumes, to current slang and obscure words. Translations from Latin, Hebrew and Aramaic, grammar treatises and even dictionaries and guides to translation make this collection rich in cultures from around the world.

Early History of the Law

With extensive collections of land tenure and business law "forms" in Great Britain, this is a comprehensive resource for all kinds of early English legal precedents from feudal to constitutional law, Jewish and Jesuit law, laws about public finance to food supply and forestry, and even "immoral conditions." An abundance of law dictionaries, philosophy and history and criticism completes this series.

Early History of Kings, Queens and Royalty

This collection includes debates on the divine right of kings, royal statutes and proclamations, and political ballads and songs as related to a number of English kings and queens, with notable concentrations on foreign rulers King Louis IX and King Louis XIV of France, and King Philip II of Spain. Writings on ancient rulers and royal tradition focus on Scottish and Roman kings, Cleopatra and the Biblical kings Nebuchadnezzar and Solomon.

Early History of Love, Marriage & Sex

Human relationships intrigued and baffled thinkers and writers well before the postmodern age of psychology and self-help. Now readers can access the insights and intricacies of Anglo-Saxon interactions in sex and love, marriage and politics, and the truth that lies somewhere in between action and thought.

Early History of Medicine, Health & Disease

This series includes fascinating studies on the human brain from as early as the 16th century, as well as early studies on the physiological effects of tobacco use. Anatomy texts, medical treatises and wound treatment are also discussed, revealing the exponential development of medical theory and practice over more than two hundred years.

Early History of Logic, Science and Math

The "hard sciences" developed exponentially during the 16th and 17th centuries, both relying upon centuries of tradition and adding to the foundation of modern application, as is evidenced by this extensive collection. This is a rich collection of practical mathematics as applied to business, carpentry and geography as well as explorations of mathematical instruments and arithmetic; logic and logicians such as Aristotle and Socrates; and a number of scientific disciplines from natural history to physics.

Early History of Military, War and Weaponry

Any professional or amateur student of war will thrill at the untold riches in this collection of war theory and practice in the early Western World. The Age of Discovery and Enlightenment was also a time of great political and religious unrest, revealed in accounts of conflicts such as the Wars of the Roses.

Early History of Food

This collection combines the commercial aspects of food handling, preservation and supply to the more specific aspects of canning and preserving, meat carving, brewing beer and even candy-making with fruits and flowers, with a large resource of cookery and recipe books. Not to be forgotten is a "the great eater of Kent," a study in food habits.

Early History of Religion

From the beginning of recorded history we have looked to the heavens for inspiration and guidance. In these early religious documents, sermons, and pamphlets, we see the spiritual impact on the lives of both royalty and the commoner. We also get insights into a clergy that was growing ever more powerful as a political force. This is one of the world's largest collections of religious works of this type, revealing much about our interpretation of the modern church and spirituality.

Early Social Customs

Social customs, human interaction and leisure are the driving force of any culture. These unique and quirky works give us a glimpse of interesting aspects of day-to-day life as it existed in an earlier time. With books on games, sports, traditions, festivals, and hobbies it is one of the most fascinating collections in the series.

The BiblioLife Network

This project was made possible in part by the BiblioLife Network (BLN), a project aimed at addressing some of the huge challenges facing book preservationists around the world. The BLN includes libraries, library networks, archives, subject matter experts, online communities and library service providers. We believe every book ever published should be available as a high-quality print reproduction; printed on-demand anywhere in the world. This insures the ongoing accessibility of the content and helps generate sustainable revenue for the libraries and organizations that work to preserve these important materials.

The following book is in the "public domain" and represents an authentic reproduction of the text as printed by the original publisher. While we have attempted to accurately maintain the integrity of the original work, there are sometimes problems with the original work or the micro-film from which the books were digitized. This can result in minor errors in reproduction. Possible imperfections include missing and blurred pages, poor pictures, markings and other reproduction issues beyond our control. Because this work is culturally important, we have made it available as part of our commitment to protecting, preserving, and promoting the world's literature.

GUIDE TO FOLD-OUTS MAPS and OVERSIZED IMAGES

The book you are reading was digitized from microfilm captured over the past thirty to forty years. Years after the creation of the original microfilm, the book was converted to digital files and made available in an online database.

In an online database, page images do not need to conform to the size restrictions found in a printed book. When converting these images back into a printed bound book, the page sizes are standardized in ways that maintain the detail of the original. For large images, such as fold-out maps, the original page image is split into two or more pages

Guidelines used to determine how to split the page image follows:

- Some images are split vertically; large images require vertical and horizontal splits.
- For horizontal splits, the content is split left to right.
- For vertical splits, the content is split from top to bottom.
- For both vertical and horizontal splits, the image is processed from top left to bottom right.

THE
Jewell House of Art and Nature.

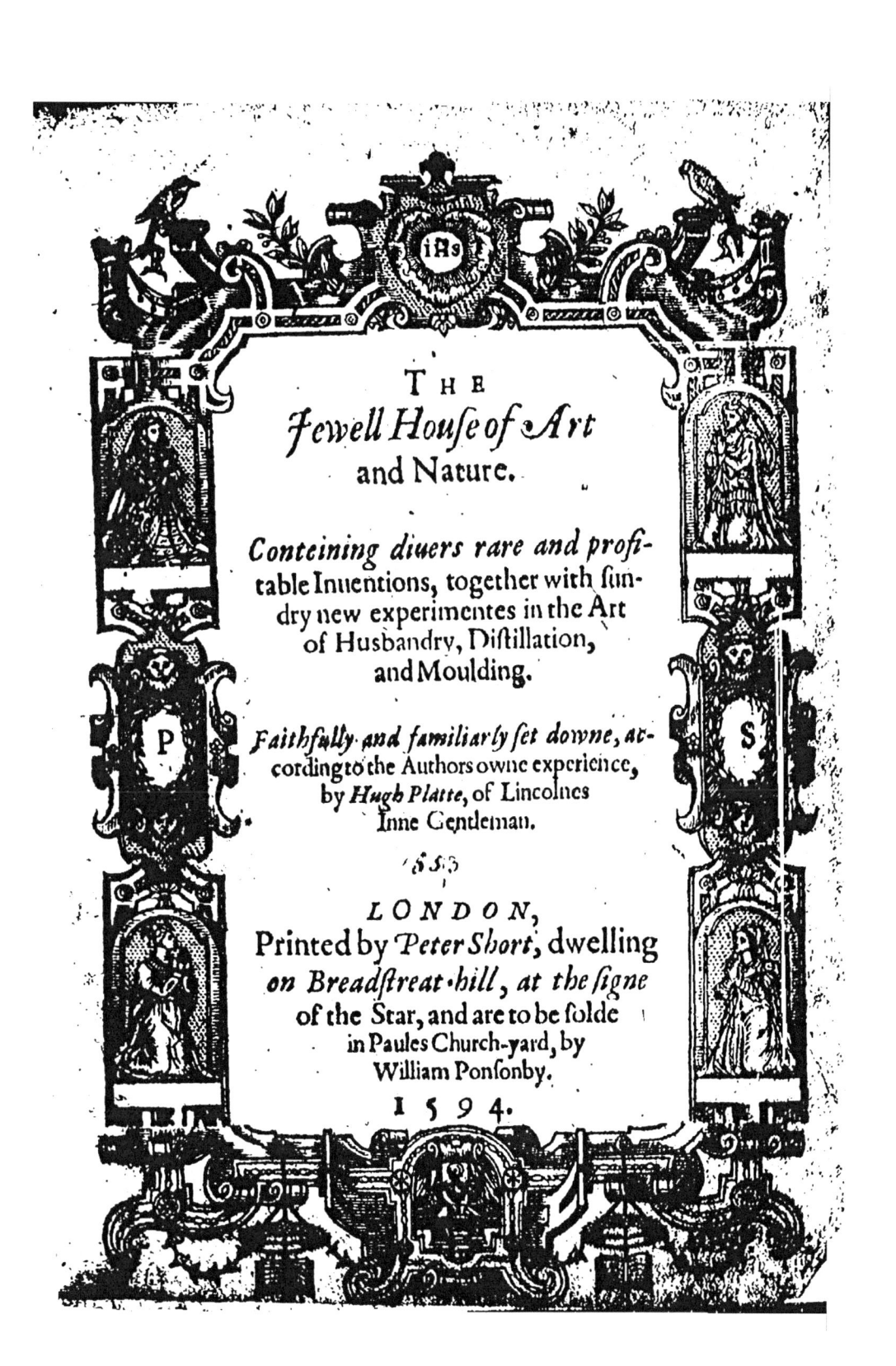

Conteining diuers rare and profitable Inuentions, together with sundry new experimentes in the Art of Husbandry, Distillation, and Moulding.

Faithfully and familiarly set downe, according to the Authors owne experience, by *Hugh Platte*, of Lincolnes Inne Gentleman.

LONDON,
Printed by *Peter Short*, dwelling on Breadstreat·hill, at the signe of the Star, and are to be solde in Paules Church-yard, by William Ponsonby.
1594.

16-76

The first Booke conteineth, diuers new and conceited experiments, from the which there may be sundry both pleasing and profitable vses drawne, by them which haue either wit, or will to applie them.

1 Sondry new and artificiall waies for the keeping of fruites and flowers, in their fresh hew, after they are gathered from their stalks or branches.

2 A perspectiue ring, that will discouer all the cardes that are neere him that weareth it on his finger.

3 How to carrie gold in a most secret manner.

4 How to keepe or preserue any foule, or other peece of flesh, sound and sweet, the space of three weekes, or one whole moneth togither, notwithstanding the contagiousnesse of the weather.

5 How to defend fresh water a long time from putrifaction.

6 A marchants compasse, whereby he may know vpon what point the wind blowes, in his bedchamber, and in the night time, without beholding the skie, or any vane abroad.

7 How to feed and fatten hens, chickens, geese, ducks, &c. in a more cheap manner, then hath as yet beene made knowne, or common to the world.

8 How to write a letter secretly, that cannot easilie bee discerned, or suspected.

9 How to brew good and wholesome beere without any hops at al.

10 How to harden leather, so as the same shall last much longer in the suckers of pumps, then it doth vnprepared.

11 A conceited chafingdish, to keepe a dish of meat long hot vpon the table, without any coles therein.

12 How to roast meat more speedilie and with lesse fire, then wee doo in our common manner.

13 To make a new peece of Walnut tree or Wainscot, to be of one selfe same colour with the old.

14 How to turne fiue spits with one hand, whereby also much fire is saued.

15 A probable coniecture at the composition of hard wax.

16 To helpe venison that is tainted.

17 A pistol of two foot in length, to deliuer a bullet point blanke at eight skore.

The Table.

18 A peece whereby to performe some extraordinary seruice.
19 To make greene wood to burne cleere, at the further end of the Ouen.
20 How to walke safely vpon an high scaffolde, without any daunger of falling.
21 A round ball of copper to blow the fire with.
22 How to erect or build ouer any brooke, a cheape woodden bridge, of forty or fifty foot in length, without fastening of any tymber worke within the water.
23 A cheape Lanthorne to carry a light in any stormy weather, without any defensatiue before it.
24 To plum vp an horse to keepe him from tiring in his trauell, and to make him soame at the bit.
25 A drinke for trauellers to bee made *Extempore*, when they want good beere or ale, at their Innes.
26 How to endure ones hand in molten lead.
27 To hold an hot iron barre in a naked hand.
28 Sweet cakes made without either spice or suger.
29 One candle to make as great a light as two or three.
30 Timber made to last long in water workes.
31 To close the chops of greene timber.
32 To graue any deuise vpon an egge-shell, and to thorough cut the same.
33 An apparance of strange formes in a glasse.
34 Inke to be carried in the forme of a powder.
35 To write both blew and red letters at once.
36 Inke kept from freezing and molding.
37 How to draw any patterne by a deske of glasse.
38 Helps for the speedy attaining of the secretary hand.
39 To helpe Inke when waxeth thicke.
40 To renew olde letters that are almost worne out.
41 To speake by signes onely.
42 Limming with colours drawne from flowers.
43 A ready way to learne the ABC.
44 To graue and inlay colours into al the mettals.
45 To make bad paper to beare inke.
46 To make an egge to stand alone without any helpe.
47 To harden the white of an egge into a gum.
48 A cheape candle or lampe for poore folks.
49 To refresh the colours of old oile pictures.
50 An excellent cement for broken glasses.
51 To drie gunpowder without danger of fire.
52 To draw fish to a certeine place in the night by a candle.
53 A baite to catch fish with.
54 To draw fish into a tramell.
55 Diuers good baits to catch fish with.

The Table.

56 A ready way to catch pigeons.
57 A worme to catch birds with.
58 To catch crowes, iackdawes, &c.
59 To kill Seapies, Seaguls, &c.
60 To gather Waspes.
61 To keepe garments and hangings from moath eating.
62 To helpe beere that sowreth or is dead.
63 To helpe a chimnie that is on fire presently.
64 To haue Seafish all the yeare long.
65 To make beere stale quickly.
66 To steale bees.
67 To make a tallow candle last long.
68 How to tell the iust number of Apples, nuts, shilling, &c, as they ly in bulke together.
69 To preuent drunkennesse.
70 An excellent tent for a Diamond.
71 Oyle or vernish made to dry speedilie.
72 To fetch out any staine.
73 To helpe wine that reboyleth.
74 How to make Bragget.
75 Clarifieng of hony in an excellent manner.
76 To make an artificiall Malmesie.
77 To keepe Gascoigne wine good, a long time.
78 To keepe Walnuts good and moist, a long time.
79 To preserue the glosse of Spanish leather.
80 To helpe smoking chimnies.
81 Tinder and matches sweet, and of a new kind.
82 An excellent mixture to scoure pewter withal.
83 To defend a horse from flies in his trauell.
84 To kill Rats in a garner.
85 To take away the offence of noisome vaults.
86 Sweet and delicate dentifrices, or rubbers for the teeth.
87 To helpe horse and man that is tender footed.
88 To keepe oysters good ten or twelue daies.
89 To keepe Lobsters, Crayfishes, prawnes, &c. good, and sweete, some reasonable time.
90 To make smooth or glistering floores or wals.
91 To make parchment transparent.
92 A cheape morter to be vsed in buildings.
93 A conceited drinking glasse.
94 To dissolue gold, and to part the same from gilt siluer.
95 To know when the moone is at the full by a glasse of water.
96 To melt downe iron easilie.
97 To put seuerall wines in one glasse.
98 The Art of memorie.
99 To make a conceited proiection either vpon Sol or Luna.

The Table.

100 To nip a glasse, Hermetice.
101 A Waggon to be drawne with men.
102 A delicate stoue to sweat in.
103 The Art of refining of Suger.

The second Booke entreateth of sundrie newe sortes of soyle or Marle, for the better manuring of pasture or arable groundes, with diuers conceits of Husbandry not heretofore published.

The third Booke conteineth, diuers chimicall conclusions, concerning the Art of Distillation, with many rare practises and vses thereof, according to the Authors owne experience.

The fourth Booke conteineth, the Art of molding, or casting of any liue bird, or little beast, hearbe, or flower, or of any patterne of mettall, wax, &c. into golde, siluer, plaister, &c.

The last part, is an offer of certeine new inuentions, which the Author wil bee ready to disclose vppon reasonable considerations, to such as shall be willing to entertaine them, or to procure some priuiledge for them.

FINIS.

Diuerse new and conceited Experiments, from the which there may be sundrie both pleasing and profitable vses drawne, by them that haue either witte, or will to applie them.

Sundry new and artificial wayes for the keeping of fruits and flowers, in their fresh hew, after they are gathered from their stalkes or branches.

CAuse new fourmes of Lead to be made, either round or square, that may fit the bignes of your flower, or fruit which you meane to keep, in euerie of which fourmes place one flower, Cherrie, Plomme, or Peare, hanging by the stalke in such maner as it grew, let these fourmes be well fitted with their apt couers, and sodered verie close with safte Soder which will runne with a small heate, so as no aire enter, bury them deep in a shady place, where the Sunne may worke no penetration. Some commend a sandie, and some a grauellie ground, aboue all other for this purpose, but if they be well sodered, I thinke any ground wil serue the turne, or if you think good, you may hang them by lines in some coole and running brooke. Or else you may put euery seuerall fruit or flower in his seuerall earthen pot well

C   leaded

The Jewel-house of

leaded within, and couered with earthen couers, well burnt & leaded likewise, cementing or closing them togither with the Goldsmiths waxe or cement, consisting of stone-pitch, rosen, powder of bricke, and such like (although some content themselues with molten Brimstone, and others with yellow waxe and rosen, molten and well wrought togither.) These litle pots you must place within greater, and these greater within vessels of wood, stopping vp euerie breathing place that you can imagine (for here I can assure you that the aire will be a player, vnlesse you can keepe it out of the Alley perforce.) If you would afterwardes burie these woodden vessels, then were it requisite to pitch them well, both within and without: but if you meane to place them onely in coole and fresh vaults, or Sellers, then may you verie well spare this defensatiue, so as the caske be strong and tight of it self. Yet some commende the keeping of fruite or flowers in Glasses made of purpose for them, to be the best of all others, so as the Glasses bee made with long neckes, and bee nipped (*hermetice*) with a paire of whote tongs, the maner whereof you shall find hereafter set downe *num.* 100. I dare not commend in anie high tearmes, the dipping of fruite in wax well tempered with some Turpentine, Pitch, Rosen, sweete suet, or Barrowes greace: where also some woulde haue the fruit first wrapped in paper, to keepe it the cleaner, although I know there is somewhat to bee performed this way in some kinds of fruit which begin to rot frō the outward partes inwardly. But if the fruit begin to rot first at the Core (as the Katherin peare, and diuers other sorts of fruit doe) then all the outwarde couers and enclosures whatsoeuer (yea though they were dipped in dissolued Ambre which is counted the purest

Art and Nature.

rest and most defensatiue garment of all the rest) will neuer be able to turne Nature out of her bias. Here also some sharpe wittes haue imagined that if spirit of wine wel rectified, were glutted with thimbibition of anie flower, vntill it coulde worke no more vpon the same, that thereby it were possible to preserue anie flower of the same kinde, a long time therein. But this is to bee vnderstoode onely of the drie leaues which bring nothing else but the Tincture and strength of the hearbe with them, and not of the moist leaues which will leaue a putrifying phlegme behind them, which in time will helpe to corrupt the spirit. Nowe me thinkes I see a whole troupe of gallant dames attending with their listning eares, or rather longing with their great bellies, to learne some newfound skil, how they may play at chopcherrie, whē cherrie time is past. Wel, to giue these Ladies some content, I will vnfolde a scroule which I had long since as carefully wrapped vp as euer any of the Sybels did their fatall prophesies, wherein I will make them as cunning as my selfe (sauing onelie that I will reserue one strange venue to foile a scholler withal if need be.) The secret is short, let one element be included within another, so as the one may haue no accesse nor participate with the other. But this paraduenture is too philosophical for women. Then receiue it Ladies with plaine tearmes into your open lappes. For want of Glasses with broade skirts (whereof notwithstanding I doe thinke there are inough to bee had if you can bee so gracious with master Iacob of the Glashouse) cause new Pewter vessels of some large content to be made and of the fashion of bell Saltsellers, with diuerse eies or hookes hanging in the inside, at the which you must fasten the Cherries, by their stalkes, and hang

them

them so as that one maie not touch an other, the skirts of which vessels you must compasse with leaden rings of such weight as may be able to presse thē downe to the bottome of some leaded panne, wherin you must place them, hauing first filled the panne almost full with fayre water prepared as is heere set downe *num. 5.* least by putrifaction of the water, the Cherryes also beginne to putrifie with it. Yet heere you muste bee carefull that the Cherryes hang within the ayre of these inner Vesselles, not touching the Water, which may happilie rise one inche or somewhat more within the innermost skirtes of them. And thus the ayre beeing kept coole, and defended from chaunge (whose alteration from heate to colde, and from moysture to drinesse, is the principall meanes of the ruinating of all mortall bodies) will preserue such Cherryes as it receyueth in charge for two whole Moneths at the least as I haue long since prooued. And peraduenture if you make choyse of sounde fruite gathered after two or three fayre dayes togither, the deaw being sufficientlie drawne from them by the Sunne, you may yet keepe them somewhat longer. But the onely pleasure of this secrete is perfourmed in Glasses through whose perspicuitie after some reasonable quantitie of water first remooued or deuided, one may discerne weekely in what plight they are. It seemeth very probable, that if Cherries as they hang vppon their braunches, and before they come to their full maturitie were included in an earthen vessell of some receipte, hauing a partie couer with a hole in the middest, deuided into two equall partes, and euerie breathing place well stopped or luted, and the Sunne sufficiently defended from the pot, that so

the

Art and Nature.

the fruit would keepe fresh a long time vpon the tree whereon it groweth. This secrete extendeth generallie to all fruite. And it is not much vnlike to the spreading of a Tent ouer a Cherrie tree about fourteene dayes or three weeks before the Cherries were ripe, practised by a Surrey knight not many yeares sithence, whereby he did greatly backward the tree in his bearing, now and then watering the tent in a sunnie day with colde water, whereby the strength of the Sun beames became verie weeake vpon the tree, and when he was disposed to ripen them speedily, he withdrew the vaile, giuing a freer passage to the hote and scorching beames of Phœbus. By the helpe of some one of these, or of some other of the like kinde and qualitie it was my happe to present vnto sir Iohn Allet L. Maior of the Citie of London 8. greene and fresh Artichokes vpon the twelfe day, with a score of fresh Orenges, which I had kept from Whitsuntide then last past, at which time I was also furnished with 200. Artichokes for mine owne prouision, which continued a seruice at my table all the lent ensuing, to the great contentment of sundry of my ghestes who would haue bin right glad to haue dined with the secret onely. It may be that at my next inpression I will impart the same, as also the true & perfect ordring of the rose tree, whereby wee may haue the flowers to bud and blow when all other roses haue made an end of bearing. Which conclusion I haue inserted in my conceyted booke of gardening, wherein I haue set down sundrie obseruations, which neither M. Tusser though hee haue written sharpely, nor Master Hill though hee haue written painfully, nor Master Barnabe Googe though hee haue written soundlye, applying himselfe in his vvhole discourse both to our soyle and Cymate, hath as yet discouered to the
vvorld,

world, though peraduenture he may know them as well as I, and reserue them for himselfe, and for his secrete friendes. All which are readie for the Presse, and doe onely attende to see if Noahs Pigeon will returne with an Oliue branch, seeing his Rauen hath as yet brought nothing with her.

2 *A perspectiue Ring that will discouer all the Cards that are neere him that weareth it on his finger.*

A Christall stone or Glasse of the bignesse of a two pennie peece of siluer, or thereaboute, beeing the iust halfe of a rounde Baall or Globe, and cutte hollow within, hauing a good foyle sweetlie conueyed within the concaue superficies thereof, and the stone it selfe neatly polished within and without, will giue a liuelie representation to the eye of him that weareth it, of all such Cardes as his companions which are nexte him doe holde in their handes, especiallie if the owner thereof doe take the vpper ende of the Table for his place, and leaning nowe and then on his elbowe, or stretching out his arme, doe applie his Ring aptlie for the purpose. I haue discouered this secret rather to discorage yong Nouesses from Card-play, who by one experiment may easily ghesse, how manie sleights & cousonages, are dayly practised in our dicing and gaming houses, not doubting but that the general publication thereof wil make the same so familiar with al men, as that I shall not iustly be charged of anie to haue taught old knaues newe schoole-pointes. This secrete is as yet meerly French, but it had beene long since either denized or made English, if there coulde haue beene found any sufficient workman amongst vs, that could

haue

haue foyled the ftone fo artificially as it ought to bee. There be fome Englifh knights that can fufficiently teftifie the truth hereof by that which they haue feen amongft the French gamfters.

3 Howe to carrie Gold in a moft fecrete maner.

MElt downe fome Golde, and mixe therewith a fufficient quantitie of Leade (but then you fhall bee forced to teft the fame before you can recouer your Golde againe,) and this is the moft fecret waie of all the reft, becaufe there will bee no fhewe or apparaunce of Golde eyther within or without, but the feparation will bee fomewhat troublefome. But if you woulde carrie golde about you in fuch manner, as that without anie other mans helpe, you maie deuide the Golde your felfe from the mettall wherein you conuey it, then caft bullets of Golde in a Piftoll molde, which you may fo aptly hang within fome molde of greater boare that maie fitte the peece which you carrie with you (which will bee alfo a good meanes to remooue all fufpicion of art) as that by powring of Leade rounde about them, they may ferue in ftead of coares to your greater bullets, which with a fmall heate are foone parted in funder. But if you would carrie coine, then dip your Angels or Crownes in molten Lead that is not ouer hote, and conuey them artlie within fome fmall and feate Leaden weightes, that may agree with the *Auer de Poiz*. Some commende the powder of Marble, mingled with molten rofen to lap angels or other coine in, before it be through cold. There be alfo diuerfe philofophicall wayes for the fecretting of *Sol* and *Luna*, but thofe are referued for higher purpofes.

How-

4. *Howe to keepe or preserue anie fowle, or other peece of flesh founde, and sweete for three weekes or one whole Moneth together, notwithstanding the contagiousnesse of the weather.*

MAke a strong Brine, so as the Water bee ouerglutted with salt, and beeing scalding hote, perboyle therein the fowle or flesh which you would preserue some reasonable time, that is to say, according to the greatnes and grosnesse therof, then hang it vp in a conuenient place, and it will last a sufficient time without any bad or ouersaltish taste, as I can testifie of mine owne experience. This I thought good to publish both for the better preseruation of mutton, Veale, and Venison, whereof a great deale in this lande is yearely lost, in hote and vnseasonable Sommers, as also for the benefite of our English Mariners, which are forced sometime to vittaile themselues in such intemperate Clymates, where no flesh will last sweet foure and twentie houres togither, by reason that they haue no meanes to make the same to take salt, which without all question will enter this way and make penetration verie speedily by reason of the hote and fierie spirite of salt thus prepared. Some doe vse to perboyle their fowle, after they haue taken out the garbage, and then do dippe them in Barrowes greace, or in clarifyed Butter, till they haue gotten a newe Garment ouer them, and then they lay them one by one in stone pottes, filling the stone pottes vp to the brim with Barrowes greace or clarified Butter, wherein they doe pricke some Cloues, and sprinckle dried salt vppon the vppermoste face thereof, placing the pottes in

some

some coole roome. Some thinke that fowle being filled ful of good wheat & after buried al ouer in wheat, will keepe good a long time. I haue also heard it verie crediblie reported, that a side of venison hath byn kept sound and sweet one whole month together, by lapping the same in a course thinne cloath, and then couering it with bay salt. Or if it were first perboiled in the aforesaid manner, and then couered with salt as before. I could here adde one line more, whereof euerie letter should be worth an angel to diuers good housekeepers in this Land, but that the same would breed both offense and detriment vnto others, for the which cause onely, I haue thought good to keep the same vnder hatches a little longer.

5. *How to defend fresh Water a long time from putrefaction.*

THis is performed by the addition of some small proportion of the oyle of Sulphur with it, incorporating them both togither, whereof I haue long since made a sufficient triall. Some commende the oile of Vitriol to the same end: and seeing my penne hath so vnaduisedly slipt into an Element of so great necessitie, I wil make the Sea-men a little beholding vnto me at their first watering, which being spent, I must leaue them to their brackish waters againe, vnlesse by the helpe of some distillatorie vessell (wherin as also in diuers other of the same kind and qualitie, I haue found maister Sergeant *Gowthrowse*, the moste exquisite and painfull practizer and performer of our times) they can make separation of the freshe part thereof on Ship-boord. Let the owner, Marchant, or Mariner, hauing sufficient leisure to make his prouision

D

dison of fresh water, before hee beginne his voiage, prepare his water in this manner. First let him fill either some Rhenish Wine fattes, sack buts, or White wine pipes, such as haue beene sawed through the midst, onelie with faire water, these halfe tubs hauing tapholes within three inches of the bottome, at the which after the water hath passed his first putrifaction, and is become sweet againe, he may then drawe it from his residence into a cleane Caske, and by this meanes it will last much longer at the Sea than otherwise; and yet if there were but two or three handfuls of salt dissolued in a pipe of the same water (which would not much offend either the tast or stomach) it would preserue it much more then the bare preparation of the water will doe in the aforesaid maner. Sir *Fraunces Drake* that *Spanish* scourge & *Magna spes altera Troiæ*, who hath sought for all the helpes which he might, either in his water or his victual, for the better comfort and reliefe of his Mariners, in one of the last conferences which I had with him, did assure me, that the most putrified and offensiue water that could happen at the sea, would by 24. howers agitation or rolling vp and downe, becom sweet and good beuerage. And Captaine *Plat* in whome sir *Frances Drake* for his good partes did alwaie repose great trust and confidence, did vsuallie carrie certein long and thicke peeces of sheet lead with him, which he would cause to bee hanged by lines at the bunghole euen to the verie center of the vessel, wherby he did attract much of the fecicall part of the water, and the Leades would become very slimie therwith. This he did with often change and iteration, alwaies clensing the leades as they grew filthie, and so with much adoo, he found the water a great deale more pleasing

then

Art and Nature.

then before. These fewe conceiptes I haue thought good to impart for the benefit of the whole Natiue of England, for the which I haue prouided more daintie cates, then it hath been hitherto acquainted with all, *I* doe onlie keepe them in my breast, vntill an honest purueyor may bee rewarded with some honest pencion. *Qre.* what proportion of spirite of Wine, or *Aqua vitæ* well rectified, will defende water from corruption.

6. *A Marchants Compasse, whereby he may knowe vpon what point the wind blowes, in his bedchamber, and in the night time, without beholding the skie or any vane, abroad.*

FAsten a large vane, to a long yron rod, let the same rise thorough the middest of the roofe or some other part, that may best agree with the roome wherin you mean to place the same, and let the yron stole thereof, come through the seeling of your chamber, and at the end of the rod, let there be a sharpe *index*, that may point vpon a table of wood (which for that purpose must be drawne, with al the parts of the wind vpon it like a mariners compasse) to that wind which bloweth. You must haue diuers staies of yron by the waie as the rodde passeth to keepe it vpright, hauing holes in the midst of them, and wrought with lappets at the sides, wherein to fasten nailes to a long post, which for the same purpose must bee placed within the garret, betweene the seeling of your chamber and the roofe thereof. Note that the *Index* and the edge of the vane must alwaies stand vpon two direct contrarie points.

7. How to feed & fatten Hens, Chickens, Geese, ducks, &c. with diuers other sorts of fowle, in a more cheap manner, then hath as yet beene made knowne or common to the world.

I Knowe diuers that haue contented themselues, to feed and fatten them with graines onelie, whereof they haue made a great benefit vnto themselues; by reason of the easy price for which they are sold. But if you take the bloud of beasts, wherof ẏ Butchers make no great reckoning, filling stone pottes therewith, whose couers may bee full of such holes, as that the flesh flies in sommer time, may easilie get in and out at the same, you shall finde the bloud by meanes of the flie-bloes and putrefaction together, wholie conuerted into white and glib worms (which the anglers call Gentils) which will fatten them exceedinglie, & make them eate most tenderlie. A Dutch man that first practised this secret in a Noble mannes house of England, (whose fowle for the tendernesse of their flesh, was highlie commended of all his gheſtes) had a yearelie ſtipend of twentie nobles conferred vppon him by his Lord, during his naturall life, for the diſcouerie of the ſecret. Yet I coulde wiſhe, that theſe wormes did firſt ſcoure themſelues; either in moſſe, lome, or bran, before they were ſcatred amongſt the fowle: And if notwithſtanding this helpe, the foode ſhall ſeeme offenſiue to our weake ſtomaches, eſpeciallie being made acquainted therwith before hand, then receiue the ſame in a better form and in a ſweeter manner at my handes, who haue alwaies deſired to giue all the grace which I might to any ſecret of good vſe. Boile this bloud with ſome ſtore of branne

amongſt

amonſt it (perhaps graines may ſuffice, but bran is the better) vntil it come to the nature and ſhape of a bloud pudding, & therewith feed your foule ſo fat as you pleaſe, and this wil be both a wholſom & a clenly feeding for them. Som commend, carrots, turnips, Parſenips and pompeons, firſt ſodden and then ſome bran or courſe pollard mingled therewith. You may feed Turkies with bruſed acrons, and they will proſper exceedinglie with them. Some to fatten their capons ſpeedily, put them into coopes wherin ech bird hath a ſeueral roome deuided from the reſt, being ſo ſtraight and narrowe as that the hen or capon may onely feed himſelfe and rooſt therein, not being able to turne his bodie, thereby perſwading themſelues that wanting motion and exerciſe he wil ſoon growe to be fat and of greace. Some do vſe to keepe fowle 2. or 3. daies without meat, til they be exceeding hũgrie, and then they giue them their fill. Others doe ſoke chippings and other cruſtes of bread in broken beere, or flatten milk, wherewith they do afterwarde feed their capons: out of al theſe a good huſwife will eaſilie chooſe both the likelieſt and the beſt.

8. How to write a letter ſecretlie that cannot eaſilie be diſcouered, or ſuſpected.

Write your minde at large on the one ſide of the paper with common inke, and on the other ſide with milck, that which you woulde haue ſecret, and when you would make the ſame legible, holde that ſide which is written with inke to the fire, and the milckie letters wil ſhew blewiſh on the other ſide. Or elſe rule two papers of one bigneſſe with lines of an equal diſtance, make the one ful of glaſſe windowes, through which you muſt write your mind vpon a ſecond

cond paper, thē fil vp the spaces with some other idle words: but if all were made to hang togither in good sense it would carrie the lesse suspition. Each friend must haue one of these cut papers to read all such letters as shalbe sent vnto him, & this maner of writing will trouble a good decipherer to bring into perfect sense. Also you may first write an ordinary letter that may carry some good sense to your friend, but let the lines be wide asunder. Then betwene these lines write your secret letter with gall water onely wherein the gauls haue bin infused but a small time (for if after you haue writtē therwith there be any sensible colour left behinde vpon the paper, you must throw away that water and make new.) This being drie and of one colour with the paper, will giue no cause of suspition, & the rather because the letter purporteth a sufficient sense already. Now for the discouery therof, you must dissolue some coppres in faire water. & with a fine calaber pensill first dipped in y̆ coppres water, you must artly moisten the interlining of your letter, and thereby you shall make it sufficiently legible. This is one of the most secrete waies that I know. But yet the finest conceited way of all the rest in my opinion, is y̆ close cariage of a letter within a lawne or Cambricke ruffe or handkirchief, which a man may weare for his necessary vse without the defacing of any one letter cōtained therein. And this serueth most fitly for a loue-letter, which may without all suspitiō of friends be easily presented in a hākirchief, to any gentlewomā that standeth well affected to her secretary. There is also a redy way without changing of the Alphabet to write ones mind speedily vpon paper, & yet the same not to be deciphered without the helpe of a rolling pinne of the same scantling with that whereon it was first written.

Art and Nature.

written. But these two latter conceits (for some reasons best knowne vnto my selfe) I may not so boldly impart as otherwise I would.

9 *How to brew good and wholsom Beere without anie Hoppes at all.*

Since my profession is this booke is in some sort to anotomize both Art and Nature, without any regard of priuate mens profits, whom it may either essentially, or accidentally touch: I am bolde therefore without crauing any leaue to do good, to renue or rather to confirm & ratifie an ancient opinion & practise, which long since in the great dearth and scarcity of hops many Brewers of this land, haue bin forced to put in vse for y̆ better supportation of their weak & declining estates. But because they failed in proportion (without the which there can be nothing cómplete or absolute) they suffered a good conceit to die in the birth. And no maruel then if wormwood notwithstāding it be a simple so highly cómended of all the anciēt & new Herbarists for his great & singular effects in physick, be in a maner vtterly abandoned of all the brewers of our time (except a few y̆ can make a difference betweene 5. s. and 5. li. charge when hops are sold for 50. s. the hundred, seeing as yet not any one of them hath so clarkly wrought vpon this simple as to couer & hide the taste therof, from y̆ wel mouthed Ale-conners of our cómon wealth. Which weaknes of theirs because it consisteth wholly in the want of a due proportion betwene the mault & other beercorn in respect of wormwood, I haue thought good to set downe a sufficient direction, for such as are wise and willing to doe good both to themselues and to their Countrie, whereby they may easily euen in one dayes practize attaine to the full perfection thereof

Supposing

Suppoſing then that your Wormewood is either cut down in the leaf before it be ſeeded, or being ſeeded that it is cut into ſhort peeces, whereby there may be made an equall mixture of the whole bulcke togither (for you muſt note that the ſeeded toppes are much ſtronger and more oyly then the reſt of the leaues or ſtalkes) make firſt a decoction of foure ounces of hops with nine gallons of water (which is the proportion that ſome Brewers in ſome ſorts of drink doe vſe) and when you haue gotten out by ebulition the full ſtrength and vertue of them, keepe the ſame apart, and begin likewiſe with ſome ſmall proportion of Wormewood to the like quantitie of water as before, and when you haue beſtowed as much time and fire herein, as you did about the hoppes, then taſte each of them by it ſelfe, and if you finde the ſame to exceed the firſt in bitterneſſe, then begin with a leſſe proportion of Wormewood, and ſo reiterate your worke, vntil you haue equally matched the one with the other, then may you ſafely proceede by the rule of proportion to a barrell, and from thence to a tun, and ſo to a whole brewing. Neither let the exceſſiue bitterneſſe of Wormewood in his preſent taſte anie thing diſmay you, for if you did but taſte the decoction of hoppes onely before the mixture of the ground mault (which doth wonderfully ſweeten the ſame) you would think it a verie vnapt liquor to be wrought vp into ſo pleaſing a drinke as our ordinarie Beere doth ſhewe it ſelfe to bee. For it is the Hoppe onelie which maketh the eſſentiall difference betweene Beere and Ale, and that by allaying of the exceeding luſciouſneſſe of the mault with his bitternes, whereby both vniting themſelues together, become a ſauorie and wholſome drinke for mans bodie. Which may which may bee as well in euerie respect perfourmed with Wormwood as with the Hoppe, yea and peraduenture with Centuarie, Artichoke leaues, or *Aloes hipatique*, as some workmasters haue confidently affirmed vnto me. And though the Hoppe be vsuall in drinke, and the Wormwood onely in medicine, whereby some may happily be perswaded, that it is inconuenient for men that are in health to drinke a medicine continually to their meate, yet let this be a sufficient answere to that obiection, that it is the dose onely that maketh the difference herein. For I can assure you in mine owne experience, and by the experience of one of the best experienced Brewers of London who yet liueth, that if you giue a double or treble quantitie of good English hoppes, to an ordinarie guile of strong Beere, you shall find the same to be a sufficient preparatiue to your bodie for the best purgation that shalbe ministred after. And this can one of the right honourable Peers of this lande sufficiently witnesse, who togither with some good part of his retinue, hauing well tasted at a dinner of such Beere, as (by the misprision of the Brewer of English hoppes for Flemish hoppes) was so ouerhopped, that both himselfe and the rest of his family that was then about him, were suddenly surprised with a great loosnesse. And this is the reason why Venice Turpentine which being ministred in a small dose is giuen for the strengthening of the backe, and to stay the running of the reines, yet if it be taken in y̌ quantitie of an ounce at once, it will purge sufficiently in diuerse bodies. So then either let there be no more taste of wormwood then there is of hoppes in our drinke, and wee shall finde no difference in effects, but such as shall commend and grace the wormwood beyond the hoppe,

E or

or else let beere be aduaunced with the hoppe to the bitternesse of wormwood wine, and so we shall finde the hop farre to exceede the wormwood in his maligne qualitie. Neither woulde I haue any man to thinke, that I doe either wrongfully intrude vpon other mens possessions, or presumptuously vndertake a charge which I cannot performe, for I am in by discent, and haue continued fiue yeares in possession at the least, and therefore am not easily to be remoued without a philosophicall action commenced against me. And because you shall farther knowe that I haue some reasonable skill in my trade, I dare vndertake without the helpe of any yeast at all, to bring ỹ woort either of Ale or Beere to his perfect workemanship (wherin it shall cõtinue at the least either six or seuen daies togither) without any intermission, & that only by a philosophicall stirring vp of the fire of nature which shall extend and spread it selfe *à centro ad circumferentiam*, till it haue digested the whole body to his perfect ripenesse or maturitie. Thus much I haue thought good to publish for ỹ credite of wormwood, and for the benefite of this Iland in sundry respectes, which I shal not need to particularize at this time because they are so commonly knowne to all men. And though I know I may bee ouerweyed either with the Fraunders Merchants, or with the great Hoppe-masters of Englande whose foundation is so deepelie laide, that a fewe loose lines can neither shake nor stirre the same: yet either knowing, or at the least perswading my selfe to maintaine the trueth, before I giue it ouer I will craue the libertie of the schooles, *quod fiat controuersia*. And in the meane time those which will not bee satisfied, of the wholesome and rare medicinable helpes of the one, togither with

the

Art and Nature. 19

the weake and feeble vertues of the other, (which was but a Hedgebirde the other daie, though nowe it bee perking so prowdly vpon his poles) I will referre them to the learned Herbals of Dioscorides, Matheolus, Doctor Turner, Dodoneus, Turnizerus, and the rest.

10 Howe to harden Leather so as the same shall last much longer in the suckers of Pumpes then it dooth vnprepared.

THis secret is so necessarie for the whole lande, as that I muste craue pardon of my especiall good friend for the discouerie thereof. Lay such leather as is well tanned, to soake in water wherein there hath beene some store of the filings of yron a long time, or else in the water that hath lien long vnder a Grindstone, into the which such yron as hath beene from time to time ground away, hath fallen, and there setled. This hath beene found to bee a secret of good vse, by one of the Pumpemakers of our time, and if thou canst pumpe out any better vses of this secrete, take them in aduauntage; and remember where thou hadst them.

11 A conceipted Chaffingdish to keepe a Dish of meate long hote vpon the Table without any coles therein.

LEt the Dish bee somewhat deepe, and cause the Chafingdish to bee made of such shape as may best receiue the same, into the which you may conuey a peece of yron red hote, the same beeing of an apt forme to lie in the bottome of the Chafingdish.

E 2   This

This will continue his heate a long time, and if you haue one other spare iron to heat as the first cooleth, you may keepe any dish of meate warme as long as you thinke good. From this ground did those warming pinnes first spring, which of some are called Froes, and being put into their cases, and those cases wrapped in linnen bagges, doe serue to heate beddes with, and to cast one into a kindly sweat. The like deuice is also vsed by others in conueying of such iron pinnes into hollow boxes of wood first lined inwardly with mettall, and iron chests, either to lay vnder their feete where they vse to write or studie in colde weather, or in their coches to keepe their feet warm. The now distressed king of Portugall caused a paire of wooden soles to bee made for a paire of shooes which he had to sit in, which he would warme at his pleasure with *Mars* well rubified.

12 Howe to rost meate more speedily, and with lesse fire then we now do in our common maner.

MAke a square and concaue boxe, or else of the fashion of a Cilinder of iron plates, or else of wood lined with those plats long inough and large inough for such and so many ioynts of meat as you meane to rost at once, within which Cilinder let the meat turne as it roasteth. For the reflexion of the heate that is gathered within the boxe will make great expedition. Note that the boxe must onelie couer the meate, because you are to leaue a fire (if neede be) to hang on a pot or kettle ouer the same fire. It must also be close on euery side sauing onely agaynst the fire, and at the sides thereof you must haue slittes to let in the spitte. I haue heard of the like deuise heretofore executed

Art and Nature. 21

xecuted by an outlandish potter in burnt clay, for he which he had his priuiledge, but his deuice wanted a couer, it was exceeding heauie, very apt to bee broken, and not so strong in reflexion as this metalline deuise, especiallie if it be kept cleane and bright.

13. *To make a new peece of Walnut tree or Wainscot to be of one selfe-same coulour with the old.*

First straine walnut rindes well putrified with some liquor, and with a sponge rubbe ouer your wood throughlie well, and after it is drie, rub the same ouer againe with good olde Linseed oile, & it wil become of an excellent brown colour: then if the other wood which you would haue match with it, do much differ frō the new in colour, you must also with fine sand, skoure off all the filth and greace of your olde wood, and then rub it also ouer with Linseede oile. Some take broken beere only. By this meanes I had an old wainescot window, that was peeced out with newe wainscot by a good workeman, and both becam verie suteable and of one colour.

14. *How to turne 5. spittes at once with one hande, whereby also much fier is saued.*

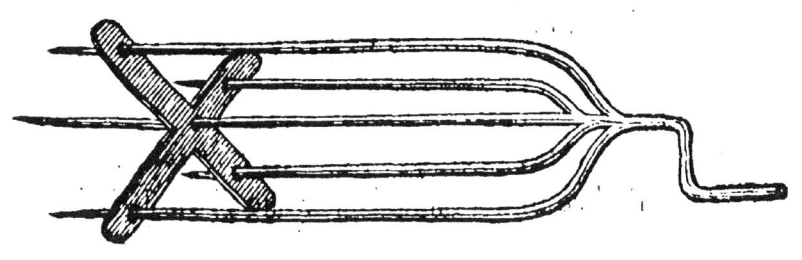

E 3   Fasten.

The Jewel-house of

FAsten 5. round spittes together, like the teeth or tines of a mole-speare, with a handle in the center of them, let them be placed in a reasonable distance the one from the other, according to the bignesse of the iointes of meat that you would roast vpon them, (I take them to be most apt for fowle) you must also haue a crosse of yron, hauing a hole in euerie corner therof, to receiue the ends of these spits, which may be propped with a staie behind that it fall not backeward. Vsing these spits, you shall not neede to rayse your fire vppon such high raunges as otherwise you shall be forced to doe, when one spit is placed directlie aboue another. This secret I haue borrowed out of Pope *Pius* the v. his kitchin.

15. A probable coniecture at the composition of harde Waxe.

I Am verilie perswaded, that the essentiall part, if not the whole bodie thereof, is made of the gum *Lacca*, peraduenture refined a little, or incorporated with some other apt bodie. For I haue sealed therewith oftentimes, and doe find the same to agree with hard wax, in the perfect taking of the impression of the seale, in the manner of the burning, in the smell, and in brittlenesse. It onely differeth in cleerenes and colour. I haue heard that the Barbarians doe make a bright and orient crimosin colour therewith vppon leather, for which purpose it is greatly sought for in England, to transport into Barbary./

16. To helpe venison that is tainted.

IF it bee much tainted cut awaie all the flesh that is greene, and cut out all the bones, and bury it in a thin

Art and Nature.

thin olde course cloth a yard deepe in the ground for 12. or 20. houres space, and it will bee sweet enough to be eaten as I am enformed by a Gentlewoman of good credit, and vpon hir owne practise.

17. *How to make a Pistol whose barrell is two foote in length to deliuer a bullet point blank at eight skore.*

A Pistoll of the afore said length and beeing of petronel bore, or a bore higher, hauing eight gutters somewhat deepe in the inside of the barrell, and the bullet a thought bigger then the bore, & so rammed in at the first three or foure inches at the least, and after driuen downe with the skowring stick, will deliuer his bullet at such distance. This of an English Gentleman of good note and for an approoued experiment.

18. *A peece whereby to performe some extraordinarie seruice either by Sea or land.*

CAuse a long barrell to be made and of the bore of a Tennis ball, of fiue or sixe foot in length and well stocked, hauing within twelue inches of the mouth thereof, a hooking iron of foure inches in length, forged to the neather part of the peece, by which hooke you may staie your peece by som raile, or other peece of timber, whereby you may safelie discharge the same, without feare of any recoile vpon you. I leaue the full vse thereof to bee found out by Martiall men. This inuention I hadde of the fine lymner of Lambith, beeing a Gentleman of good conceipt in all ingenious deuises.

The Jewel-house of

19. To make greene wood to burne cleere, at the farther end of the Ouen.

IF you burne greene wood in an ouen, it burneth somwhat cleere toward the mouth of the ouen but commonly black & deadish at the further end, wherby the ouen is neuer sufficientlie heated to bake well. You shall find a remedie thereof in this manner. Deuide the mouth of the ouen into foure equall partes, and cause a bar of yron to be made as long or somewhat longer than the mouth of the ouen, & in bredth one exact fourth part thereof. Fasten this bar ouerthwart-wise in the middle point of the ouen mouth, and this will make a partition, betweene the fire and the aier, so as the ayer will passe vnder the bar to kindle the fire, and the flame will issue ouer the barre, and so the smoke which before did choke the fire will also haue his passage.

20. How a man may walke safelie vpon a high scaffold or peece of Timber, without danger of falling.

THis is easilie performed by wearing of a paire of spectacles, whose sightes must be made so grose, as that he which weareth them may not discerne any thing a farre off, but at hand onely. For it is the sight onely of the steepenesse of the place, that bringeth the feare, and ouerturneth the braine. By this means I haue heard that the English man which displayed an ancient vpon a scaffold neere the top of the pinacle of Paules steeple, did helpe himselfe in his desperate attempt.

Art and Nature. 25

21. *A round ball of Copper or latton, that will blow the fire verie stronglie, onely by the attenuation of water into ayre, which deuice will also serue to perfume with.*

MAke a round ball of Copper or Latten, of y̆ bignesse of a small bowle, soder thereunto a rounde pipe or necke, of three or foure inches in length, and somwhat lesse than a goose quil, at the end whereof, in the manner of an elbowe, soder on a lesse pipe no bigger than a straw, whose vent in the ende may not much exceed the bignes of a pinhole, let al the ioints and sides be sodred with siluer soder, heate the same well in the fire, and then put it into a vessel of cold water, and it will sucke some of the water vnto it, you may heate the same so often, till by the peize thereof you may bee assured that it is more then halfe full. Then set this ball vpon a few glowing coles, and you shall finde the same to giue a very strong blast against the fire which you mean to kindle, directing the nose of these bellowes towards the same. I make no question, but that it is possible with a verie small helpe to melt dovvn either gold or siluer with these bellows, and that the same may be made so large as that they wil blow one whole houre together, without anie intermission. If you make a little round ball of siluer in this maner, only with a small and streight pipe, rising out of the bodie therof, you may put some

F   rose-

rosewater or some other sweet senting water therin, and therewith perfume your chamber, and by this meanes a small quantitie of sweet water will be a long time in breathing out.

22. *How to erect or build ouer any brooke, or small riuer, a cheape and woodden bridge, of 40. or 50. foote in length, without fastening any timber work within the water.*

PEece the timber work in such sort, as that it may resemble an arch of stone, make the ioints strong, and binde them fast with crampes or dogs of iron, let this bridge rest vpon two strong pillers of wood at either end, both being well propped with spurres, & at either ende of your bridge make a strong buttresse of bricke, into the which you must let your pillers and spurres, that by no meanes they may shrinke or giue backewarde, then planke ouer your bridge and grauell it and it will last a long time. This is already in experience amongst vs.

23. *A cheape Lanterne, wherein a burning candle may be carried, in any stormie or windie weather, without any horne, glasse, paper, or other defensatiue, before it.*

MAke a foure-square box, of 6. or 7. inches euerie waie, and 17. or 18. inches in length, with a socket in the bottome thereof, close the sides well either with doue tailes or cement, so as they take no aire, leaue in the middest of one of the sides a slit or open dore, to put in the candle, which from the bottome to the toppe thereof may containe 6. or 7. inches in length,

Art and Nature.

ngth, and twoe and a halfe in edth, place your candle in the cket, and though it stand open nd naked to the ayre without ny defense, yet the winde will ue no power to extinguish the me. The reason seemeth to be cause the box is already full of re, whereby there is no roome place to conteine any more, ither can the ayre finde any orough passage, by reason of e closenesse thereof. The soc- t would be made to screw in and out at the bottom d then you may put in your candle before you fa- n the socket. This is borrowed of one of the rarest athematicians of our age.

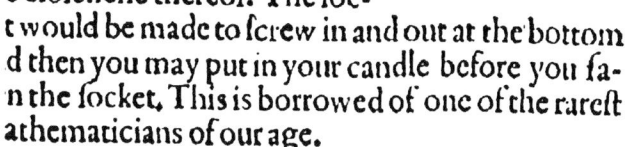

. How to plom vp a horse, and to make him fatte and lustie, as also howe to keepe a Iade from tiring by the way, and to make him to foame at the bit.

TAke *anula campana*, Comminseed, Turmericke & annis seeds, of each a pennieworth, and seeth m well (with three heades of Garlike amongest m well stamped) in a gallon of Ale, then streine it d expresse as much of the substaunce as you may ll wring out, and giue your Horse to drinke ther- loud-vvarme a full quart at once, then ride him til be hot, then stable him, litter him well, and currie a vntill hee bee colde, doe the like two or three minges together, and so turne him to grasse, and will thriue woonderfullie in a short time. Some nmend a handfull of grunsell sodden in the afore-

F 2 said

saide ale with the rest of the ingredientes. But if you keep him in the stable, giue him to eat in his prouender the rootes of *anula campana* with some commen seedes both beaten togither, or ỹ *anula campana* smal shred, for 14. daies together, and it wil make a leane Iade to thriue more in one moneth, then otherwise he would doe in three. And when you ride abroade vpon a hired Hackney, carie a good quantitie of the powder of *anula campana* with you in some leather bag, and when others doe baite their horses in their ordinarie manner, your horse being first well walked, littered, and rubbed, giue him a handfull of this powder in a quart of strong ale with a horne, and tie his head high to the rack, and you need to giue no other or verie little prouender vntil night, then let him bee well meated, and giue him in the morning two peny worth of bread, and his ale with the powder, but water at night. This a friend of mine yet liuing, did learn of a good fellow that had beene a ranke-rider in his daies, by whose meanes though his hackney tired at Bristow, yet this companion for his better encoragement, seeing him out of all heart, by reason that hee was like to lose so good companie as then was gathered together, he exchaunged Horses with him, and brought the Hackney (by the meanes aforesaide) verie quicke and liuely vppe to London. Also if you tie a prettie bunch of Peni-royall about the bit within the Horses mouth, the Horse champing thereon, will foame gallantlie, and trauell with muche more courage. Another Gentleman, who also attendeth vppon a verie Honourable personne, tolde me, that whensoeuer hee founde any Iade to tire vnder him, hee woulde presentlie take off his Saddle, and with a good quantitie of *Arsesmart* (which is an hearbe

that

that groweth almoſt in euerie Ditch and ſtanding
Water) rubbe him well on the backe vnderneath
the Saddle, and aftervvarde lay a good quantitie of
Arſeſmart vnder the ſaddle, and ſo ride him any reaſonable iourney. Theſe ſecrets I thought good to diſcouer for the benefite of all Engliſh trauellers, and I hope they are true becauſe my authours are aliue, and ſpeake of their own experience, and not by bare report from others, they doe alſo carrie great probabilitie with them. But nowe from the horſe to the rider.

§ *A ſpeedie or preſent drinke which trauailers may make for themſelues, (ex tempore) when they are diſtreſſed for want of good Beer or Ale at their Inne.*

TAke a quart of good water put thereto fiue or ſix ſpoonfuls of good *Aqua cōpoſita,* which is ſtrong of the Anniſ ſeedes, & one ounce of Sugar with a branch of Roſemarie, brew them a pretie while out of one pot into another, and then is your drinke prepared. Or if you leaue out Sugar it will be pleaſing inough. I haue bene crediblie enformed, that diuerſe gentlemen of good credit when they trauell abrode, and cannot like the taſte or reliſh of their drinke, that they vſe no other then the aforeſaide compoſition, and finde the ſame both to refreſh and coole them verie well, neither are they troubled with the rawnes of colde water, by reaſon that it hath receiued ſome correction from the *Aqua Compoſita*, and that the Anniſ ſeedes doe giue a delicate taſte vnto it. It were not amiſſe for all ſea-men to carrie ſome ſtore of *Aqua Vitæ* with them, that when their Wine, Sider, Perrie, and Beere are ſpent, they may tranſmute their water into the ſaid drinke.

F 3   26 How

The Jewel-house of

26 *How any man may safely put his finger or hand into molten lead, without any danger of burning.*

TAke of quickesiluer one once, Bole Armoniack of the best two ounces, Camphire half an onnce, common *Aqua vitæ* two ounces, first beate, and then mingle all these well togither with a pestle in a brazen morter, then annoint your hands al ouer thrughly well with this ointment, & be sure that your hands are cleane without itch or scabbe. I did see a Dutchman called Haunce, a prety nimble Chimist, who after he had set some lead on the fire in a melting pot, till it became blewish and exceeding hot, hee stirred the same first with his forefinger vp and downe, pretending to see whether it were not too hot to endure in the palme of his hande, and afterwards telling his fellow that it was of a good temper, he caused him to poure the same out being some half pound in weight into the palme of his hande, first prepared as before, and presently he poured it into his other hand, and so out of one hand into another fiue or sixe times togeether, till in the ende he threw the same cold vpon the ground. This hee did for a pot of the best Beere in a garden in Southwarke about ten or twelue yeeres sithence, in the presence of my self and diuers others, at which time I writ the receit euen as I did both see him make it, and vse it my selfe, disbursing the charge both of the Beere, and the ingredients.

27 *How any man may hold a hot iron barre in his hande without burning his flesh.*

DIppe your hand in molten glewe (take heede the glew be not too hot) & presently strew the powder

Art and Nature. 31

der of horne burnt to ashes vpon the glew, then dip your hand againe in the glew, and strew more of the said powder thereon. Note that the thicker your bar is, the thicker crust you must make vpon your hande. This I learned of an olde and skilfull man that yet liueth, and assured me that hee had made often triall thereof. *Qre.* if this be not a good deuise to defende mantletrees, and other peeces of timber that stande neer the fire from burning. Take an equal proportion of fish-glew, and Alom, mingle them well together, the glew being first dissolued in wine vineger, then parget ouer whatsoeuer thou wilt with this composition, and throw the same into the fire, and it shall not burne. This out of the secrets of *Wickerus* 110. See *Cardane de rerum varietate.* 644.

28 *Sweet and dilicate Cakes made without either Spice or Sugar.*

Slice great and sweet Parsnep rootes (such as are not seeded) into thin slices, and hauing washed and scraped them cleane, then drie them and beate them into powder, searcing the same through a fine searce, (*Qre.* if there might not be som means found out for the grinding of them, whereby to make the greater riddance or quantitie,) Then knead two parts of fine flower with one part of this powder, and make some cakes thereof, and you shall finde them to taste verie daintilie. I haue eaten of these cakes diuerse times with verie great good liking.

29 *How with one candle to make as great a light as otherwise with two or three of the same bignesse.*

Cause a round & double Glasse to bee made of a large size, & in fashio like a globe, but with a great
round

roundé hole in the toppe, and in the concaue part of the vppermost Glasse place a Candle in a loose socket, and at some hole or pipe which must bee made in the side thereof, fill the same with spirite of Wine or some other cleare distilled water that will not putrifie, and this one Candle will giue a great and wonderfull light, somewhat resembling the Sun beames. Note that this Glasse is not much vnlike to those Wine drinking bolles that haue false bottoms, wherein Sacke, or Claret wine may bee conueyed with faire water onelie in the vppermost part of the Cup, whereby a plaine meaning man may easilie be deceyued. This conceipt of a Candle, a Gentleman of good account, and my especiall good friend did learne in Venice, where hee was shewed the secrete for a fewe French Crownes. *Qre.* What light a Candle woulde shewe if it were placed in a large Cilinder like vnto a halfe Lanterne, all of Latten kept bright and glistring, the same being inwardly garnished with diuerse steele Looking-glasses, so artificially placed as that one of them might reflect vnto another. I knewe an expert Ieweller, dwelling (whilest he liued) in the Blacke-friers, who had a Glasse with a round bellie, and a flat backe standing vpon a foote, with a Lampe placed so at the backer part thereof, as that the light thereof was iust opposite to the center of the bellie through which (the Glasse being first filled with spirite of Wine) there would so brim and glittering light appeare, as that by the helpe thereof he would graue anie curious worke in golde as well at midnight as at the noone day.

30 How

30. Howe to make great postes and peeces of timber that are to be driuen into the earth, or piles for water works to last much longer then otherwise they would.

I Haue heard that the Venetians whose houses doe stand vpon piles of wood, do vse to burne or scorch the timber in a flaming fire, continually turning it round with some engine, vntill they haue gotten a blacke and hard colie crust vpon it, and so they finde it to last some hundreds of yeares, as it hath beene reported vnto me. A Kentish knight of good woorth did also assure me, that they vse to burne in this manner the endes or poyntes of their postes, which they driue into the grounde when they make their pales and other enclosures. This secret carieth great probabilitie with it, for that by this meanes the outwarde part of the wood is brought both to such a hardnesse and likewise to such a drinesse, *vt, cùm omni putrefactio incipiat ab humido*, for want of moysture and sappinesse, neither the Element of earth, nor yet of water can make any penetration into it.

31. To make all the choppes and cleftes of greene timber to close againe.

ANnoint or supple well the greene timber which you doe expose into the ayre, with the fatte of powdred beefe broth, and soake it well with sponges or pensils into the cliftes or choppes thereof, do this twice ouer, and you shall finde the same to answere my report. Some Carpenters doe vse to close vp the great choppes of Wood with Greace and Sawdust mingled together, but the first I take to bee the better way, for that I haue thereby seene the timber to come so close togither, as if it had neuer beene windshaken at all, but note that the timber must bee thus prepared in time, and whilest it is greene.

32 How to graue any armes, posies, or other deuise vpon an egge shel, & how to through-cut the same, with diuers works and fancies, which will seem very strange to such as know not the maner of the doing thereof.

Dippe an egge in suet being molten, first the one halfe, and then the other, holding the same betweene your thumbe and forefinger when you dippe it, let the same coole in your hand, and beeing colde, with a sharpe bodkin or some other instrument of iron, worke or graue in the suet what letters or portrature you wil, taking away the suet clean, & leauing the shell bare at the bottom of your worke. Then lay this eg thus engraued in good wine vineger or strong alliger in a Glasse or stone Pottinger, for some sixe or eight houres, or more, or lesse, according to the strength and sharpenesse of the Vineger, then take out the egge, and in water that is blood warme dissolue the suet from the egge, then lay your egge to coole, and the woorke will appeare to bee grauen in the shell of a russet colour. *Sæpius probatum*. And if the egge lie long inough in the vineger after it is so grauen, and couered with suet as before, the letters will appeare vpon the egge it selfe being hard sodden, or else if you care not to loose the meate, you may picke out the same when the shell is through grauen, and so you shall haue a straunge peece of worke perfourmed. Those two latter conceiptes I learned of late, but I haue not prooued them, but in all likelihoode
they

Art and Nature.

they should seeme to bee true.

33 An apparance of strange formes in a Glasse.

GRind an Angell weight of fine leafe golde, with two ounces of *Sal armoniacke* vpon a marble till you can scarcely discerne any golde, then take two parting Glasses each of them containing a pinte, in the one put the ground golde with foure ounces of good strong water, and in the other glasse put foure ounces of Mercury with eight ounces of *Aqua fortis*, set both these glasses in warme ashes vpon some furnes, till both the bodies be dissolued, then take a parting glasse of a quart, and whilest the substances being dissolued are yet warme, poure the same into your quart glasse, but first you must put in your strong water wherein the Mercury was dissolued (I write according to the practize which I did see) and then poure the other water vpon that, and presently you shal see an extreeme thick blacknesse, which a Dutch Alchimist and practiser of phisicke that died of ẏ last yeres plague (vpon the discouery therof) wold maintain to be that *nigrũ nigro nigrius*, so much spoken of amongst the philosophers, & after a while when the water began to cleare, then he termed it *cœlũ christallinũ*, after that did appeare a continual rising & falling as it were of flakes of snow which continued certaine houres, & then as it were a hil al couered with pearle, & that he called *sepulchrũ Mosis*. Al which composition hauing stood one night, there appeared diuerse spires like blades of corn or grasse but of a whitish colour in the bottome of the glasse, yet in the end, by a reuerberatory furnesse hee turned al this great matter into a precipitate, and therefore it must needes bee a Philosophicall woorke, that did ende in so great an *arcanum*. Yet the same if it bee truelie perfourmed is woorth the beholding, if it were to no other end, then to put vs in minde of Democritus his *Atomi*, which concurring together, at length engender bodies. There is a like woorke to bee perfourmed in siluer, whereby I haue seene seuerall fourmes and shapes of things somtime to spring vp suddenly, and somtimes in a night or two, the same somtime representing trees, shrubs, hedges, and flowers, and diuerse other shapes, and notwithstanding many practises to find out the reason of the differences of these forms, I could neuer yet make any one forme twise, but that Nature would play so infinitly, and at her owne pleasure herein, as though I did obserue a iust proportion of all the ingredients of this magisterie, yet (because she found some difference of peize when shee weyed them in her owne ballance) I had alwayes a seuerall and differing forme from the last which I made.

34 A portable ynke to be caried in the forme of a powder in any paper, leather purse or boxe.

IN Foster lane or amongst the refiners of golde and siluer, get a large panne, such as they make their testes of bone ashes in, it is a deep dish made of burnt clay; into this put so much of the fattest and best coppres that you can get, set the same vpon a treuet ouer a reasonable fire of charcole, at the first it will dissolue into a water, & after by continuing of your fire it will grow drier and drier, stir the same continually with a wooden spattle into the midst of the pan, and keepe it from burning or hardning to the sides of the pan, and when it is throughly calcined into a whitish

powder

powder and before it become redde, take it from the fire, then weigh out of this calcined coppresse one part, one part of the best gals wellpowdred, and half a part of the cleerest gum *Arabicke* well powdred also, searce them all through a fine scearce, the finer the better, and it will not be amisse if you vse a lawne searce herein. Keepe this powder in close boxes and in the warmest places of your house, and when you wil write therewith, put some of the powder into a spoone, adding thereunto some water, wine, beere, or vinegar, and stir it well together a prettie while, and when it hath set'ed a little, you may write therewith, and as it drieth, it will growe blacker and blacker vpon the paper till in the ende it become verie legible. This I haue often proued. Some commend dry Litmas scraped in water, and forced to a solution, wherwith to write in stead of a blew Inke. But I thinke it not amisse, first to dissolue some Gum *Arabick* in the water to keepe your inke the better from sinking. These sortes of inkes are verie good for the sea, because glasses are subiect to breaking and though you put your inke in leaden pots, yet in time it wil thicken exceedinglie, and then euerie man knowes how troblesome it wil be to the writer. I could here set down some other sorts of inkes that be not common, wherof some will fall from the paper in a few daies, and others would corrode or fret the paper in peeces, but because I know but one good vse of them all, and for that I feare so many bad vses, or rather abuses, would follow if they were known and made common, I will rather seeme ignorant of them, then become an author or helper vnto badde men in their bad purposes.

35. How to write both blew and redde letters at once, with one selfe-same Inke and pen, and vpon the same paper.

PVt the quantitie of a Hasell nut of Lytmas blewe to three spoonfuls of conduit water, wherin some Gumme *Arabicke* is dissolued, and when it hath setled the space of one hower, if you write therewith you shall haue perfect blewe letters, and if you dip a pensill in the iuice of Lymmons, that is drained from his residence, and do wet some part of the paper ther with, and after let your paper drie againe, and then write vpon the place where the iuice of the lymmon was laid, with your former blew inke, the letters will suddenlie become red, and in all the rest of the paper the letters will be blew. And so you may also make partie letters and other fansies, if you wet your paper accordinglie. *Sæpius probatum.*

36. To keepe Inke from freezing and moulding.

PVt a few drops of *Aqua vitæ* therein, and then it wil not freeze in the hardest Winter that can happen, and in Sommer time if you put salt therein it will not waxe mouldie as I haue beene crediblie informed.

37. How to draw any grose pattern of any Beast, fowle, Tree, Fruit, Flower, Personage, or other picture whatsoeuer.

YOu must haue a deske of the cleerest and euenest glasse that is to be bought, yet I haue seene our

Art and Nature. 39

Suffex glaffe to ferue the turne fufficientlie (and fom vfe the skinne of an abortiue Lambe, finelie dreffed and ftreined ftiffe vppon a frame) vppon this Deske you muft faften the patterne at the foure endes with a little wax, vpon the which patterne, lay the fineft paper that you can get for money, and wax that alfo vpon the patterne as before. Then place your deske with the back therof againft a brim or perfect light, that hath no other oppofit nor fide light to hinder it, and I thinke it beft of all againft a window where the fun shineth) and the pattern wil shewe all the lineaments thereof very perfectly through the fine paper, vpon y̆ which you may trick, either with a fine pointed cole, black lead, or pen. *Qre.* Of a fufficient light to be placed vnder the deske by feuerall lampes, if thereby alfo in a darke night, you may not difcerne howe to performe your worke perfectlie. Some in fteade of this deske doo oyle a paper and lay it vpon a patterne, and draw thereon with blacke lead, and then prick the pattern full of holes & fo pounce it vpon another paper. And fome haue paterns of beafts,

birds,

birds, flowers, &c. prickt out in paper, and those they pounce also vpon other paper. And this is a good & readie waie for him that is not skilfull in the Arte of drawing, to garnish any plot which he hath taken of any Manor, parke, close, &c. with Trees, hedges, deer, houfinges, &c. But there is a waie by a perspectiue glaffe (which becaufe it is confecrated vnto Arte, I dare not profane the fame too much by deliuering it into vnhallowed hands) whereby a young fcholler may by one houres demonftration exactlie draw and fet downe the lineamentes of any liue perfonage, Beaft, or other fowle whatfoeuer, being placed at any reafonable diftance from him, and fo of any ftatelie edifice or building, fort, bulworke, or fortification, and of al manner of engines, whatfoeuer the wit of any worke-maifter is able either to actuate in the great or to performe in modell onely. Yea al manner of drawne patternes whatfoeuer, bee they neuer fo great, may by the helpe of this glaffe (wherof I haue gotten the vfe at the hand of my deare friend) be leffened and brought within as narrow a Compaffe as a man would reafonablie wifh or defire. And whofoeuer fhall aduifedlie practife by the helpe of this glas, may in one moneths fpace be able to drawe any patterne by hand onely, without praying in aide of the fame any more. So likewife it is poffible by waie of reflexion, for any man to behold in a looking glaffe, and that alfo in his priuate ftudie, al the geftures and actions whatfoeuer any perfonne fhall make or performe, in any roome or corner of his houfe, as alfo to fee euen in the bottome of his feller, whatfoeuer is done vpon the top of Paules fteeple, or any other fteeple within London, fo as his dwelling bee within the Citie or the Liberties therof, or within any competent

Art and Nature.

petent number of miles distant from the same. But because I doo see that euerie Author is in danger to be censured according to the particular iudgement of euery Reader, and because *Stultorum plena sunt omnia*, I will not extend the credit of this secret to his vttermost bounds, but this shall bee sufficient for the weake faith that reigneth in the world at this time.

38. *Some helpes for the speeditr and true making and breaking of any letter, as also how a learner may write straight, and giue some prettie grace vnto his letters.*

FOr the speedier attaining to any written hand, let some perfect wrighting maister, (and I knowe not whom I should heere commende before mine olde Schoolemaister, Maister *Conradus*, that teacheth oueragainst saint *Anthonies* schoole) deliuer a few copies written, or rather broken in this manner. Let him diuide or breake each letter into so many partes, as he hath cause to make any little pause or addition before hee finish the same, which is nothing else but the vndooing & disioining of the same, that a yong scholler may the better see, which waie the same was made vp and brought togither. As for example, the Secretarie small a, hath six partes before it bee made vppe, the b. c. and d. haue foure and some more, and some lesse, and for the better vnderstanding of my whole meaning, I would haue caused the whole Al-

H phabet

phabet to haue beene cut, and so printed in this manner, but that I could not staie the doing of it, and also
for that I knew, that maister *Conradus* will sufficiently
performe the same with his pen, to any that shall bee
willing to requite his paines; and hee hath alreadie
written some such coppies for my children. Also it
giueth a great grace to your writing, if the whites of
certeine letters bee made of one equall bignesse with
the o. supposing the same were all round, as the white
of the b. of the a. p. y. v. w. x. q. d. g. and s. And for
the writing straight, and true breaking of the letters,
cause a paper to bee ruled all ouer, with great lines,
drawne with a text penne, vpon which ruled paper,
you must laie a leafe of the finest paper that can bee
gotten, such as they doe commonlie sell for two shillings, foure pence the queere, and let the scholler
write vpon the shadowe of the text lines, or else if the
neather paper be ruled full of small lines, when hee
writeth vpon the fine paper, let him haue care, that
those small lines may cut or deuide all those letters
which he maketh, in the middest, and hee shall finde
great vse thereof. Some draw the letters first in black
lead or red inke, and then let their scholler run ouer
them with blacke inke, till they haue brought their
hande in vre with the shape and fashion of the Letters. There is no doubt, but that some willing and
carefull Schollers will finde some of these helpes, as
good as the Ace of heartes in their wrighting, thogh
other heedelesse Drones, will scarce make the Ace
of Diamondes of the best meanes that any maister
or Teacher shall discouer.

Art and Nature. 43

39. A Gall water very necessarie to mingle with your Inke, as it groweth thick in your standish or inkhorne.

Slice or beat some of the best Galles, and put them in a glasse of faire water, and when they haue giuen some reasonable tincture to the water, you may mix the same with your inke as it thickneth: this is a more kindlie waie, then to vse either faire water, beere, or vineger in stead thereof. But when the water beginneth to be ouer olde and out of date, you must then throw away the same and make fresh.

40. How to renew olde letters, that be almost worn out of sight.

THis is performed by rubbing them ouer carefully with the gall water aforesaid being wel prepared, for that will strike a fresh hew again into the old and outworne Coppres. These two secrets I learned verie lately of a skilful & well conceipted gentleman, who hath made some practises thereof himselfe, and the first I can warrant by mine owne triall.

41. How to speake by signes only without the vttering of any word.

DEuise 24. signes, whereof euerie one may represent some one of the 24. letters, but place your vowels for the more readines in this maner, First A. vpon the tip of your thumb on the left hand: E. vpon ỹ tip of your forefinger on the same hand, & so of the rest, so as when you lay the *index* or forfinger of your

H 2 right

right hand on the tip of your thumb on the left hand, the party with whom you shal conferre in this maner may alwaies note the same for an A. the rest of the letters which be consonants, may be vnderstood by touching of seueral parts of your body, or seueral gestures, countenances, or actions, as an heire for a B. a crosse made on the forehead for a C. a phillip for a D. and so of the rest. I haue seene a gentleman togither with a gentlewomā that were very ready in their conceited alphabet, to deliuer their mindes each to other in this manner, when as not any of the standers by vnderstood either word or letter of their meaning. And I hold the same a necessarie arte to be practised of such as doo naturallie lacke their speech, whereby they may be vnderstood of others, which otherwise could haue no mutual conference with them.

42 How to paint or limne with the colours that are taken from hearbs or flowers.

Some drie the leaues of hearbes or flowers, which carrie any deep colour in them, and if there be seuerall colours vpon one leafe, they deuide them, and keep each colour by it self, grinding the same vpon a Marble, and after keepe it in close glasses or leaded pots, sufficiently defended from the aire. If you grind the leaues of a white rose with a little Allome, it will giue a yellow colour, and so wil the purple part of the leafe of the flower deluce, ground with a little lime, yeeld a good and perfect greene. Some expresse the iuice of herbs or flowers, and then euaporat either in balneo or in the sun so much as wil ascend, spreding ỹ rest thinly vpō the bottoms & sides of small dishes, & after, then set ỹ same in the sun to dry, & then grind it

with

with gumme water as they haue cause to vse it. Some vse the moist, and some the drie leafe with faire water, and so soone as the beautiful hew of the leaues begin to vade, they draine away the water, and make an addition of fresh leaues thereunto, and so change their leaues often, that they may purchase to themselues nothing else but the liuelie and bright tincture of euerie hearbe or flower. Those two colours of the Rose, & Flower-deluce I learned of master Bateman sometime the person of Newington a most excellent lymner.

43 A readie way for children to learne their A B C.

Cause 4. large dice of bone or wood to bee made, and vpon euerie square, one of the small letters of the crosse row to be grauen, but in some bigger shape and the child vsing to play much with them, and being alwayes tolde what letter chaunceth, wil soone gaine his Alphabet, as it were by the way of sport or pastime. I haue hearde of a pair of cards, wheron most of the principall Grammer rules haue been printed, and the schoolmaster hath found good sport thereat with his scholers.

44 To graue and inlay colours into Sol, Luna, Mars, or Venus, to shew in the nature of an Ammel.

First couer your mettall with a crust of waxe, and with a fine sharpe toole when the same is cold, cut out the shape or proportion of what letters or other portraiportrature you please, and of some reasonable largenesse, then poure some strong water in those emptie places, and when you find them deep inough grauen, mingle Orpiment and Masticke melted togither for a yellow colour, and Vermillion with Masticke for a red, and so of all other colours. Now when your Mastick hath bin molten together with any of the aforesaid colours, let it coole, and beat the same into powder, and lay of that powder within the grauing, & after lay the mettal vpon the fire, til the mastick melt, & it will remain fast and firme therein a long time. This of a Iew that yet liueth for ought that I know.

45 To make bad paper to beare ynke in some reasonable manner.

RVb your paper wel ouer with the fine powder or dust of Rosen and Sandrach mingled in equall parts before you write therwith. Note that you must tie the powder hard in a rag of Laune or thin Cambrick, and therewith rub the paper throughly well. This is a necessarie secret for students, whereby they may note in the margentes of their bookes if the paper should happen to sinke, which is an especiall fault in many of our late yeere bookes of the Law.

46 To make an egge to stande vpon an ende without anie helpe at all.

THere is an olde tale of a good workeman who made an egge to stand in salt vpon an ende, but here the same is more artly performed, and yet without any such supportation. Holde an egge in your right hande, and with your fist giue three or foure good strong blowes vppon your lefte arme, or
vse

Art and Nature

vse anie other deuise by agitation or shaking, vntill you haue broken the yolke, and so made the white to mingle confusedly with it, and then it will presently stand vpon the broad end on an euen table. It should seeme that before the breaking of the yolke, that the yolke did hang playing or totteting within the white, whereby the egge could not be made to stande speedilie without this deuise. And yet I heard a Gentleman whom I dare beleeue in a greater matter than this, affirme that hee hath diuerse times caused an egge to stande alone by peyzing it to and fro betweene his handes, till in the ende it stoode vpright without anie other helpe. But the first is the readier way.

47 To harden the white of an egge into an artificiall gum

BEate the whites of diuerse egges into a thinne and cleare Oyle or water, put the same into bladders, and hang them in your kitchin Chimney where a fire is vsually kept in the day time, and in a few dayes the same will become as hard as gum Arabicke. This I haue often proued. Some performe the same in the Sun onely. Qre to what vse this gum will serue.

Multa ouorum albumina simul exagitabis, ih vesicam impleas, inde in ollam aquæ plenam feruentis immittas, ac diu coqui sinas, detrahe, & per nonnullos dies desiccari curabis loco tamen non puluerulento, & sic lapidescit vt in vitri duritiem transeat. Vide vesicam in bro. de secret. fol. 53. aut Iean Baptist. Portam. locis istius secreti.

Heere wee may note the diuerse and sundrie effects wrought by the seuerall degrees of fyre. We see a continuall whote fire dooth roast an egge till it it become extreeme hard, but yet the nature of foode remaining, an intermissiue heat bringeth forth a gum altogither vnfit for nourishment, and a gentle or natural heat engendereth a chicken that is good meat, but not before it hath receiued some alteration by an outward and elementall heat. I will not vrge this philosophicall point of fire any further, only I wish that he that is a true maister of this element, were my maister also for a time.

48. *A cheape Candle or Lampe for the poorer sort to vse in their howses.*

Dip Candleweeke in molten rosen, then wet your hands in water, and after you haue dipped euery weeke, you must stretch it out at length, or streighten it betweene your fingers, and so lay them to coole vpon a halfpace or floore of stone. I thinke the refuse of olde ropes and cordage would be a very profitable weeke for this purpose. This conclusion although it haue beene in some sort already published by meane persons both in towne and countrie, and giuen ouer by the inconueniance of the excessiue smoke onely which annoieth the whole room exceedingly wherin it burneth, yet mee thinkes that during the deare price of tallow candles, the poore might make some shift or other with them, as either by setting the candle within the Chimney, or else in a Candlesticke ouer the mantletree with a large wide tunnell made of wicker, and couered with paper, and hauing an elbow which might passe through some large hole into the chimney whereby the smoke may be auoided. These candles I know will not exceed halfe the price of the woorst weeke candles that are to bee boughts,

But

But for those that can content themselues with the light of a Lampe (and I am sure the same will serue for watching Candles, and yet bee much easier in price) let them buy Rape Oyle, which for the moste part is to bee had after two shillinges the Gallon, and therwith maintaine their Lamps, vsing a small weeke of a fewe foldes onelie, or rather a Candle-rush in the Socket of their Lampe, and so they shall finde that one pint of oile wil last them an hundred hours, whereas a pound of watching candles will bee spent in threescore, or threescore & ten houres at the most, and yet they are dearer by one pennie in the pound. Note that the weeke or rush must stande a little sloping in the nose of your Lampe. Or if you would vse your Lampe in steade of a watching candle, and to maintaine a light onely, then may you take a prettie large beere Glasse, placing your weeke vpon a wier, being platted like a trefoile in the bottom, the wier it selfe being first thrust through a litle round flat peece of Leade of the bignesse of a two pennie peece of siluer, to make it stande the steddier. The weeke must be fastened to the wier with a thred of Cotten losely bound about it. When you haue placed this weeke in the middest, then poure in either oile or suet round about it, and so kindle your Lampe, and it will giue some light also through the Glasse. Note that your Glasse may not be too large, least that the week grow to a cole before the Oyle can consume away fast inough to giue it passage vnto fresh weeke thereby to maintaine his light the better. But if you woulde haue your Lampe to last the longer, but to giue no light at the sides, nor greatly at the toppe, then set your Glasse in a deepe Bason or potte of water, thereby to keepe the Oyle the cooler, and so it will

I   also

also last the longer. And it is not amisse, nay it is verie requisite to put in some water into your Glasse before you put in the Oyle, thereby to keepe the oile from burning. Neither can I heere omit or passe ouer in silence that one more speciall vse of a Lampe than anie Candle can affoorde, which is the safetie of your light from beeing caryed to and fro in the nighttime with Rattes and Mise, which haue oftentymes set Mattes on fire with the flame of a Candle as they haue sought to conuey it into their Nestes. Neither woulde I willingly studie by anie other Candle, because it continueth so long in one equall light, without giuing that offence to the eye which the Candle dooth by his present blaze after it is newlie topped, and by his dimnesse if it bee not often topped; If it were possible to haue store of that Oyle of Beech-maste (which a late Writer dooth vndertake to produce in great quantitie from the Nutte, and which I haue knowne expressed in England, but not with such yeelde, the difference whereof maie peraduenture bee found in the distinct natures of the English and the Naple Nut) or of that *Oleũ Palmæ*, which is taken at this daye to bee the Oile that issueth out of the Date tree, the burning whereof is most sweete and delicate in a Lampe, as I can testifie by the triall of sundrie nightes wherein I vsed no other watching Candle in my bedde Chamber. Let this suffice to haue spoken of Lampes for this time, and vntill I may obtaine more leysure and more libertie to lighten a newe Lampe that will giue more light then a Cresset in some of the darkest corners of this lande.

Art and Nature.

49 Howe to refresh the colours of olde peeces that bee wrought in oyle.

Some vse to beate the dust off them with a Foxe taile, or with a brush of feathers, and after rubbing them ouer with a Spunge and warme Vrine. This way was commended vnto mee by master Bateman, sometime parson of Newington, a man whom for diuerse good partes that were in him, I can neuer sufficiently commend. Others rubbe them ouer lightly first with a Spunge and faire water, and after there commeth no more soile then with a spunge and good old Linseed oile, wherin somtimes for the speedier drying they do put some burnt Alom or powder of glasse finelie ground. Some do vse first to wash ouer the pictures with sope, and presently after they be drie to vernish them ouer. Note y̌ all this is intended in pictures not vernished before. *Vide postea, num. 72.*

50 An excellent cement for broken Glasses.

Take one part of Virgin-wax, and two parts of the teares or cleare drops of Masticke, and cement therwith. But the better way is if you beat the whitest fishglew you can get with a hammer till it begin to waxe cleare, and then cut the same into verie small and short peeces, suffring the same to dissolue vpon a gentle fire in a little leaded pan with a fewe drops of *Aquavita*. Then let some other that standeth by, hold both the peeces y̌ are to be cemented ouer a chafing-dish of coles till they be warme, & during their heat lay on the dissolued glew with a fine pensil, then bind the glasse with wier or packthred, & let it rest till it be cold:

The Iewel-house of

colde. With this cement I did see a Dutch Ieweller (dwelling then in the Blackfriers, but since departed this world) cement two of her Maiesties christal cups that were broke. Some comend vnsleakt lime, wheat floure, and the white of an egge. Others like fishglew, with *Aqua vitæ* and Ceruse, or with the teares of Masticke, *Aqua vitæ*, and Ceruse. A singular workeman did highly commende vnto mee Rennish wine, and Isinglasse or fishglew for this purpose.

51 How to drie gunpowder without all danger of fire.

Although I do not hold this for any great secrete, yet becauſe there hath much miſchiefe & ſpoile of men happened onely by the retchleſſe drying of powder, I haue thought it requiſite and neceſſarie in that reſpect, and for the preuention of all daungers to come, to publiſh the ſame. Cauſe then a veſſell either of Lead, Pewter, Latten, or Copper to be made, hauing a double bottome, betweene which bottomes you maie conuey ſcalding water at a pipe, which water may alſo bee heated in another roome, for the more ſafetie agaynſt the fire, and then you may lay your powder vpon the vppermoſt bottome till it bee drie, and when the water beginneth to coole, you may let it out at a Cocke in the bottome of the Veſſell, and ſo giue paſſage for more ſcalding water into the Veſſell by an other Cocke which may be faſtened in the pipe that runneth into the veſſell. Or hauing a little pipe in the ſide, you may from time to time with a funnell poure in ſcalding water at your pleaſure, & this is done both with leſſe coſt, and alſo leſſe circumſtance. I do vſe when I would dry my powder in haſt, to heat a fireſhouel by diſcretiõ, & thẽ

I lay

Art and Nature.

I lay a paper thereon a prettie while, and if I see that the paper burne not nor take fire, then I doe spreade my powder vpon the paper, stirring it vp and downe till it leaue smoking. And this I haue alwaies found to be a verie readie and a safe way. Some dry their powder in a stoue, where no fire can come neere to endaunger it.

52. To draw Fish to a certaine place in the night time, by a light or candle.

PVt so much filed lead into an vrinall as will make it sinke, and vpon the lead strew some hearbes, and vpon those hearbs some glo-worms, couer the glasse with a corke and lute it well, and about the necke of the vrinall tie a string, which must bee put through a great corke that may keepe the vrinall swimming in the water at what deapth you please. Note that with some pipe or quill, you must conuey some ayre into the glasse, for else the glo-wormes will die, and then I thinke their shining brightnesse will vanish awaie, and therefore those perpetuall lights are meerelie fabulous and fantasticall that are drawne from these distilled wormes and Mercurie togither. Some nip or lute a glasse hauing crude Mercurie therein, and so hang it in the water as before. Also a candle helde either euen with the water, or sunke a little way into the water, will amaze and drawe the fishes vnto it, so as if you haue a little hoope net, vpon the ende of a cane or pole, you may easilie take them, and bring them to the brinke-side. All these experimentes are best performed in a darke night.

53. A Bait to catch fish with.

TO halfe a hotte halfe penie white loafe, take one ounce of Cocle seed (*Qre*, if *Coculus indiæ* be not better) one ounce of Henbane seed finely powdered, temper the same wel with strong *Aqua composita* into a past, then diuide your past into small peeces, of the bignesse of a graine of wheate, and cast in a handefull of them at once, somwhat aboue the place where the fish doe haunt, if it be in a riuer. This serueth especiallie when you see the fish to flote, but for the cheuen you must make your baites as big as cherrie stones, and put them in little coffins of paper, & then throw them vpon the water. This secret I haue not proued.

54. How to driue fish into a Tramell.

PItch a tramell ouerthwart a riuer where there is good store of fishe, then goe vpwarde against the streame a prettie waie from the net, and as you come downeward againe with the streame, throw in some lime stones here and there dispersedlie, on both the sides of the riuer. These vnflaked limestones wil make such a crackling in the water, that no fish dare return backe againe vpon them, but will run forwarde and mash themselues in the tramell. This *I* had of *Iohn Hester*, one of the most auncient chimists of my time in London, in exchange of one other secret which I disclosed vnto him. Yet some be of opinion, that you must hurle in whole handfuls at once now and then, whereby the fish hearing so great a noise, and tasting the strength thereof in the water, may bee the more affrighted.

55. Diuers good baites to catch fish with.

Fill

Fill a sheepes gut with smal vnsleakt limestones, and tie the same well at both endes, that no water get therein, and if any pike deuoure it (as they are rauening fish and verie likelie to doe) she dieth in a short time, you may fasten it to a string if you please, and so let it flote vpon the water. Also the liuer of euery fish is a good baite to catch any fish of the same kind. Past made of vvheate flower, a little saffron and some suger, and tempered with water, is a good baite to angle withall for roche, dase, &c. Also if you gather dunghill wormes, or from vnder a block, and take the earth from them, and put them into fine clean mosse, suffering them to scowre themselues three or foure daies therein, the fysh will bite the better at them.

56. A readie waie to catch Pigeons, and other great birdes.

Make small coffyns of paper, (such as the Confitmakers vse to put their confites in) not exceeding the length of ones finger, past the sides & endes with some starch, clip the vpper part of them round with a paire of sheeres, then annoint the inside of the vppermost skirts of them round about with birdlime in the forme of a ring, and after you haue procured the pigeons to haunt a place, by making of a shrap a day or two before, lay of these coffyns heere & there with a few peason in euerie one of them a little sloping or declining, and strewe some other peason amongst them. And when the Pigeon pecketh at the pease within the coffyn, shee is immediatlie masked or hooded, not seeing which waye to flie. And so you shall fynde verie good sport, and take them easilie.

57.

57. A Worme to catch birds with.

THere is a great opinion conceiued of a Worme that hath many feet, and is found in a horse-mill, where corne is ground, most commonlie vnder the ground where the horse treadeth, and is exceeding sweet, place this worme with lime twigs about her, where she may be seen, and you shal soone take birds therewith. But I take this rather to bee the worme wherein the Nightingale dooeth so much delight, which is found in a mil-case, or where Bakers vse to boult their meale.

58. How to catch Pigeons, Crowes, Iacke-dawes, and Magpies.

FOr the taking of pigeons, you must make a shrap three or foure daies together, laying lose lines amongest the pease vntill the Doues bee acquainted therwith, then in som euening tie at those lines great store of strings, which with a needle before, you must thrust through the pease, being first sodden softe for the purpose, and at the end of euery string tie a little knot, when a pigeon hath swallowed downe one of these pease, together with the string, she cannot possiblie get it vp againe, but she is easilie taken. Perhaps some other birdes may also be taken in this manner. It is not amisse to hide the threeds neare the pease with grasse, earth or straw, or some such like matter. Also if you throw gobbets of flesh or cheese curds abroad in the fieldes where there be store of Rookes, Crowes, Dawes, or Magpies, within the which there is conueied some of the powder of *Arsenicke* or
subli-

Art and Nature.

sublimate, you shall soone dispatch your barnes and other Garners of corn, of al these wastfull birds. But take heed that none of your hogges doo eat of these dead birds, least they happen to poison them also.

59. How to kil Seapies, Seaguls, & other rauening waterfowle.

Some be of opinion that if in the winter time, you doe streine ouerthwart a riuer or brooke, where fowle doe haunt, some strong line or whipcorde, at the which you may also hang diuers other smaller threads, baited with garbage vpon hookes, of an apt size for them, that so they will hang themselues, and be easily taken. Also for the taking of store of seapies, you may lime some twigs which may be fastened at small fishes, and then laie the same vpon large leaues, so as the lime touch not the water, and the sea pie striking at the fish is taken with the lime twigs. And hauing taken one or twoe of them, then clippe their winges and so leaue them in the water, and all the seapies thereabout that are within hearing, wil come to helpe them, and continuallie flie houering ouer them, so as hauing your peeces charged you may discharge at the whole flocke as fast as you can charge, for they wil not be driuen awaie.

60. How to gather great store of Waspes together, so as you may destroy them all.

Some honie put into a pipkin, and the same placed ouer a gentle fire, the windowes of the roome being set open, will by the sent and vapour thereof, draw all the Waspes that are neere the place within

K   any

The Jewell-house of

any reasonable compasse, into the roome where you haue bestowed the pot. Note that this must be done in an apt season of the yeare, when as there bee store of waspes, and in some place where they haunt greatlie. Also the waspes will soone resort to an earthen pot, wherein there is some raw flesh, and when you haue drawne some store of them together into the pot, then couer it and set it on the fire vntill you haue destroyed them all. This latter secret I hadde out of *Cardanus de rerum varietate, pag. 294.* but the first is more naturall and commaundeth farther off. Also if you set store of iarre glasses in your Orchard, and about your house, where you see the greatest haunt of them, with some decoction of honie and water, or water and suger, or any other sweet wine or composition in them, leauing these pottes or glasses three partes emptie, they will not forsake these sweete liquors, vntill they haue drowned themselues therein.

61. How to keepe garments of cloth, or hanginges of Tapistrie, Dornickes, Saie, &c. from mouth-eating.

BRush your apparell with an ordinarie brush, and so likwise your hangings, or else you may vse a brush made of a figge frale, vntill you haue gotten all the dust out of them, then brush them ouer throughlie wel twice or thrice euerie yeare as they hang, with a brush made of wormwood tops. And yet I thinke it to be the surer waie, if they were also wel rubbed with wormewood on the backsides. I haue heard that it is an vsuall practise amongst the Italians here in England in summer time to cause great store of Walnut tree leaues to be hoong vpon a thread, so as one may

not

Art and Nature.

not touch another, and when they are throughlie drie, then strewe them in their Chestes and Presses, amongst their cloathes and other furniture of their chambers and beds, and within the seuerall foldes of euery garment.

62. To helpe beere that beginneth to soure or is dead.

Some put a handfull or two of ground malt into a barrell of beere, and stir the same and the beere wel together, and so make it to worke afresh and become good againe. Some do burie sower beere 24. houres in the earth, and thereby recouer it. Others adde new strong beere to the old, and so the dead beere is forced sometimes to worke againe to a new head. Some fetch it againe with chalke or lime, and some with Oyster-shels, and some throw a handfull of salt into a barrell of dead beere. A Ladie in this lande hath alwaies vsed to put in a handful of ote-meale into euery barrell of beere, when it was first laide into her seller, whereby hir drink did alwaies carrie with it a quicke and a liuely tast. It is also very good to tilt your beere, when the vessel is little more then halfe drawn off, for so you shall draw your beere good euen to the latter end.

63. To helpe a chimney that is on fire, presentlie.

When you see the chimny on fire, forthwith get a large thick blanket or couerlet, and with y help of twoe or three persons, let the same bee held close both aboue and below vnto the mouth of the chimney, so as no ayre may enter, and if you canne come easilie to the toppe of the Chimney, couer the same close also, either with a fitte boorde, or else

The Jewell-house of

with wet woollen cloaths, & so the fire wanting aire wil presentlie go out and be smothered.

64. To haue store of Seafish for the prouision of ones table, without repairing to the sea for them.

SYr *Edward Hobbie* (as I haue heard) hath stored certeine dikes in the Ile of Sheppey, with sundrie kindes of Sea-fish, into which dikes by sluces, he doth let in from time to time, change of sea-water to nourish them.

65. To make ale or beere to become stale in a short time.

BOttle ale, or bottle beere, being buried somewhat deepe in the ground, in a coole or shadie place, becommeth stale enough to bee drunke in 48. howers space, as I haue beene assured by an honest and sober Courtier.

66. How to steale Bees.

IF you place a Bee-hiue somwhat before swarming time in the midest of a great beech tree, so close as that it may not be discerned for feare of stealing, the Bees wil resort vnto the same, especiallie if it bee first wel sprinkled within with water and honie.

67. How to make a tallowe candle to last much longer, then it doth in our vsuall manner.

A *Neopolitane* hath written, that salt mingled with oile will make it to double his lasting, but I thinke the practiser herof wil find it somwhat troblesome to make a good solucion of salt in oile. For oile is an improper subiect to reteine salt. I haue heard an Irish practici-

Art and Nature. 61

practitioner affirme, that if tallow candles be made about Alhallontide of good stuffe, and presently laide in colde water by the space of 24. houres together, and then hung vp to drie in a coole and windie place vpon their stickes, that by this meanes onely they will last much longer than otherwise they would, and burne also much sweeter. But I am sure that if there be a true counterpeize giuen to a short tallow candle, (such as is vsually called the Goldsmiths candle) and the same afterwards let down betweene ones fingers into the midst of a pale or tub of water, so carefully, as that the flame be not extinguished in letting the same fall into the water, it wil last as long as two candles of the same length and bignesse, alwayes supporting it selfe aboue the water, by a thin crust or webbe, which it worketh about the flame in the nature of Camphire, which continueth his burning in the water (being once set on fire) vntill it haue wrought a passage or entrie for the water into it selfe.

68 How to tell the iust number of Apples, Nuts, Shillings, &c. as they lie in bulcke togither, how great so euer the heape be.

CAuse the owner of them to dispose of the whole heape in this maner. First will him to lay downe two, then let him double that number likewise, and so continue in the rule of duplation vntill Hee can double no longer, laying all the odde ones apart by themselues, then shall you easily ghesse by the present view of the whole number, how many there are in the whole heape. For either they must be 2. 4. 8. 16. 32. 64. 128. &c. and which of these numbers soeuer it bee, euery reasonable eye will ghesse, the bulk of the one number dooth so much surmount the o-

K 3 ther.

The Jewel-house of

ther. The like also may be done in trebling, and now and then doubling or trebling, the more to obscure the conceipt.

69 *How to preuent drunkennesse.*

DRinke first a good large draught of Sallet Oyle, for that will floate vpon the Wine which you shall drinke, and suppresse the spirites from ascending into the braine. Also what quantitie soeuer of newe milke you drinke first, you may well drinke thrise as much wine after, without daunger of being drunke. But howe sicke you shall bee with this preuention, I will not heere determine, neither woulde I haue set downe this experiment, but onely for the helpe of such modest drinkers as sometimes in companie are drawne, or rather forced to pledge in full bolles such quaffing cōpanions as they would be loth to offend, and wil require reason at their hands as they terme it.

70 *An excellent tent for a Diamond.*

BVrne Iuorie in a crusible or melting potte, being close luted, into a blacke powder, then take a little of the fine powder thereof, and mingle it with a few drops of the exrtacted Oyle of Masticke, and in the setting of the stone you must haue care that it touch not the tent.

91 *How to make Oile or Vernish to drie speedily.*

THis is done first by boyling of the oile to the consumption of the one halfe, or one third thereof, and then by the putting in the ashes of the backbones of Shads or Mackerell. Also diuerse Shaddes

heades

Art and Nature. 63

heades dried in the winde, and hung vp in a darke place, will glister like Glow-wormes.

72 A strong Lee that will fetch out any steyne as also refresh an olde Oyle Picture, and make it verie faire againe.

TAke of the ashes of the Vine one handfull, of white coppres and burnt allom of each the quantitie of halfe a Walnut, put thereto a pint of conduit water, infuse the same vpon the said substances in an Ipocras bagge, & reiterate the water vpon them 4. or 5. times till it grow verie strong, set the said water on the fire, and put thereto the quantitie of an hasill nut of good Sope, then take the saide Lee so hote as you may well endure your hande therein, and after you haue taken off the dust from the picture with some brush or foxe taile: rub ouer the picture with a splinge till it come to a good lustre with the said Lee, and when the colours please you, then with faire water wash off the said Lee againe, and the peece or picture though neuer so olde will become verie fresh. *Qre.* if this secrete do not onely extend to such oile peeces as are not vernished. Some rub ouer pictures or Tables with an Onion cut through the midst. This secrete with the preceedent I had of a Dutch mountbanke, aud they came so hardly from him as if hee had beene extreemly costiffe. *Vide antea. num. 49.*

73 To helpe Wine that reboileth.

IF anie sweete Wines happen to reboile in the hot part of the Summer (as I haue often seene, and as manie Vinteners to their great losse haue oftentimes

times felt) then Placentius willeth a little peece or cantle of Cheese to be put into the vessell, and presently a strange effect will follow. *Hoc ex anchora famis & sitis.* I beleeue that the corporation of Vintners would giue twentie pound yearely to haue this secrete warranted to bee true. For the best remedy which they haue, is to draw the wine of from the lee into other cleane caske, thereby perswading themselues to coole the wine, and to stay the boyling thereof. But after a while the inward fire oftentimes beginneth a fresh workmanship, and frustrateth all their labour. I would esteeme him for a learned Vintner, and worthie to haue the next auoydance of Bacchus his chaire, that could giue me the true reason of this reboyling of wines. But because I haue allotted so great a place of honour to him that can but shewe the reason onely thereof, therefore I will not presume nor professe to knowe the cause efficient, but I durst vndertake to perfourme the remedie, if I thought my rewarde would not bee somewhat like vnto his, that within this few yeares taught diuerse of the companie how to draw out of a Hogges-head of wine lees, 10 gallons of cleare wine at the least, which beeing trickt, or compassed, or at the least mingled with other wine, hath euer since by diuerse Vintners beene retailed for wine, whereas before it was wholie solde for lees to the *Aqua vitæ* men. And this is the reason why there hath neuer since been the like store of lees to make *Aqua vitæ* of, as before the discouerie of this conceit, and that the lees of many Cellors which before were liquid, are now become stiffe like paste, and may verie well be wrought vp into the forme of bals. And if I be not deceiued, the first practize thereof began in Pater noster row, and within these few yeares,

but I

but I feare by this time, it is a parcell of manie mens Creedo that wil neuer be left til the worlds end. Wel, the poore fellow got hardly a good sute of apparell amongst diuerse of them to whom hee disclosed the secrete, although some one of them could tell which way presently to raise 30 or 40.li. *per annū* vnto themselues. And therefore I see it is no offring of skill in these dayes to Vintners. But the better course were to take a Tauerne and get a Hollibush if France were more open, and a litle more freed of the excessiue impost, and so to draw wines as artificially as the best of them. For I can assure you I haue almost the whole art as it is this day in vse amongest the Vintners, written in a prettie volume entituled, *Secreta dei pampinei*. And if I durst here so boldly as I could, both truly & largely write of those iumbling sleights, that are too often practized in our naturall wines by some of the Coopers of London, to the great benefite of the Marchant and Vintner, although themselues, poore soules, get nothing thereby but the hooping of the vessels, and now and then a Can of wine for their labours, a man would wonder from whence such great varietie of iugling should growe or spring, and howe these plaine fellowes that neuer read their Grammer, nay scarcely know their A,B,C, should be able to run through Ouids Metamorphosis as they doe at midnight. And yet I cannot altogither blame either the Cooper, or the Vintners man for practising of these alterations, transmutations, and sometimes euen real transubstantiations, of white wine into Claret, & old lags of Sacks or Malmesies, with malassoes into Muskadels. For we are growne so nice in taste, that almost no wines vnlesse they be more pleasant than they can bee of the Grape will content vs; nay no colour vnlesse it bee perfect, fine and bright, will satisfie our wanton eyes, whereupon (as I haue beene creedibly enformed by some that haue seene the practize in Spaine) they are forced euen there to enterlace now and then a lay of Lime with the Sacke grape in the expression thereby to bring their Sackes to bee of a more white colour into England then is naturall vnto them, or then the Spaniardes themselues will brooke or endure, who will drinke no other Sackes them such as be of an Amber colour. This makes the Vintners to tricke or compasse all their natural wines if they bee a little hard, with Bastarde to make them sweeter, if they pricke a little they haue a decoction of honie with a few Cloues to deceiue the taste; if they be clowdie or not perfect fine, they giue them either the white or the yellow parrell, according to the naturall colour of the Wines, wherein they must vse Egges, Milke, Baysalt, & Conduit water well beaten and laboured together with a stubbed rodde, and then wrought soundlie together with a parrelling staffe, which parrell for the most part in one night (vnlesse the Wines happen to haue a flickering Lee) will cause them to fine, whereby you may presently drawe at certaine. But this is daungerous vnlesse it bee in a house well customed, for that the Wine may not lie too long vpon his parell. And some Wines will not endure long after you haue racked them from their parell. Note the wholesomnesse of these Lees to make *Aqua vitæ* withall. But when the Wines doe rope or beginne to faile or faint in themselues, either in substaunce or in colour, either by age, by the fault of Caske, soyle, salt water, or other accident, then manie tymes the Vintener is driuen to his hard shiftes, and then

hee

hee helpeth himselfe with Allome, with Turnsole, Starch, and with manie other Drugges, and aromaticall ware which hee fetcheth from the Apothecarie, the particulars whereof I coulde set downe and applie euen as they haue beene a long time (till within these fewe yeeres.) practized in one of the most autentique Tauernes of my time. But my purpose is onely to put some in minde of their grosse night-woorkes which discouer themselues by Candlelight at their Celler Windowes, whishing them to leaue all vnwholesome practizes for mans bodie, least if they shoulde heereafter against my will force mee to publish them to the worlde, I shoulde drawe my Countrey men into such a liking of our Royston Grape, that in the ende they woulde for the most part content themselues with their English and naturall drinke, without raunging so farre for forreine Wines.

74 The making of a Bragget, which is manie times mistaken for a Muskadell by the simple sort of people.

PVt one part of smal Alewoort that is blood warm with one part of clarified Honie according to the maner set downe num. 75. but put no Cloues therein in the clarifying. For the making of one Hogesheade of this Bragget which is aboute 63. Gallons, you must take nine Gallons of this clarified Honie, and 54. gallons of strong new ale: when your clarified hony hath stood one day, then mingle the same with your newe *Ale* in a Hogshead, first filling your Hogshead halfe full before you put in your honie, and then hang this aromaticall cōposition following in a long slender bag in the midst of the vessell vz. of Cinamon three ounces, ginger three ounces, grains 3. ounces, colianders one ounce, cloues one ounce, nutmegs one ounce, long pepper halfe an ounce, *Cardamomum* one ounce and a halfe, liquerice one ounce, then fil vp the vessell almost full with the rest of the new ale (yet some commend rather the putting in of the spices confusedlie then in a bag) bee sure to haue foure or fiue gallons or more of the same newe ale, to fill vp the hogshead as it purgeth ouer continuallie. There is a lesser hole neere the bung hole in beere hogsheads, which must stande open whilest it purgeth, you must also be carefull in the beginning to giue some little vent to the hogshead whilst it worketh: in three or foure moneths, it will bee readie to drinke. You must haue a hazell sticke of the bignesse of a good cudgell, so great as may well enter in at the round bung-hole, and when your hogshead is about three quarters full, put in this stick, being sawed croswise at the end about one cubite in length, (the Vintners call it their parrelling staffe) as the aptest toole for this purpose. Beat with the said staffe the new ale and the honie togither a good prettie while, & when you haue finished this agitation, fill vp the vessel with the rest, and let it purge as before. If you finde your muscadell too thicke, after it hath stood 3. or 4. monethes, you may take a cane or pipe, made of Tinne plates, that will reach into the midst of the hogshead or somewhat more, stop the ende thereof and make some holes in the sides, and with a funnell you may poure more newe ale into the Cane, and so make it thinner. This Cane is an apt instrument to conueie any liquor or composition into a vessell of wine without troubling of the same, or turning vppe the lees,

wherby

whereby you may draw the same fine presently.

75 Howe to clarifie honie so that the taste thereof shall be much altered.

PVt a gallon of water blood-warme to a gallon of honie, put in your honie first, and with a sticke take the depth thereof in the vessell wherein you boile it, and then put halfe an ounce of beaten cloues bound in a linnen cloth therein, and let them boile with the water and honie on a gentle fire till all the water bee consumed, which you shall ghesse at by the marke on the sticke. Your hony must be pure and simple not mingled with woort, flowre, or other bad composition, euen as it is gathered vpon the breaking vp of the hiues. It is a worke of two or three hours, and the elder the honie is the better it serueth for this purpose. You must remember to take away the skum as it riseth. Som boile this honie a little higher to a more consistencie, and preserue fruit therewith in stead of sugar. These two receits I had of an Oxeford scholler, who assured me that hee had often made proofe therof in the Citie of Oxford, and I know the man to be both of good conceipt, and verie carefull in the commendation of any secrete to his friend otherwise then may well stand with his owne credite.

76 A Receipt for the making of an artificiall Malmesey.

TAke four gallons of conduit water, into the which put one gallon of good English honie, stirre the honie well till it be dissolued in the water, set this water in a copper pan vpon a gentle fire, & as there ariseth

times felt) then Placentius willeth a little peece or cantle of Cheese to be put into the vessell, and presently a strange effect will follow. *Hoc ex anchora famis & sitis.* I beleeue that the corporation of Vintners would giue twentie pound yearely to haue this secrete warranted to bee true. For the best remedy which they haue, is to draw the wine of from the lee into other cleane caske, thereby perswading themselues to coole the wine, and to stay the boyling therof. But after a while the inward fire oftentimes beginneth a fresh workmanship, and frustrateth all their labour. I would esteeme him for a learned Vintner, and worthie to haue the next auoydance of Bacchus his chaire, that could giue me the true reason of this reboiling of wines. But because I haue allotted so great a place of honour to him that can but shewe the reason onely thereof, therefore I will not presume nor professe to knowe the cause efficient, but I durst vndertake to perfourme the remedie, if I thought my rewarde would not bee somewhat like vnto his, that within this few yeares taught diuerse of the companie how to draw out of a Hogges-head of wine lees, 10 gallons of cleare wine at the least, which beeing trickt, or compassed, or at the least mingled with other wine, hath euer since by diuerse Vintners beene retailed for wine, whereas before it was wholie solde for lees to the *Aqua vitæ* men. And this is the reason why there hath neuer since been the like store of lees to make *Aqua vitæ* of, as before the discouerie of this conceit, and that the lees of many Cellors which before were liquid, are now become stiffe like paste, and may verie well be wrought vp into the forme of bals. And if I be not deceiued, the first practize thereof began in Pater noster row, and within these few yeares,

but I

Art and Nature.

but I feare by this time, it is a parcell of manie mens Creede that wil neuer be left til the worlds end. Wel, the poore fellow got hardly a good sute of apparell amongst diuerse of them to whom hee disclosed the secrete, although some one of them could tell which way presently to raise 30 or 40. li. *per annū* vnto themselues. And therefore I see it is no offring of skill in these dayes to Vintners. But the better course were to take a Tauerne and get a Hollibush if France were more open, and a litle more freed of the excessiue impost, and so to draw wines as artificially as the best of them. For I can assure you I haue almost the whole art as it is this day in vse amongest the Vintners, written in a prettie volume entituled, *Secreta dei p.mpinei.* And if I durst here so boldly as I could, both truly & largely write of those iumbling sleights, that are too often practized in our naturall wines by some of the Coopers of London, to the great benefite of the Marchant and Vintner, although themselues, poore soules, get nothing thereby but the hooping of the vessels, and now and then a Can of wine for their labours, a man would wonder from whence such great varietie of iugling should growe or spring, and howe these plaine fellowes that neuer read their Grammer, nay scarcely know their A,B,C, should be able to run through Ouids Metamorphosis as they doe at midnight. And yet I cannot altogither blame either the Cooper, or the Vintners man for practising of these alterations, transmutations, and sometimes euen real transubstantiations, of white wine into Claret, & old lags of Sacks or Malmesies, with malassoes into Muskadels. For we are growne so nice in taste, that almost no wines vnlesse they be more pleasant than they can bee of the Grape will content vs, nay no colour vn-

L   lesse

lesse it bee perfect, fine and bright, will satisfie our wanton eyes, whereupon (as I haue beene creedibly enfourmed by some that haue seene the practize in Spaine) they are forced euen there to enterlace now and then a lay of Lime with the Sacke grape in the expression thereby to bring their Sackes to bee of a more white colour into England then is naturall vnto them, or then the Spaniardes themselues will brooke or endure, who will drinke no other Sackes them such as be of an Amber colour. This makes the Vintners to tricke or compasse all their natural wines if they bee a little hard, with Bastarde to make them sweeter, if they pricke a little they haue a decoction of honie with a few Cloues to deceiue the taste, if they be clowdie or not perfect fine, they giue them either the white or the yellow parrell, according to the naturall colour of the Wines, wherein they must vse Egges, Milke, Baysalt, & Conduit water well beaten and laboured together with a stubbed rodde, and then wrought soundlie together with a parrelling staffe, which parrell for the most part in one night (vnlesse the Wines happen to haue a flickering Lee) will cause them to fine, whereby you may presently drawe at certaine. But this is daungerous vnlesse it bee in a house well customed, for that the Wine may not lie too long vpon his parell. And some Wines will not endure long after you haue racked them from their parell. Note the wholesomnesse of these Lees to make *Aqua vita* withall. But when the Wines doe rope or beginne to faile or faint in themselues, either in substaunce or in colour, either by age, by the fault of Caske, soyle, salt water, or other accident, then manie tymes the Vintener is driuen to his hard shiftes, and then

hee

hee helpeth himselfe with Allome, with Turnsole, Starch, and with manie other Drugges, and aromaticall ware which hee fetcheth from the Apothecarie, the particulars whereof I coulde set downe and applie euen as they haue beene a long time (till within these fewe yeeres) practized in one of the most autentique Tauernes of my time. But my purpose is onely to put some in minde of their grosse night-woorkes which discouer themselues by Candlelight at their Celler Windowes, whishing them to leaue all vnwholesome practizes for mans bodie, least if they shoulde heereafter against my will force mee to publish them to the worlde, I shoulde drawe my Countreymen into such a liking of our Royston Grape, that in the ende they woulde for the most part content themselues with their English and naturall drinke, without raunging so farre for forreine Wines.

74 *The making of a Bragget, which is manie times mistaken for a Muskadell by the simple sort of people.*

PVt one part of smal Alewoort that is blood warm with one part of clarified Honie according to the maner set downe num. 75. but put no Cloues therein in the clarifying. For the making of one Hogesheade of this Bragget which is aboute 63. Gallons, you must take nine Gallons of this clarified Honie, and 54. gallons of strong new ale: when your clarified hony hath stood one day, then mingle the same with your newe *Ale* in a Hogshead, first filling your Hogshead halfe full before you put in your honie, and then hang this aromaticall cōposition following in a in a long slender bag in the midst of the vessell vz. of Cinamon three ounces, ginger three ounces, greins 3. ounces, colianders one ounce, cloues one ounce, nutmegs one ounce, long pepper halfe an ounce, *Cardamomum* one ounce and a halfe, liquerice one ounce, then fil vp the vessell almost full with the rest of the new ale, (yet some commend rather the putting in of the spices confusedlie then in a bag) bee sure to haue foure or fiue gallons or more of the same newe ale, to fill vp the hogshead as it purgeth ouer continuallie. There is a lesser hole neere the bung hole in beere hogsheads, which must stande open whilest it purgeth, you must also be carefull in the beginning to giue some little vent to the hogshead whilst it worketh: in three or foure moneths, it will bee readie to drinke. You must haue a hazell sticke of the bignesse of a good cudgell, so great as may well enter in at the round bung-hole, and when your hogshead is about three quarters full, put in this stick, being sawed croswise at the end about one cubite in length, (the Vintners call it their parrelling staffe) as the aptest toole for this purpose. Beat with the said staffe the new ale and the honie togither a good prettie while, & when you haue finished this agitation, fill vp the vessel with the rest, and let it purge as before. If you finde your muscadell too thicke, after it hath stood 3. or 4. monethes, you may take a cane or pipe, made of Tinne plates, that will reach into the midst of the hogshead or somewhat more, stop the ende thereof and make some holes in the sides, and with a funnell you may poure more newe ale into the Cane, and so make it thinner. This Cane is an apt instrument to conueie any liquor or composition into a vessell of wine without troubling of the same, or turning vppe the lees,

wherby

Art and Nature. 69

whereby you may draw the same fine presently.

75 Howe to clarifie honie so that the taste thereof shall be much altered.

PVt a gallon of water blood-warme to a gallon of honie, put in your honie first, and with a sticke take the depth thereof in the vessell wherein you boile it, and then put halfe an ounce of beaten cloues bound in a linnen cloth therein, and let them boile with the water and honie on a gentle fire till all the water bee consumed, which you shall ghesse at by the marke on the sticke. Your hony must be pure and simple not mingled with woort, flowre, or other bad composition, euen as it is gathered vpon the breaking vp of the hiues. It is a worke of two or three hours, and the elder the honie is the better it serueth for this purpose. You must remember to take away the skum as it riseth. Som boile this honie a little higher to a more consistencie, and preserue fruit therewith in stead of sugar. These two receits I had of an Oxford scholler, who assured me that hee had often made proofe therof in the Citie of Oxford, and I know the man to be both of good conceipt, and verie carefull in the commendation of any secrete to his friend otherwise then may well stand with his owne credite.

76 A Receipt for the making of an artificiall Malmesey.

TAke four gallons of conduit water, into the which put one gallon of good English honie, stirre the honie well till it be dissolued in the water, set this water in a copper pan vpon a gentle fire, & as there ariseth any skumme take it off with a goose wing or a Skimmer, and when it hath simpered about an hour, then put in a new laid egge into the water, which will sinke presentlie, then continue your first fire without any great encrease, and also your skimming so long as any skim doth arise, and when this egge beginneth to floate aloft and sinketh no more, then put in another new laide egge, which wil sinke likewise, & when that second egge doth also swim aloft with the fyrst egge, let the water continue on the fyre a *Pater noster* while, then take it off, and beeing colde, put the same into some roundelet, fylling the roundelet brim ful. And in the middest of this roundelet hang a bagge, wherein first put some reasonable weight or peize, and to euerie eight gallons of liquor two nutmegges groselie beaten, twentie Cloues, a rase or two of Ginger, and a sticke of Cynamon of a fynger length. Set your roundelet in the sunne, in some hot Leades or other place, where the sunne shineth continuallie for three whole monethes, couering the bung-hole from the raine, and now and then fylling it vppe with more of the same composition as it wasteth. This I learned of an English trauayler, who aduised me to make the same alwaies about the middest of Maie, that it might haue 3. hot moneths togither to work it to his ful perfection. But least this way should happen to faile you, I haue thought good for thy better securitie, to set down mine owne fansie, for the easier stirring vppe of this Malmesey to his workmanship. Let your vessel bee such as hath alreadie conteined some muste or other liquor that hath wrought therin (for he that knoweth not the vse of a worker is but a slender Artist) stop the same very close and lay it in a conuenient Seller til it haue wrought

suffy-

sufficientlie, but in the working giue the caske vent by degrees, for feare of afterclaps. Or elfe you may eafilie procure the fame to worke, by adding of fome yeaft or ferment vnto it, and fetting it warme, according to the vfuall manner of ale and beere.

77. *How to keepe Claret wine, or any other wine good, many yeares together.*

AT euerie vintage you muft drawe off almoft a fourth part out of the hogfhead, and then rowle it vpon his Lee, and after fyll it vp with the beft newe wine of the fame kind, that you can get. Your caske muft be bound with iron bandes or hoopes, and alwaies kept full and tight. I haue heard that an Effex knight vfeth this practife, and hath Wine of nine or ten leaues (as they terme it) which is fo many yeares olde.

78. *To keepe Wall-nuts greene and moift a long time, fo as you may pill the kernell.*

TAke the ftampings of Crabs after the veriuice is expreffed from them, lay your nuts therein one by one, fo as they touch not one another, and fo make *ftratum fuper ftratum* till your veffell be ful, thefe will laft fome two or three moneths as I haue beene credibly enformed by a gentlewoman that hath made proofe thereof.

79. *How to keepe the gloffe of Spanifh Leather fhooes, or buskins, a long time.*

The

THe blacking of a Lampe tempered with the oyle of Almondes or some other sweete oile, is verie good for this purpose. I know a gentleman that doth vse to rub his spanish leather shooes with the backeside of a peece of freese-leather, but you must haue care to keepe this kinde of leather verie drie. Some maintaine the glosse of this leather, with a peece of black veluet onely.

80. How to helpe smoking Chimnies.

IF the Chimnies bee large, and carrie some good length and breadth with them, then may you erect or builde a false back & sides to your smoking chimnies, so as there may be a distance of three or four inches betweene the olde backe and the new, raise this new worke a foot aboue the mantletree. Warranted by a Gentleman of Ireland, being a great practiser in artificiall conclusions, &c.

81. Tinder and match of a new kind and sweet.

TAke the light & thin shauings of drie fir boords, light them with a candle, and when they are almost burnt, put them out as you woulde doe Linnen rags, after the flame is past, in a stone pot. Then laie another thin shauing thereon, and with a steele and flint stone strike fire into this tinder, and blow therein till this new shauing doo kindle and so light your candle, and then put out this last shauing in some reasonable time, and it will helpe to increase your Tinder. This I haue seene a Dutch Ioiner vse oftentimes in the lighting of his Candle. Note here that your

match

match and your tinder is all of one substance or matter. Also you may make sweete matches to your ordinarie tinder in this maner. Cut or thwite a number of small Iuniper stickes, with sharpe points like picke toothes, and dip them but a little waie, and that very lightly in Brimstone, and when the brimstone is spent the Iuniper will burne sweetlie.

82. *An excellent mixture, to make pewter bright withall and to take out the staines.*

TO a gallon of strong bucke Lee, put halfe a pound of blacke sope, and a reasonable handefull of the dust of Flaunders tile, which you shall make by rubbing one against another. Boile them well together til they become like pappe or birdlime. This will last a whole yeare. You must onely haue care to bestowe good labour vpon the vessel if you meane to vse this scowring.

83. *To defend a Horse from flies in his trauaile.*

STeepe *Arsmarte* in water, making the water verie strong of the hearbe, and therewith wash your horse before you meane to trauell.

84. *To kill Rats in a Garner.*

BE sure there be no holes in the bottome or sides of your garner, or any where else, sauing aboue the boords which you must place shelving wise, or in the maner of a penthouse throughout the garner, about halfe a yard or two foote from the corne, so as when the Rats haue leaped downe into the bulke of corne, then they shall not be able to rise or bolt vp againe before you haue sped them.

85. How to take away the offence of noisome vaults.

MAke the vent thereof vpwarde as large or larger then the tunnell downward, and carrie the same vp to a conuenient heigth, for so the offensiue ayre as fast as it riseth hath issue and stayeth not in the passage

86. Sweet and delicate dentifrices or rubbers for the teeth.

DIssolue in foure ounces of warme water, three or foure drams of gumme Dragagant, and in one night this wil become a thicke substance like gellie, mingle the same with the powder of Alablaster finely ground and searsed, then make vp this substance into little round rowles of 4. or 5. inches in length. Also if you temper roset or some other colour that is not hurtfull with them, they will shew full of pleasing veines. These you may sweeten either with rosewater, ciuet, or muske. But if your teeth be verie scalie, let som expert Barber first take off the scales with his instrument, and then you may keepe them cleane with the aforesaid rowles. And heer by those miserable examples that I haue seene in some of my nearest friendes, I am enforced to admonish all men to bee carefull, how they suffer their teeth to be made white with any *Aqua fortis*, which is the Barbars vsuall water, for vnlesse the same be both well delaied, and carefullie applied, a man within a few dressings, may be driuen to borrow a ranke of teeth to eate his din-

Art and Nature.

...er with, vnlesse his gums doe helpe him the better.

87. *To helpe either man or horse that is tender in the foote or hoofe, whereby they cannot endure any great trauell.*

Let him that traueleth much and hath this infirmitie, put in each sock before he draw on his hose a new laid egge somewhat groselie broken, and so let him trauell vpon them. So likewise you must put in two egs a little beaten into either hoofe of the horse, and clap cow dung vpon them, and then wrap them well one night that they fal not out, and after you may trauel him any reasonable iourny. This is much vsed in Italie.

88. *How to keepe Oysters good 10. or 12. daies.*

Some hold opinion that if you barrel them vp whilest they are new and quick at the Sea side, putting some of the brackish water where they are taken amongst them, that so they wil last manie daies good. Qre. Of dissoluing of some salt in fresh water til it bee of one strength with the brackish, which conteineth some eighteenth or twentith part of salt, peraduenture it wil not be amisse to change your brine now & then. Some pile them vp in smal roundelets with the hollow parts of the shels vpward, casting salt among them at euerie laie which they make. This is a good deuise to send them far into the Countrey, where oysters are deintie and sold by tale.

89. *To keepe Lobsters, crayfishes, Prawnes, Shrimpes, &c, sweet and good for some few daies.*

These

The Iewel-house of

THese kind of fyſh are well noted to bee of no durabilitie or laſting in warme weather, yet to prolong their daies a little (though I feare I ſhall raiſe the price of them by this diſcouerie amongeſt the Fiſhmongers, who onely in reſpect of their ſpeedy decay doo now and then affoord a penieworth in them) if you wrap them in ſweet and courſe rags firſt moiſtened in ſalt water, and then burie theſe cloaths in Callis ſande, that is alſo kept in ſome coole and moiſt place, I knowe by mine owne experience, that you ſhall finde your Labour well beſtowed, and the rather if you lay them in ſeuerall cloathes ſo as one doe not touch the other.

90. An artificial compoſition, wherwith to make ſmooth gliſtering and hard floores, or to plaiſter wals with.

TEmper Oxe-bloud and fine clay together, and lay the ſame in any floore or wall, and it will become a verie ſtrong and binding ſubſtance, as *I* haue beene told by a gentleman ſtranger, who affirmed vnto me that the ſame is in great vſe in Italie.

91. To make parchment cleere and tranſparent, to ſerue for diuers purpoſes.

MAke choice of the fineſt and thinneſt parchment you can get, ſcrape the ſame ouer with a knife till it become verie thin, (but firſt you muſt wet it wel in water) then ſtraine it vpon a frame, and faſten it well, and when it is drie oile it all ouer with a penſill, with the oile of ſweet Almonds, oile of turpentine, or oile of ſpike, ſome content themſelues with linſeed oile, & when it is thorow dry, it will ſhew very cleere, & ſerue

in

Art and Nature.

in windowes in steade of Glasse, especially in such roomes as are subiect to ouerseers. You may draw anie personage, beast, tree, flower, or coate armour vpon the parchment before it bee oyled, and then cutting your Parchment into square panes, and making slight frames for them, they will make a prettie shew in your windowes, and keepe the roome verie warm. This I commend before oyled Paper, because it is more lasting, and will endure the blustring and stormie weather much better then paper.

92 A profitable and cheape morter for building, wherin either no Lime, or small store of Lime shall bee requisite.

A Wise, wealthie, and ancient Sopeboyler, dwelling without Algate, hath for the better encouragement of others, long since erected a faire and stately edefice of brick for his owne habitation, vpon the good successe whereof he hath also verie latelie built one other house of some charge and good receipt, the morter whereof did consist of two loades of waste sope ashes, one load of lime, one load of loame, and one load of Woolwich sand. So likewise one other of the same facultie, being likewise of good credite and great experience, hath vsed onelie loame and sope-ashes tempered and wrought together in stead of morter, whereby he hath laid both the foundations, chimneys, and their tunnels in his dwelling house in Southwarke, and they haue endured those stormes alreadie which haue ouerturned manie other both new and olde tunnels that hath beene built with the ordinarie morter. It may be that many lime-men, and some of those Bricklayers that are in fee with them may bende their force against this newe practize, and labour to discredite the same by all meanes possible, but there is no reason that can holde agaynst experience, nor no malice so great, but that trueth in her time shall bee able to vanquish. And if these three tryals shall not bee thought a competent number to giue credite to a new inuention, I will vppon reasonable request and warning, backe and confirme them, with threescore more at the least, which I can produce alreadie made and executed within the Citie of London and the Suburbs thereof, insomuch that who soeuer will take a carefull view of all our late buildinges that consist of Brickwoorke (especially within the Suburbs of the Citie) hee shall finde great store of these waste ashes to be imployed in them.

93 A conceipted drinking Glasse wherein many sortes of fish will seeme to swim vp and downe.

IN the middest of a good large drinking-glasse, and of a bole fashion, let a short piller of Glasse arise, vpon the which a rounde Globe or Ball of Glasse must be placed, vpon which Ball there must bee diuerse sortes of small fishes well drawne and limned, then fill the Glasse either with water, or with white, or Rennish Wine, and the least motion that can happen, either to the Wine or water, will make the fishes seeme to play vp and downe within the Glasse.

94 Howe to dissolue golde, or to part it from guilt siluer, without melting downe the siluer.

Dissolue

Dissolue some *Sal Armoniacke*, in some good *Aquafortis*, whose fæces (fixes the Goldsmiths vnproperly tearme them) haue beene first striken down with some fine siluer, or else still by retort the saide *Aquafortis*, from good store of Baysalt first calcined, set some of this water in a parting glasse vpon warme imbers, and put therein your guilt siluer, and it will stand in the forme of a golden water. You may gather your golde againe either by euaporation of the water, and so the golde will settle in the bottome, or else if you put Mercurie therein it will amalgame with it, which Mercurie will soone flie awaie in fume, being put into a Crusible, and leaue the Golde behinde. I doe hold this to bee a verie profitable secrete for the Goldsmith, vnlesse the Mercurie in the first guilding of the siluer doe conuey some part of the Golde so farre within the siluer, as that the water can make no sufficient penetration vnto it. For by this meanes all the charge of testing and parting wil be saued, which (as I take it) will not bee much lesse then foure pence vpon euerie ounce. But whereas it hath beene obiected by some Refiners, that by this meanes there will be much golde lost (especially in such auncient plate as hath beene made and perhaps melted down againe before the arte of refining which is of a *puisne date* was found out, for that this water doth only take holde of such gold as doth enuiron the outside of the siluer) I holde this to be a weake obiection to discourage any man from the practize of this solution, for that in such plate as either carieth no touch, or so old a touch as the buier shall not bee acquainted withall, he may follow the old refining rules: and in such guilt plate as hath beene made since the arte of refining

hath

hath first beene vsed amongst vs (which is the most vsuall plate that is bought and sold in these dayes) he shall finde the same a most beneficiall practize, if the first doubt may be salued. Which may easily be proued in one ounce or two of guilt siluer, making a straite obseruation howe much golde was bestowed thereon.

95. Howe to knowe when the Moone is at the full by a glasse of salt water.

IT hath beene creediblie reported vnto me, that if an ordinarie drinking glasse bee filled brim full, a little before the full of the Moone, that, euen at that instant when the Moone commeth to the full, the water will presently boile ouer.

96 How to melt downe the filings of yron, nailes, or other small peeces of yron with a small fire.

TO three partes of yron put one fourth part of Antimonie powdred, in a crusible or melting pot, set the same in any ordinarie fornesse, and blowe a little with a paire of bellowes, (or else for your more ease you may vse a winde fornesse) and you shall finde the same to melt verie speedily. This way you may easily cast both Musket and Caliuer bullets of yron.

97 How to put seuerall liquors or Wines in one Glasse, without mixing.

TAke a Beere glasse of six or eight inches in height, and being of one equall bignesse, from the bottom to the toppe, then powre therein some faire water,

an

Art and Nature. 81

an inch or two in height, vpon the which lay a round trencher that is almost equall in compasse with the Glasse. Then out of a long spowted Glasse or pot, poure gently some milke vppon the Trencher, and after that some Rochell or Connyacke white wine, and then some Gascoigne Claret wine, and after Sacke, and so you shall haue each liquor or wine to flote vpon the other without mingling togither, because the fall thereof is broken by meanes of the gentle pouring vpon the trencher. Some holde opinion that the same may also bee perfourmed with a round toste. But I thinke that you must haue a speciall care herein, that the heauiest liquor do lie in the bottome, and that you proceed from lighter to lighter, so as the lightest or most aereous or fierie bee placed vppermost, for each thing desires to bee in his naturall place.

98 The Art of memorie which master Dickson the Scot did teach of late yeres in England, and whereof he hath written a figuratiue and obscure treatise, set downe briefly and in plaine termes according to his owne demonstration, with the especiall vses thereof.

YOu must make choice of some large edifice or building, whose Chambers or Galleries bee of some reasonable receipt, and so familiar vnto you, as that euerie part of each of them may present it selfe readily vnto the eyes of your minde when you call for them. In euerie of these roomes you must place ten seuerall subiectes at a reasonable distaunce one from the other, least the neerenesse of their placing shoulde happen to confound your Memorie. Your subiectes must consist of Decades, whereof the first

The Iewel-house of

THese kind of fysh are well noted to bee of no durabilitie or lasting in warme weather, yet to prolong their dates a little (though I feare I shall raise the price of them by this discouerie amongest the Fishmongers, who onely in respect of their speedy decay doo now and then affoord a penieworth in them) if you wrap them in sweet and courfe rags first moistened in salt water, and then burie these cloaths in Callis sande, that is also kept in some coole and moist place, I knowe by mine owne experience, that you shall finde your Labour well bestowed, and the rather if you lay them in seuerall cloathes so as one doe not touch the other.

90. An artificial composition, wherwith to make smooth glistering and hard floores, or to plaister wals with.

TEmper Oxe-bloud and fine clay together, and lay the same in any floore or wall, and it will become a verie strong and binding substance, as I haue beene told by a gentleman stranger, who affirmed vnto me that the same is in great vse in Italie.

91. To make parchment cleere and transparent, to serue for diuers purposes.

MAke choice of the finest and thinnest parchment you can get, scrape the same ouer with a knife till it become verie thin, (but first you must wet it wel in water) then straine it vpon a frame, and fasten it well, and when it is drie oile it all ouer with a pensill, with the oile of sweet Almonds, oile of turpentine, or oile of spike, some content themselues with linseed oile, & when it is thorow dry, it will shew very cleere, & serue

in

in windowes in steade of Glasse, especially in such roomes as are subiect to ouerseers. You may draw anie personage, beast, tree, flower, or coate armour vpon the parchment before it bee oyled, and then cutting your Parchment into square panes, and making slight frames for them, they will make a prettie shew in your windowes, and keepe the roome verie warm. This I commend before oyled Paper, because it is more lasting, and will endure the blustring and stormie weather much better then paper.

92 *A profitable and cheape morter for building, wherin either no Lime, or small store of Lime shall bee requisite.*

A Wise, wealthie, and ancient Sopeboyler, dwelling without Algate, hath for the better encouragement of others, long since erected a faire and stately edefice of brick for his owne habitation, vpon the good successe whereof he hath also verie latelie built one other house of some charge and good receipt, the morter whereof did consist of two loades of waste sope ashes, one load of lime, one load of loame, and one load of Woolwich sand. So likewise one other of the same facultie, being likewise of good credite and great experience, hath vsed onelie loame and sope-ashes tempered and wrought together in stead of morter, whereby he hath laid both the foundations, chimneys, and their tunnels in his dwelling house in Southwarke, and they haue endured those stormes alreadie which haue ouerturned manie other both new and olde tunnels that hath beene built with the ordinarie morter. It may be that many limemen, and some of those Bricklayers that are in fee with them may bende their force againſt this newe practize, and labour to diſcredite the ſame by all meanes poſſible, but there is no reaſon that can holde agaynſt experience, nor no malice ſo great, but that trueth in her time ſhall bee able to vanquiſh. And if theſe three tryals ſhall not bee thought a competent number to giue credite to a new inuention, I will vppon reaſonable requeſt and warning, backe and confirme them, with threeſcore more at the leaſt, which I can produce alreadie made and executed within the Citie of London and the Suburbs thereof, inſomuch that who ſoeuer will take a carefull view of all our late buildinges that conſiſt of Brickwoorke (eſpecially within the Suburbs of the Citie) hee ſhall finde great ſtore of theſe waſte aſhes to be imployed in them.

93 A conceipted drinking Glaſſe wherein many ſortes of fiſh will ſeeme to ſwim vp and downe.

IN the middeſt of a good large drinking-glaſſe, and of a bole faſhion, let a ſhort piller of Glaſſe ariſe, vpon the which a rounde Globe or Ball of Glaſſe muſt be placed, vpon which Ball there muſt bee diuerſe ſortes of ſmall fiſhes well drawne and limned, then fill the Glaſſe either with water, or with white, or Renniſh Wine, and the leaſt motion that can happen, either to the Wine or water, will make the fiſhes ſeeme to play vp and downe within the Glaſſe.

94 Howe to diſſolue golde, or to part it from guilt ſiluer, without melting downe the ſiluer.

Diſſolue

Dissolue some *Sal Armoniacke*, in some good *Aquafortis*, whose fæces (fixes the Goldsmiths vnproperly tearme them) haue beene first striken down with some fine siluer, or else still by retort the saide *Aquafortis*, from good store of Baysalt first calcined; set some of this water in a parting glasse vpon warme embers, and put therein your guilt siluer, and it will [stand] in the forme of a golden water. You may gather your golde againe either by euaporation of the water, and so the golde will settle in the bottome, or else if you put Mercurie therein it will amalgame with it, which Mercurie will soone flie awaie in fume, being put into a Crusible, and leaue the Golde behinde. I doe hold this to bee a verie profitable secréte for the Goldsmith, vnlesse the Mercurie in the first guilding of the siluer doe conuey some part of the Golde so farre within the siluer, as that the water can make no sufficient penetration vnto it. For by this meanes all the charge of testing and parting wil be saued, which (as I take it) will not bee much lesse then foure pence vpon euerie ounce. But whereas it hath beene objected by some Refiners, that by this meanes there will be much golde lost (especially in such auncient plate as hath beene madd and perhaps melted down againe before the arte of refining which is of a *puisne date* was found out, for that this water doth only take holde of such gold as doth enuiron the outside of the siluer) I holde this to be a weake obiection to discourage any man from the practize of this solution, for that in such plate as either carieth no touch, or so old touch as the buler shall not bee acquainted withall, he may follow the old refining rules: and in such guilt plate as hath beene made since the arte of refining

hath

hath first beene vsed amongst vs (which is the most vsuall plate that is bought and sold in these dayes (he shall finde the same a most beneficiall practize, if the first doubt may be salued. Which may easily be proued in one ounce or two of guilt siluer, making a straite obseruation howe much golde was bestowed thereon.

95. Howe to knowe when the Moone is at the full by a glasse of salt water.

IT hath beene creediblie reported vnto me, that if an ordinarie drinking glasse bee filled brim full, a little before the full of the Moone, that, euen at that instant when the Moone commeth to the full, the water will presently boile ouer.

96. How to melt downe the filings of yron, nailes, or other small peeces of yron with a small fire.

TO three partes of yron put one fourth part of Antimonie powdred, in a crusible or melting pot, set the same in any ordinarie fornesse, and blowe a little with a paire of bellowes, (or else for your more ease you may vse a winde fornesse) and you shall finde the same to melt verie speedily. This way you may easily cast both Musket and Caliuer bullets of yron.

97. How to put seuerall liquors or Wines in one Glasse, without mixing.

TAke a Beere glasse of six or eight inches in height, and being of one equall bignesse, from the bottom to the toppe, then powre therein some faire water,

an

an inch or two in height, vpon the which lay a round trencher that is almost equall in compasse with the glasse. Then out of a long spowted Glasse or pot, poure gently some milke vppon the Trencher, and after that some Rochell or Connyacke white wine, and then some Gascoigne Claret wine, and after sacke, and so you shall haue each liquor or wine to lie vpon the other without mingling togither, because the fall thereof is broken by meanes of the gentle pouring vpon the trencher. Some holde opinion that the same may also bee perfourmed with a sound toste. But I thinke that you must haue a speciall care herein, that the heauiest liqnor do lie in the bottome, and that you proceed from lighter to lighter, so as the lightest or most aereous or fierie bee placed vppermost, for each thing desires to bee in his naturall place.

8 The Art of memorie which master Dickson the Scot did teach of late yeres in England, and whereof he hath written a figuratiue and obscure treatise, set downe briefly and in plaine termes according to his owne demonstration, with the especiall vses thereof.

YOu must make choice of some large edifice or building, whose Chambers or Galleries bee of some reasonable receipt, and so familiar vnto you, as that euerie part of each of them may present it selfe readily vnto the eyes of your minde when you call for them. In euerie of these roomes you must place in seuerall subiectes at a reasonable distaunce one from the other, least the neerenesse of their placing shoulde happen to confound your Memorie. Your subiectes must consist of Decades, whereof the first hath first beene vsed amongst vs (which is the most vsuall plate that is bought and sold in these dayes) he shall finde the same a most beneficiall practize, if the first doubt may be salued. Which may easily be proued in one ounce or two of guilt siluer, making a straite obseruation howe much golde was bestowed thereon.

95. *Howe to knowe when the Moone is at the full by a glasse of salt water.*

IT hath beene creediblie reported vnto me, that if an ordinarie drinking glasse bee filled brim full, a little before the full of the Moone, that, euen at that instant when the Moone commeth to the full, the water will presently boile ouer.

96 *How to melt downe the filings of yron, nailes, or other small peeces of yron with a small fire.*

TO three partes of yron put one fourth part of Antimonie powdred, in a crusible or melting pot, set the same in any ordinarie fornesse, and blowe a little with a paire of bellowes, (or else for your more ease you may vse a winde sotnesse) and you shall finde the same to melt verie speedily. This way you may easily cast both Musket and Caliuer bullets of yron.

97 *How to put seuerall liquors or Wines in one Glasse, without mixing.*

TAke a Beere glasse of six or eight inches in height, and being of one equall bignesse, from the bottom to the toppe, then powre therein some faire water,

an

an inch or two in height, vpon the which lay a round trencher that is almost equall in compasse with the glasse. Then out of a long spowted Glasse or pot, poure gently some milke vppon the Trencher, and after that some Rochell or Connyacke white wine, and then some Gascoigne Claret wine, and after Sacke, and so you shall haue each liquor or wine to flote vpon the other without mingling togither, because the fall thereof is broken by meanes of the gentle pouring vpon the trencher. Some holde opinion that the same may also bee perfourmed with a round toste. But I thinke that you must haue a speciall care herein, that the heauiest liquor do lie in the bottome, and that you proceed from lighter to lighter, so as the lightest or most aereous or fierie bee placed vppermost, for each thing desires to bee in his naturall place.

The Art of memorie which master Dickson the Scot did teach of late yeres in England, and whereof he hath written a figuratiue and obscure treatise, set downe briefly and in plaine termes according to his owne demonstration, with the especiall vses thereof.

YOu must make choice of some large edifice or building, whose Chambers or Galleries bee of some reasonable receipt, and so familiar vnto you, as that euerie part of each of them may present it selfe readily vnto the eyes of your minde when you call for them. In euerie of these roomes you must place in seuerall subiectes at a reasonable distaunce one from the other, least the neerenesse of their placing shoulde happen to confound your Memorie. Your subiectes must consist of Decades, whereof the first

is a

is a man, and the fifth a woman, or rather the wife of that man which beginneth the Decade. And by this meanes your first, your fift, your tenth, your fifteenth, and your twentieth subiect, &c. Both forwarde and backewarde is easily brought to minde. The rest of the subiects in euerie Decade may be such as are meerly differing the one from the other, vnlesse you shall like to haue some few of them resembling the profession of him that beginneth the Decade. As for example, if you begin with the Souldier, you may take a Drumme and a Target for two of the subiectes in that Decade. But if you place too manie subiectes of one nature within one Decade, you will finde them verie troublesome to remember. These subiectes woulde bee such as are most apt either to bee agents or patients, vppon whatsoeuer you shall haue cause to place in them. And therefore a fire, a Dunghill, a Carte, a paire of Bellowes, a Tubbe of water, an Ape, a Shippe, a night-gowne, a Milstone, and such like, are apt to make your subiects of, wherein you may place all such thinges as you woulde remember, and as Maister Dickson tearmed it, to animate the *vmbras* or *ideas rerum memorandarum*. But heerein euerie man may best please his owne witte and memorie. Nowe to proceede to the placing of these tenne subiectes, in their tenne locall roomes, you maie beginne with a Souldier, whome you may place euen in the doore or entrance confronting with a sterne and warlike looke all such as shall offer to enter that roome, whereof hee taketh the charge, you maie also imagine him with Flaske, Touch-boxe, Morion, Peece, Sworde and Dagger, &c. Because you may happilie haue occasion in the placing of some harde woorde, to vse

some

me one of these more fitlie then the other. Your seconde place maie bee your Bed-steed, (if that do happily stande next your doore) at the heade whereof, you maie by a strong imagination place an exceme burning fire, and at the feete thereof a great and smoaking Dunghill. In your Chimney (if that likewise bee next your bed, and of a competent distance from the bedde) you maie imagine a Tubbe full of water. Then in your window beeing the next the place you may imagine Bellona staring with her fierie eies, and portraied in all points according to the usual description of the Poets. Then vpon your court cubbarde, you may place an Ape with her clogge, and in an other Window (if your Chamber haue two Windowes) a Shippe vnder saile with all her tackle. Vpon your Chaire you may imagine a night-gowne furred with Foxe skinne, hauing wide sleeues, and great pockets belonging to the same. Then vppon your Table standing in the middest of the roome, you may place a Millstone, or a Drumme, and in the top of the seeling ouer your Table, a Target, a sword, or a Lute hanging downwarde. And if you want places, you may make either side of your windows to be one, and so of your Chimney: But heere you must haue an especiall care beginning at the doore of your Chamber to take the places round about the chamber according as they lie, and that before you fall to the practize of this arte you may perfitely (as your *Pater noster*) remember euery place, and what subiect you haue placed therein; which you shall the better performe if you make a full and a liuely description of euerie subiecte in your minde before you place the same. Nowe hauing gotten all these subiectes, with their seuerall pla-

N 2 ces,

ces memoriter & adunguem, suppose you are to remember a Cat, a Lute, and a hande, you must alwayes remember to place your first worde whatsoeuer it bee, and howe vnapt so euer it bee in the first subiect, and the seconde woorde in the seconde subiect, and so forwarde. And therefore you may imagine your Cat scratching the Souldier by the face, till the blood runne downe his cheekes, he himselfe swearing and staring and strugling with her. Your Lute beeing layde in the fire, you may imagine the same burning to coles, and all the strings cracking in sunder to your great greefe. Then you may imagine for the better remembrance of your third word, a hande raking in the dunghill till it become foule and lothsome in sight. In the like maner you may passe through the whole decade. And if you haue more words or *Capita rerum* to remember then ten, you must beginne with the next decade of your locall subiectes wherein you may place other tenne woordes, and so you may proceede to what number you list, hauing subiectes inough to receyue them. Beholde heere that great and swelling Arte, for the which Maister Dickson did vsually take of euerie Scholler twentie shillings, making one whole Moneths discourse of the Theorique part thereof, but in the practique hee coulde scarcely tell which way to bestowe a full houre in demonstration. And yet to deliuer my censure hereof, according as I haue found therein, I must of necessitie confesse, that although it doe neither answere his great promises, nor the expectation of those his Schollers, whose good opinions he did entertaine so long with such golden hopes in the bettering of their weake memories, that yet notwithstanding the same is verie sufficient

Art and Nature.

cient to procure an assured and speedie remembrāce of any 10. 20. 30. or 40. principall thinges more or lesse, that we shall take in charge to perfourme, and therfore verie necessarie for him that is charged with many errandes, and would discharge them all in such order as they are deliuered vnto him, as also for the remembrance of all such pleasant tales and histories as shall passe in table talke, from conceipted wits. In which two especial vses, I haue often exercised this Art for the better helpe of mine owne memorie, and the same as yet hath neuer failed mee. Although I haue heard of some of Maister *Dickson* his schollers, that haue proued such cunning Card-players heereby, that they coulde tell the whole course of all the Cardes, and what euery gamester had in his hande. So readie we are to turne an honest and commendable inuention into meere craft and cousenage. And if there be any that doe either make doubt of this art, or shal thinke that I haue dealt too compendiouslie in so large a Subiect, I will according to my ancient promise, be at al times readie, and that freely, aswell in this as in any other secret which I haue disclosed alreadie, or shal hereafter by any publique impression disclose vnto my Countrey men, be readie to manifest the same by plaine tearmes, or manuel demonstration, to their best contentment.

99. *How to make proiection, either vppon* Mercurie, Venus, *or any of the rest of the base bodies, with a medicine so exalted, as that one shal extend vpon a hundreth, either* ad album, *or* ad rubrum, *and abiding both the touch, malleation and coppell, the golde being 24. Carots high, and the siluer 12. ounces fine.*

A multis amatur Alchimia & tamen virgo est.

I Coulde neuer yet receiue any sufficient warrant or allowance from the true and ancient chimical Philosophers of al former ages, for the manifesting of so great a secret as I haue now in hande, in any plaine or naked tearmes. And that made *Geber* to take holde of this Posie, *Secretum tuum non reuelabis cuiquam.* And *Comes Treuisanus*, dooth so religiouslie holde and maintaine the secretting both of the Philosophers matter, their fire, the Colours, time and proportion that is to be vsed in the great worke, as that he breaketh out into this strong coniuration, of al such happie Alchimistes as haue alreadie accomplished their golden desires in this Art. *Quod si materiam, pondus, aut colores noueris, adiuro te per Deum viuum ne cuiquam reuelaueris.* But because I purpose not to prophane or violate those Sacred groundes of Nature in this discourse, but onely to particularize a fewe proiections, I hope that both my pardon and my fault shal carrie one date, and therefore I will proceed the boldlier in my purpose. It is a worlde to see, how euerie Arte hath gotten his Counterfeite in these daies. Howe Logike is turned into Sophistrie, Rhetorique into flatterie, Astronomie into vaine and presumptuous Astrologie, that ancient and diuine science of Alchimie into Cementations, Blaunchers, and Citrinations, ending commonlie either in coosenage, quoinage, or in *Capistro*, which made *Petrarke* to giue a Caueat in these wordes. *Caue Alchimiam, semper rebus aliquid defuerit, dolis nihil.* And againe. *Chimista qui tibi auram suum spondet, cum tuo auro improuisus aufugiet.* This made *Chawcer* in his time to play so plesantlie

vpon

vpon the Alchimists hollow cole, & this hath made me to touch or glance at a few other sleights of later date, therby to admonish al yong gentlemen and others to take heed of al these mercenarie hirelinges, *Qui cum aliis mille aureos promittant, ipsi drachmam petunt. Locus poscit fabulam.* A subtile marchant sorting himself of late, with an old smokie Alchimist for his better credit, as they became fellow trauellers in the higher parts of Germanie togither lighting by chance vpon a young crewe of marchants that were wel monied, and ready for any rich prize that should be offred vnto them, especially for *Iasons* barke that was laden with the golden fleece, after some salutation had, and a few words of course enterchangeablie passing betwixt them, this cunning companion of the alchimists began to parlie with them in this maner. My maisters and friends, you seeme to be men of honest parentage and condition, and most happily to be here met both for your owne good and ours. So it is, that if you will performe that secresie which is requisite in so weightie a matter as I am in purpose to commende vnto you, I will make you the moste royall Marchantes of the whole Worlde. Neither shall any of you make the hazzarde or aduenture of one Deniere, vntill with your owne eyes and handes you shall haue seene and made a sensible proofe of this my friendlie offer. It is but in vaine to vse manie wordes amongst friends. You shall make a perfect proiection your selues vpon Mercurie, *ad omne examen*; and because my selfe and my partener will bee free from all suspition of deceipt, you shall bringe the Crusible, the Coales, and also the Quicke-siluer with you, and wee will but onelie

deliuer

deliver you one graine of the medicine which shall extend it selfe vppon a full ounce of Mercurie, which you your selues shall likewise let fall into the crusible. A man would thinke that this were plaine dealing, and that vnlesse these men were wilfullie bent to cosen themselues, that it were impossible, to deceiue so many young eies, that watched so carefully for them selues. But now to the practise. The fire being kindeled, one of them setteth on the Crusible by direction of the Alchimist, vnder the nose of a paire of goldsmithes bellowes, who told him that for the better fixation of the Mercurie, there muste a reuerberatorie blast be made now and then with the bellowes, after the Mercurie was once warme in the melting pot. Now this Impostor had before conueied into the nose of the bellowes, an ounce or somwhat more (to supplie that which the Mercurie with his fume should carrie awaie with him) of Sol so subtiliated by often reiteration of *Aqua Regis* vpon it, as that it becam almost an impalpable powder, which when the Marchant by the appointment of the Chimist, had blowne amongst the Mercurie, he was willed to drop in the medicine, being wrapped vppe in a smal paper, and then to leaue the crusible in the fire, vntill the medicine and the Mercurie were both incorporated together, and that the Mercurie were sufficientlie tincted into Sol, and within one halfe hour (after he had first caused them to melt downe an ounce of fine golde in an other crusible, and to put the same to the first worke, for the better fusion of the powder) he willed to be taken out of the fire and conueyed into an ingot, and the same being colde became twoe ounces of perfect Sol, abiding both the hammer, the test, and the horne of Antimonie. It is not to bee doub-

doubted, but that these yong gallants were right ioyful of this good successe, desiring nothing more then to become Lullistes, offering to exchange their freedome both of the olde Haunce and of the newe, for this multiplying Art. Now this geere worketh like wax, and the Alchimist demaundeth 2000. dollers, for the prouision of coles, furnaces, saltes and Minerals, but especiallie to engrose all the Mercurie, that could be gotten, least either it should rise to an excessiue price, or be transported into Spaine, for the refining of the Indian oare. The money is foorthwith deliuered by weight, becaufe there must bee no time lost in the telling, with a charge to vse all expedition that could be for the gathering of the Mercurie together that was to be gotten far and neere. The substāce of this historie is already deliuered, I will not stande long vpon the circumstance. The Alchimist hauing fingered the monie, beginneth to erect furnaces, and enterteineth them with a few distillations, calcinations and sublimations, teaching them howe to make *Lutum Sapientiæ, Aquam seperationis, aquam regis, oleum vitrioli, salis, & sulphuris,* to congeale Mercurie with the spirit of Saturne, to make *saccarum Saturni,* to whiten their teeth withall, to blanch copper with *Arsenick,* to melt one part of Luna with 3. parts of Venus together, and then to forge plate thereof, and by a certen ebulution, to make the same diuerse times to touch equall with our best starling, or higher according to the finenesse of the siluer that was mingled with Venus, all this (with an infinite number of spagiricall experiments) was performed, both to passe away the time without tediousnesse, whilest the Philosophers egge (which required 10. moneths digestion, was hatching in *Cælo philosophorum*) as also

O   to

to gain ẏ more credit with the marchants, wherby a man of these single gifts, might not be feared or mistrusted of his flight, which both he & his companiō were dailie practising, and in the ende finding good opportunitie they put the same in execution, leauing them that had most need to blow at the cole. I doo verelie beleeue that if the old D. of Florence were aliue againe, he would haue outbidden the marchants for this secret, whose distillatorie vessels, furnaces, & other chimicall instrumentes, were all of siluer as I haue heard it often reported. But now to giue a few Items more against these Impostors, before I conclude, Let euery man that is besotted in this Art, and dependeth whollie vpon other mens practises (himselfe not beeing sufficientlie acquainted with those great and hidden Maximes of nature) take heed also of all false and double bottomes in Crusibles, of all hollowe wandes or roddes of yron, wherewith some of these varlettes doe vse to stirre the mettall and the medicine together, of all Amalgames or Powders, wherein any Golde or Siluer shall bee craftilie conueyed, of Sol or Luna, first rubified and then proiection made vpon it, as if it were vppon Venus hir selfe: but speciallie of a false backe to the Chimney or furnace, hauing a loose bricke or stone closely ioynted, that may bee taken awaie in an other Roome by a false Sinon that attendeth onely the Alchimistes hemme, or some other such like watch-worde, who after the medicine and the Mercurie put together in the Crusible, enterteineth *Balbinus* with a walk and with the volubilitie of his toung, vntil his confederate may haue leysure enough to conuey some Gold or Siluer into the melting potte, which were able to deceiue the best sighted Argus in the world.

By

By these fewe legerdemaynes, I hope many thousandes will be sufficientlie warned, of these wandring & roguing Alchimists, who since the death of Cuckow, Stannie, and Feates; and the rest of that rable, are become the verie Iuglers of the Lande, yea infinitelie woorse than they: For that our auncient Iuglers would shewe all their iugling trickes for a groat or a Teastern, and though nowe and then they made shewe to transmute siluer into Counters, or money out of one mannes hande into an others, yet in the ende, euery man returned with the Coine which he brought in his pursse againe, whereas these Rascalles doe not onelie conuert other mennes monie wholelie into their owne purses, but procure also a great losse and expence of time, which might haue beene many waies better, but no way worse employed, and can neuer bee redeemed againe. Wherefore to conclude with *Petrarch*, *Dic vt ea sibi præstet quæ promittit aliis, primumque suam pellat inopiam. Est enim ferè mendicum genus hominum, cumque se pauperes fateantur, ditare alios volunt, quasi aliena illis quam propria molestior sit paupertas: sic vt miseri se alios misereri dicere soleant impudenter, & ignotis etiam interdum magna promittere: O turpis promissio, & O stulta credulitas.*

100. *Howe to nippe or close a Glasse with a paire of hot tongues, which is commonlie called* Sigillum Hermetis.

PLace a violl or other glasse hauing a long necke, in a pan of ashes, suffering one inch of the neck only to peer aboue y̆ ashes, then lay charcole round about the neck, & close to y̆ same (som do also couer the viol

O 3 with

with a round glasse fitted to the mouth, both to keep out the ashes and also the extreame heate of the fire from striking downward into the belly of the glasse, couering also the verie toppe or sumitie of the glasse with charcole, two or three inches aboue the same, then make fire at the toppe and let it kindle of it selfe downeward, and if that heat be not sufficient, vse also the blast of the bellowes, for you must force the neck of the glasse euen to a heat of fusion, and when it is readie to melt, then nip the same close together with a paire of tongs beeing red hot, which for the same purpose must be kept in a strong glowing fire, and if you can take it in his iust time, you shal close the sam so stronglie, that it is impossible for any ayre to issue out. You may safelie keepe any distilled oile or water in a glasse so nipped. But take heed how you keepe the iuyce of any strong or fierie plant, as also of any decoction that is apt to worke it selfe into a bodie, as new must, or the strong worte either of ale or beere, least you doe not onelie mispend your time, lose your liquor, and breake your glasse, but also get a shrewde turne your selfe, if you happen to be within gun-shot. For there be certein wilde spirits within, who can indure no imprisonment, but if they can find no waie, they will make waie, bearing out before them both locke, bolt, and hinges, and yet they are such as the Philosopher can not want, though the vulgar sorte know no vse of them.

Art and Natures 93

101 *A Wagon to bee drawne with men in steade of horses.*

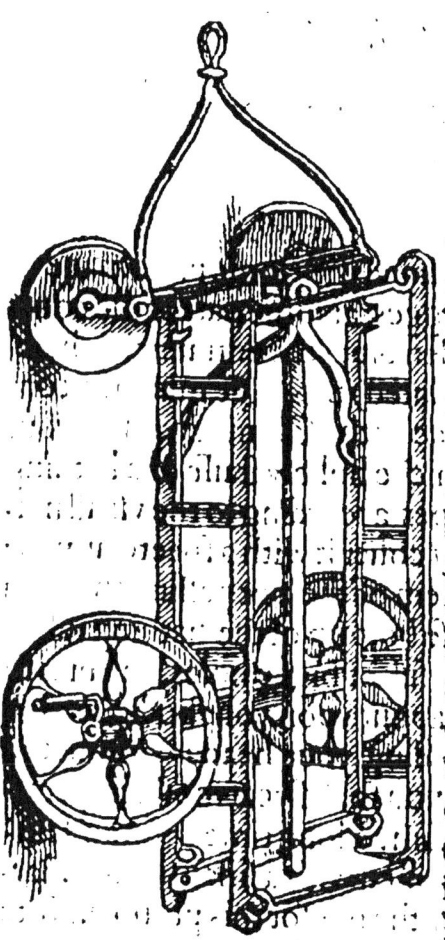

THe ioynts and other parts of this wagon are so knit togither with hookes & pinnes, as that it may easily bee disioynted and taken in sunder; whereby many of them may be couched in a narrow roome, and will lie close togither in a ship. It is to bee drawne with six men, whereof two of them muste labour at the fore-cariage thereof, and at either wheele other two, which must woorke by winding of the handles, (which are of purpose fastened both to the Naue of the wheele, and axletree) either forward or backward as occasion serueth. The vse therof is to conuey their vittails and other necessaries from place to place when the mariners or souldiers haue cause to land in some coūtries where the place affoordeth no horse or other beastes that are fit for labour or cariage. I know not the Authour of this inuention, but because it came so happilie to my handes, and carieth some good conceipt

with

The Iewel-houſe of

with it, I thinke it neceſſarie to be publiſhed amongſt other ſerviceable deuiſes for the ſea.

102 A delicate ſtoue to ſweate in.

PVt into a Braſſe potte of ſome content, ſuch proportion of ſweete hearbs, and of ſuch kinde as ſhal bee moſt appropriate for your infirmitie, with ſome reaſonable quantitie of water, cloſe the ſame with an apt couer, and well luted with ſome paſte made of flowre and whites of egges, at ſome part of the couer you muſt let in a Leaden pipe (the entraunce whereof muſt alſo bee well luted) this pipe muſt bee conueyed through the ſide of the Chimney where your pot ſtandeth, in at a thicke hollow ſtaffe of a bathing tub croſſed with hoopes according to the vſuall maner, whereby you may couer it with a ſheete at your pleaſure. Nowe the ſtem of the pot paſſing through the pipe vnder the falſe bottom of the bathing tubbe which muſt bee bored full of bigge holes, will breath ſo ſweet & warme a vapour vpon your bodie, as that (receyuing aire by holding your heade without the tub as you ſit therein) you ſhall ſweat moſt temperatly, and continue the ſame a long time without fainting. And this is performed with a ſmall fire of Charcole maintained vnder the pot for this purpoſe. Note that the room would be cloſe wherin you place your bathing tub, leaſt any ſudden cold ſhould offend you whileſt your body is made open & porous to the ayr.

103 The Arte of refining of Sugar.

MAke a verie ſtrong Lee of vnſleckt Lime wherein diſſolue as much courſe Sugar as the Lee will beare,

beare, then boyle the same a little, and presently put in the whites of egges first beaten into Oyle, which will make it to giue vp a scumme, which must bee taken away as long as anie ryseth. Then poure all the liquors through a great woollen cloth bagge, and so the filth will remaine behinde in the bagge, then boyle the liquor againe, till it bee ripe, which you shall knowe by taking two or three droppes of the liquor and putting them vppon a plate of colde yron, letting it coole, which when it is congealed a little like salt, or as a meane betweene sirruppe and hard Sugar, then take the lyquour from the fire, and poure out the same into the earthen Potte or Moldes made for the same purpose, hauing a hole in the smaller ende which muste bee stopped for one night after, and after that night open it, letting all the substance remaine in the Potte, vntill the syrruppe beginne to leaue dropping (into the nether Pot wherein the Moldes stande) or droppe verie sloulie at the little hole, this Syrruppe (as I take it) is that which they call *Malassoes*,) Then take Potters Claie, and Clay the broade endes of the Potte ouer therewith, and as that Claye sinketh downe, by reason of the shrinking of the Sugar, fill them vp with more Clay, repeating the dooing thereof till the Sugar shrinke no more. Then take the Sugar-loaues out of the Moldes, and put them in a Stoue, till they bee drie and harde, and after binde them vppe in Papers according to Arte. Note that if the Sugar after the first boyling, and beeing powred out into the Moldes and beginning to congeale, appeare to bee ouer-black or foule, and shall not become white at the first in the same Moldes, but some fecicall part remaine therein,

therein, then it must be newe boyled with Lee in all pointes *vt supra*, till it bee perfectly white. Also the clay must be potters clay, tempered like pappe in water, and the same must runne through a Colander ful of holes vppon the bottome of the Suger loafe, for the softnesse of the Sugar will not suffer the pressing downe of any stiffe clay. This receipt though happily it want some of the circumstances in the Arte of refining, yet it shoulde seeme the matter of substaunce is sufficiently vnfolded herein. I had the same of a Gentleman of good Worship and a great artist.

FINIS.

Diuerse new sorts of *Soyle not yet brought* into any publique vse, for *manuring both of pasture* and arable ground, with sundrie concepted practises *belonging therunto.*

Faithfully and familiarly set downe by H. Plat of Lincolns Inne Gent.

LONDON
Printed by Peter Short.

1594.

A Philosophicall discourse as well vpon the Common, as vpon the vegetatiue and fructifying Salt of Nature.

Hauing found by sundrie obseruations, drawn from experience her selfe the vndoubted mother of all true and certaine knowledge, that all sorts, and kindes of Marle, or soyle whatsoeuer, either knowne or vsed alreadie for the manuring, bettering of all hungry and barren grounds, or as [yet] concealed, and kept in the bosome of Nature, [fro]m the common and vulgar sort of people, do draw [th]eir generatiue and fructifying vertue from that ve[ge]table salt (which M. *Bernhard Palissy* in his learned [an]d philosophicall treatise, *de la nature des eaux, & [fon]teines*, dooth so often tearme by the name of a [fift] element, (whereon all our auncient Philosophers [di]d scarcely dreame) I haue thought good, because I [w]ould not seeme fantasticall, and ouerweening in [m]ine owne conceite, as if I were the first broacher of [th]is opinion: before I proceede to anie practicall dis[c]ouerjes herein, first to set downe that short & sweet [di]scourse of *Franciscus Valesius* in his booke *de sacra [p]hilosophia, cap. 34.* vpon the miracle contained in [th]e fourth booke of the kings and second Chapter, [an]d then to amplifie the same by some of those mani[fes]t experiments which are common in this land al[re]adie, and by some others of more value, and yet of [litt]le charge, although as yet not knowne, or at the [lea]st not published by any former Authour.

In

The Iewel-house of

In the fourth Booke of Kinges, and second chapter. 19, 20, 21, and 22. verse, it is thus written. And the men of the Citie (that is of Hierico) saide vnto Elisha, Beholde sir, the dwelling of this Citie is pleasaunt as thou thy selfe seest: but the Water is naught, and the grounde barren. Hee saide, bring mee a newe Cruse, and put salt therein. And they brought it him. And hee went vnto the Spring of Waters, and cast the salt therein, and sayde, thus sayeth the Lorde, I haue healed these waters: there shall not come hence foorth either death, or barrennesse. So the Waters were healed vnto this day according to the saying of Elisha which he spake.

Wherevpon Valetius entreateth in this maner. There is no doubt but that this, as also diuerse other signes, and tokens were shewed vnto the people of Israel by way of figure, as Saint Paule dooth testifie, and that the same dooth signifie some other purifying, and cleansing of waters, and that it was done in token of some Sacrament. But whether there bee anie regarde to bee had of Nature in this myracle or no, wee are at this present to consider, and examine. For I haue oftentimes obserued euen in the perfourming of myracles, that for the most part, it pleaseth God to vse some naturall cause, and that vppon manie, and excellent reasons him moouing thereunto. Wherefore seeing the barrennesse of the earth is cured by the Waters, it is manifest that there is nothing else meant in this place, but that the Waters were of such kinde, and qualitie, as that the earth beeing watered therewith, became barren by their corruption. And it seemeth by al probabilitie that this fault was in their saltnesse, both

because

Art and Nature.

because it is an ordinarie accident to many waters, whereby they are made vnholsome to be drunk, and because that, of all other thinges dooeth most of all make the earth vnfruitfull; wherevpon it grew into a custome with our auncient forefathers, that all such ground as became forfeit and confiscate vnto the Crowne, by reason of any high and capitall offence committed, should be ploughed and sowed with salt, which we read to haue beene doone by *Abimelech*, in the ninth Chapter of the booke of Iudges, when he had destroyed the cittie of the Sichemites, and in the Psalme it is said: He hath destroyed a fruitfull land with saltnesse, for the wickednesse of the inhabitants. And therfore saltnesse is a principall meanes to make the ground vnfruitfull, and the sowing of salt thereon bringeth forth barrennesse, and a curse vpon it. But how then commeth it to passe, that if the waters of Iericho, did hereby both become vnsauorie for the people to drinke, and vnprofitable for the encrease of the earth: that there should be any naturall vertue in salt, to helpe and sweeten them, especiallie when S. Iames saith in his Epistle and third chapter. My brethren, can the fig tree bring forth grapes, or the vine bring forth figs? So neither by the same reason, can salt make waters to be fresh & sweet. Neither can it bee denied, but that as contraries are remedied by their contraries: so likewise that the faults of al things are increased by their like and semblable Natures. Therefore one of these two must of necessity fal out, that either in the myracle of *Elisha*, there was no regard had of nature at al, but that there was a meere contrarie course to nature vsed, thereby to make the myracle the greater (for we read of y̨ like often in the holie Scriptures) or else that the fault of these waters

A 3 was

was not in their saltnesse, but rather in some other rotten and putrified corruption, which as in all other things, so in water most especially is corrected by the addition, and mixture of salt. For salt beeing of an hot and drie nature, and by solution being verie apt to incorporate therewith, consumeth all the putrified vapors, or partes thereof, and correcteth all the putrifaction which it findeth, and it maketh all good Waters to keepe sweet and sounde the longer. For the Marriners themselues can witnesse, that such waters as be somwhat brackish, be the best for long voiages, because they will last longer than others: and therfore they do often water their ships from springs that bee neere the sea. And furthermore those that doe search more narrowlie into the nature and property of all things, doo constantlie affirme, that such springes as be offensiue in smel, or that carry any bad or corrupt tast with them, are no waie better to bee purified & clensed, then by casting of salt into them. Therefore this seemeth verie probable, for that (besides all which I haue alreadie alledged) waters doo become most deadlie and contagious, by their putrified and offensiue smels, rather than by their saltnes. Yea the saltnesse of the waters (vnlesse it be extream, as in the Sea of Sodome, which for that it engendreth no liue thing, and also destroyeth whatsoeuer falleth into it, it is called by the name of the dead sea) doth neither tend to destruction, neither is it offensiue to the fertilitie of the ground (but rather beeing meanely brackish, and thereby also it selfe not subiect to putrifaction, as wee may behold in the sea) it maketh the waters themselues most fruitfull. Neither is there any place in the whole world where that generatiue vertue doth more abound, or where there is

more

Art and Nature.

more infinit generation & multiplicatiō of creatures, then in the wide Ocean. And I doo verely beleeue y͏̄ the spirit of God which in the beginning did spread it selfe vpon the waters (which I doe hold to be a certen fire) did make them to be of that nature, that is to say, thicke and salt, and by that reason they are much more apt for the generation of all creatures, then any fresh waters whatsoeuer. Now then euery kind of saltwater is not hurtful to plants, neither is it hurtfull to al alike, but there be certen plantes which prosper best in saltwaters, & those springs, which be somwhat brackish are rather vnfit to make drinke for mans body, then to water the grounds. For nothing is more vnsauory in our drink then salt, because that our thirst doth naturallie desire to bee satisfied with that which is cold and moist, wheras these watering dewes doe rather represent a food, then a bare drinke to y͏̄ earth, for they giue a kind of norishment vnto plantes, neither do they offēd vnlés they be ouersalted like brine. So that according to the measure of saltnesse, these brackish waters be either good or hurtful to al kind of vegetables, for if they sauour of the excesse then they burn, and dry vp the ground, and so make it barren, but if they bee moderatelie salt they agree well with diuers plantes, and bee not verie hurtfull vnto any.

So likewise all other liuing Creatures by the extreamitie of saltnesse are destroyed vtterlie, as wee see by the Redde Sea, for they are euen partched awaie therewith, but if that the same bee more temperate (as in all other Seas) many Creatures are ingendered thereby, and doe growe into huge and mightie bodies, and bee more sounde then any other Creatures, and many of them beeing dead, may

The Jewel-house of

may bee kept a long time, although I am not ignoraunt, that some kindes of fishes cannot endure the least saltnesse that may be, neither can they continue, or liue but in the fresh water onely, and some others againe doo thriue and prosper in either of them: such is the great varietie of natures. But vnto man, and to diuers other land Creatures, the eating of much salt is very contagious, because it maketh the bloud salt, and it breedes barennesse to mans bodie by the extreame siccitie thereof, and it maketh our seed or nature too sharpe, but the same being moderatly taken, is very stirring in our bodies, and prouoketh them to venerious actes, whereby it helpeth to the generation of mankind.

And therefore me thinks, that al those controuersies about the seuerall natures of salt, are but friuolous wherein some doo contend that it engendereth barrennesse, and death, and therefore it was vsed to bee throwne vpon cursed groundes, and others woulde haue the same to be of a fruitful and incorrupt nature, which made the Poets to faine, that Venus was born in the sea, by meanes of the sperme of the Gods that fel into it, and so they called hir ἀφροδίτην of the some or froath of the sea. And here by the waie I wil make bold also, to insert the opinion of that learned, and great Magitian *Io. Bap. Por. 347.* who writing vpon the helpes of conception saith, that salt doth greatlie further procreation, for it doth not onely stir vp lust, but it doth also minister fruitfulnesse. And therefore the Egyptians did vse to feed their bitches with salte meates, when they found them vnapt for generation. And Plutarch doth witnesse, that ships vpon the seas are pestred and poisoned oftetimes, with exceeding store of mice. And some hold opinion, that the

females

females without any copulation with the males, doe conceiue onely by licking of salt. And this maketh the Fishmongers Wiues so wanton, and so beautifull. Which caused the Egyptian priests (by the report of Plutarch) most religiouslie to abstaine from salt, and salt meates, for that they found them verie stirring, and prouoking to venerie. Wherefore since the nature of salt is to defend and take away all putrifaction, which leadeth euery thing vnto destruction, it seemeth vpon good reason that this was the salt of the waters of Iericho, and that *Elisha* did hold a naturall course in correcting of them: God himselfe exalting aboue nature that naturall propertie which hee had first giuen vnto salt: For otherwise, neyther so small a proportion of salt, woulde haue sufficed to haue purified so great a quantitie of Waters, neither could these waters haue lasted sweet vntill this daie. Thus farre *Valetius*.

Nowe that we may yet haue a farther, and more inward speculation into the nature of salt, it shall not be impertinent to our purpose, to set downe and gather, all those obseruations, which I haue also culled and gathered out of twoe larger Treatises, the same being euen wrung out of the bowels of the earth, by that learned husbandman, maister *Bernard Palissy*, whereof the one is entituled, *Des sels diuerses*, and the other *De la marne*, wherby all those that be ẏ true infantes of Art, may receiue a full light into nature, which dooth heere present hir selfe in all hir royaltie, with her *Cornucopia* in her hande, and the ignoraunt Farmers may also gleane with them, a fewe lose and scattered eares, to make so much breade of, as may relieue their hungrie bellyes. And hauing performed this collection, I will sette downe such particular ler practises, as haue their full warrant from these two Theorickes, and may serue in diuers partes of this land, either for arable, or pasture groundes, where the ordinarie soile or dung doth faile vs.

A philoso-phicall discours vpon salt.

There are so manie sortes and kindes of salt (saieth Maister *Bernard*) that it is impossible for any man to number them all, and farther I tell thee that there is not any one thinge in the worlde, which dooeth not participate of this salt, whether it be man, beast, tree, plant, or any other kinde of vegetable, yea euen the mettals themselues, and that which is more, there is not any kind of vegetable whatsoeuer, that coulde growe or flourishe, without the action of salt, which lieth hidde in euerie seede, and besides all this, if the salt were deuided from the bodie of any liuing man, or from the stones which are wrought vppe into strong buildinges, or from the principall postes, the Rafters, and the beames of any house, they woulde all fall to powder, in lesse than the twinkeling of an eie. The like may bee said, both of yron, steele, gold and siluer, and all other mettals. And therefore hee that woulde knowe of mee howe many kindes of salte there bee, I shall bee forced to answer him that there be as many, as there be seuerall sortes of tastes, or sents.

Diuersitie of salts.

Coppres is a salt, Niter is a salt, vitrial is a salt, allom is a salt, Borras is a salt, Suger is a salt, Sublimate is a salt, Saltpeter is a salt, the salt gem, *Le Sahcor*, the Tartar, sal Armoniacke, all these are diuers kindes of saltes, and if I would take vppon me to name them all, I shoulde neuer make an ende. The salt which the Alcumistes call *Sal Alcali*, is extracted from an herbe, which groweth in the salt marishes of the Isles

Art and Nature.

Isles of *Xantoigne*. The salt of Tartar, is nothing els, then that salt of the reasons which giueth the taste and sauour to the Wine, and defendeth it from putrifaction, and therefore I say yet againe, that the sauour of all things proceedeth from salt: which alone causeth the vegetation, perfection, maturitie, and the whole good that is conteined in euery thing that nourisheth.

And although there bee diuers sortes of these and other vegetables, whose saltes be more fixed and of harder solution, than the salt of the Vine, *& du salicor*, neuerthelesse I say, that in all manner of Trees, and plantes, there is more or lesse of this salt, *videlicet*, so much as is sufficient for them: aswell as in those others before mentioned, for otherwise manie kindes of Ashes woulde not serue to whiten linnen cloathes: by the effect of which ashes thou mayest easilie vnderstand that there is salt in all thinges. And thou art not to thinke, that the ashes bee of strength to whiten, but onelie by the vertue of their salt, for otherwise the selfe-same ashes might serue diuerse times.

The properties of salt.

Salt the strength of ashes.

But in so much as the salt which is within the saide ashes, commeth to bee dissolued in the water, wherin they boile, it penetrateth the linnen, and by his vertue sharpenesse, and biting, all the filthe and soile of Cloth is dispearsed, mollified, and carryed downewarde with the Water, which afterwardes becommeth a Lee, because that therein resteth and remayneth all such salt as was in the ashes before, beeing now dissolued by the action of the water, and the ashes by this meanes hauing lost their saltnesse, haue not any more strength to whighten anye

other

other linnen, and men cast them out into the streetes as altogither vnprofitable. Marke yet one other example. When the salt-peter-men seeke to drawe out the salt peter from the earth, they worke in the same manner as is before set downe for the making of the Lee, and when they haue gotten out the salt peter, both the ashes and the earth, out of which they haue now taken the salt, are altogither vnprofitable: for that there is no more salt lefte which was the principall worker.

And yet for thy better instruction, consider those men which tan the hides of beasts, they take y̆ barkes of Oake, and hauing dried and broken them, they lay them amongest the hides in their tanning fats: and when the hides haue remained their full time with those barkes, they cast them awaie as a thinge of no further vse (although I knowe that in diuers places where fewell is deere, they vse to make cloddes, or turfs of them, in the likenesse and forme of cheeses, which they cause to be dried, and so burne them for want of other fiering) but the ashes of them are nothing woorth, because the salt of them is already spent.

Dooest thou not vnderstand heereby, that it is not the barke, that hath hardned and tanned the leather, but the salt which is conteined therein? For otherwise the same barkes woulde serue againe, but because the salt is dissolued it is soaked into the Leather, by reasonne of his moysture, which hath made an attraction thereof to serue his own turne. It is also to bee noted that in al kinde of woodes, the salt is in a manner wholelie in the barkes, and that such wood as is barked dooeth neuer yeelde any strong ashes. Mounsieur Sisly Duke Mountpen-
sier

sier his Phisition shewed vnto mee vppon a certaine time a sticke of Sinamon, which was about foure foote in length, and an inch thicke. I tasted of the vttermost barke thereof, and it had the liuely, and naturall sauour of the best and strongest Cinamon, whereas in al the rest of the sticke, there was no more taste then in a stone. And this is the reason why the Tanners account of nothing else but the barkes, because of the salt which is in them, for otherwise the rest of the wood being wrought into powder, might serue their turne as well. And for further proofe that there is some salt in euerie thing, we read that the Egyptians were woont to vse Niter, and other Aromaticall bodies, about the dead bodies of their kings, and princes, which wee doe call enbawming: which Niter is a preseruing salt, that defendeth from putrifaction. And their flesh so embaulmed is called *Mumia*, which the Egyptians doe finde to bee verie medicinable, and for my part I thinke the same more wholsome then potable golde. There be some in our time that woulde faine imitate that ancient manner of enbaulming, and seeke to make a kinde of *Mumia* of their bodies who haue suffered death for some capitall offence, but they falle herein, and their *Mumia* doth soone corrupt, and putrifie, for want of such excellent Aromaticall drugges as those ancient Egyptians vsed. For now it is generally holden, that all those sweet smelling simples, all the Rubarbe, Gums, and other Aromaticall ware, are greatly sophisticated before they come to our handes, and our common salt is not of that vertue to preserue things withall, as those aromaticall drugges which come from the blessed Arabia, and other hote Countryes. And that euerie thing hath some salt in it, it is manifest,

Glaſſe of all kinds of aſhes.

ſeſt, for that it is poſſible to make Glaſſe of all kinds of Aſhes, although ſome ſortes of them bee of harder fuſion or melting than others. And were there not ſome ſalt in all trees and hearbes, it woulde bee a thing moſt impoſſible to make Glaſſe of them. The ſecrete vertues alſo which lid hid in ſalt confirme the

The vertue of Salt.

ſame. For ſalt whiteneth all thinges, it hardeneth all things, it preſerueth all things, it giueth ſauour to all things, it is that Maſticke that gleweth all things together, it gathereth and knitteth all mineall matters, and of manie thouſand peeces it maketh one maſſe. This ſalt giueth ſounde to all thinges ; and without the ſounde no mettall will ring in his ſhirle voyce: Salt maketh men merrie, it whiteneth the fleſh, and it giueth beautie to all reaſonable creatures, it entertayneth that loue and amitie which is betwixt the Male and Female, through that great vigour and ſtirring vppe which it prouoketh in the engendring members, it helpeth to procreation, it giueth vnto creatures their voyce, as alſo vnto Mettalles. Salt is the cauſe that manie ſmall pibbleſtones beeing ſubtlelie powdred, become one maſſe, whereof they make our drinking Glaſſes, and all other ſortes of Table-veſſell; and by the power of ſalt, all ſubſtaunces maie bee brought into tranſparent bodyes. And it is ſalt that maketh all ſeedes to flouriſh, and growe, and although the number of thoſe men is verie ſmall, which can giue anie true reaſon whie dungue ſhoulde doe anie good in arable groundes, but are ledde thereto more by cuſtome than anie Philoſophicall reaſon, neuertheleſſe it is apparaunt, that no dungue, which is layde vppon barraine groundes, coulde anie way enrich the ſame, if it were not for the ſalt which the ſtrawe

and

and hay left behinde them by their putrifaction. And therfore al these simple sots which leaue their muck-heaps abroad, and subiect to the weather, shew them selues to bee but meane husband men, and that they neuer tasted of any true naturall philosophie. For the raine which falleth vpon these dungue-hils, flowing downewarde into the vallyes, dooth also carrie with it the salt of the dungue which dissolueth it selfe with the moysture: whereby the soyle beeing afterwarde laide abroad vpon the land, dooth little or no good vnto it. But if thou wilt not giue credite vnto my speech, yet marke howe the labouring Hinde, when hee carryeth his dungue to the feelde, howe in discharging of his loades hee leaueth it in certane heapes together, and a while after hee commeth to spread it all ouer the ground, and layeth the same in equall leuill, and afterward when the same feeld happeneth to bee sowed with corne, thou shalt alwayes finde the corne to be more greene and ranke in those places where the same heapes were first layde (after they haue ben there some reasonable time) then in anie other place in all the ground besides, and this commeth to passe by reason that the raine which fell vppon them, hath caried euen the salt through them, and conueied it into the earth that was vnder them. Whereby thou maist easily gather that it is not the dung it selfe which causeth fruitfulnes: but the salt which the seed hath sucked out of the ground. And herevpon it commeth to passe that all excrements as wel of man as beast, serue to fatten & inrich the earth. But if any man will plow, and sow his ground yearely without dunging the same, the hungry seede in time will drinke vp all the salt of the earth, whereby the earth being robd of her salt, can bring forth no more fruit,

muckheaps ought to be couered.

All excrements enrich ground

fruit, vntill it bee dunged againe, or suffered to lie fallow a certaine time: to the ende that it may gather a newe saltnesse from the cloudes, and raine that falleth vpon it. But I speake not here of common salt, but of the vegetatiue salt. For there bee many that hold opinion, that there is no greater enemie to all seeds then salt, and that because in ancient time when any wicked, or desperate villain had committed any notorious crime that deserued death, hee had sentence giuen him to haue his house raced, his ground turned vp, and sowed with salt, that it might neuer after bring forth fruit againe. I know not whether there bee any Countrie whose salt dooth not agree with corne: but I am sure that vpon the little hillockes in the salt Marshes of *Xantoigne*, men doe mow as good grasse as in anie other place that euer I came in. And those hillockes doe come of the groundes and washinges throwne vp from the bottome of the same Marshes, which are as brackish as the sea water, and yet neuerthelesse I did neuer see any fayrer corne in my life then groweth in them. And therefore I know not why our Iudges haue taken occasion to sowe salt on the offenders groundes, to bring a curse vppon them, vnlesse there happen to bee some such Countrie where salt is the meere enemie of all seedes. But to continue our first course, and to proue that salt is no enemie, either to the vegetatiue, or sensatiue natures. We see that the Vines of the countrie of *Xantoigne* which are planted in the midst of the salt marshes, doe bring forth a kinde of blacke reason, which they call *Chanchets*, and whereof there is a wine made that is nothing inferiour to our Hipocras, in which they vse also to dippe their toasted bread, as they doe in Ypocras. And these Vines are so fertile that one
plant

plant of them dooth bring foorth more fruite, then sixe of those that growe in Paris. See nowe what reason I haue to thinke that salt is so farre off from beeing an enemie to Nature, that on the other side it doth rather helpe the goodnesse, sweetnesse, maturitie, generation, and preseruation of the said Vines. And not onely salt dooth giue his ayde, and helpe herein, but also the ayre it selfe, by his salt exhalations. In the aforesayde Islandes, and within the salt Marshes, there is a salt hearbe founde called *Salicor*, whereof the most beautifull Glasse of all other is made, and there is also gathered that *Xantonique* Wormewood, so called of the Countrey where it groweth. The same hearb hath this propertie, that if one doe boyle the same, and with the decoction thereof doe temper a little meale, and make it into paste, and so frie the same either in larde or Butter, and eate thereof, it will expell, and driue out all such Wormes, as are either within the bodies of men, or children. And before I vnderstood thereof, I had six children that died of the Wormes which I did manifestly perceiue as well in the anatomizing of their bodies, as also for that oftentimes they voyded them at their mouthes, and when they were drawing to their ende, these Wormes woulde issue at their nosthrils. My purpose is not hereby to proue that common salt doth agree with all kinde of plants, but I am well assured that the salt Marshes of *Xantoigne*, doe bring foorth all maner of fruites that are planted there, and the same so pleasaunt, as in no place more where I haue trauayled.

All wilde hearbes, thornes, and thistles, doe prosper so exceedingly there, as no where better, which is a sufficient confutation to those which would haue salt to be enemie to all plants. For if it were an enemie to plants, it should also bee an enemie to the nature of man, which the Burgonions will by no meanes confesse; for if they were so perswaded, they woulde neuer haue ordained that salt shoulde bee put in the mouthes of their infants at their baptisme, whereupon they are tearmed the powdred Burgonions. Neither will the beastes agree that salt is an enemie vnto them, for the Goates will deuoure as much thereof, as you will giue them, and they seeke out purposely for brinish walles, agaynst the which men haue made water, euen to licke them. And the Pigeons when they happen to find an olde wall whose temper was made of Lime and Sand, and beginneth once to molder away, they will neuer leaue it, nor bee driuen from it.

Now some simple Clowne that neuer knew what learning ment, will perhaps imagine, that they feede vpon the sande, but that is but a blind conceipt, for it is not digestible, whereas this is the verie potable Golde of the Pigeons, and therefore wee are not to thinke that they seeke for ought else then the Lime that is in the morter, and that for the saltnesse thereof. And if they happen to swallow one graine of sand, it is against their willes.

The Oisters for the most part are also nourished by salt, and their shels are compounded of it which they themselues haue wrought vp, and it is very apparant that it is so, for that their shels being cast into the fire, do make a crackling much like to common salt. And if salt bee of that vertue as to woorke an erection of those engendring parts (as I haue said before) it is a thing most certaine and well approoued, that Oisters themselues are of the same operation: which approueth

ueth my former allegation, that those Oysters are for the most part nourished with salt. But for a further confirmation, that salt is not enemie to anie vegetatiue nature, let vs a little beholde the worke of the plaine countrimen of *Ardenna*, in diuers places wherof they cut down woods in great quantitie, and those they couch & range in the earth in such sort, as that there may be drawne vnto them some aire from belowe, then they lay great number of cloddes of earth vpon the same wood, yet such as are full of swarth, and grasse, and afterwardes they kindle the Wood which lyeth thus couered with the turfe, and after they haue burned them all togither sufficiently, they disperse them ouer the face of the whole ground, as wee vse to doe in our dongue, then they plough it, and sowe Rie there, where nothing else but Wood grew before, and the Rie commeth vp aboundantly, and this they do euerie sixteene yeares. And in some partes but sixe yeres, and in some parts but four yeres onely, wherby the ground being spared so long, bringeth foorth afresh as much wood, and as great as at the first. And of this wood they fell so much as is sufficient to enrich the ground for one yeares crop, and burne the same with their turfes together as before: and so consequently euery yeere vntill the number of sixteen yeeres be expired, and then they begin again at the first peece of ground which they had ploughed 16 yeeres before, in the which they find the wood of as great a growth as in the beginning. Hereby it is manifest, that the rusticall opinion of those clownish people of that Countrey is vtterly false, who thinke that the heate of these fires, and the ashes, are the onelie cause which maketh their cold countries fruitfull, whereas in deede it is the salt of these trees,

C 2 hearbs,

salt to be enemie to all plants. For if it were an enemie to plants, it should also bee an enemie to the nature of man, which the Burgonions will by no meanes confesse, for if they were so perswaded, they woulde neuer haue ordained that salt shoulde bee put in the mouthes of their infants at their baptisme, wherevpon they are tearmed the powdred Burgonions. Neither will the beastes agree that salt is an enemie vnto them, for the Goates will deuoure as much thereof, as you will giue them, and they seeke out purposely for brinish walles, agaynst the which men haue made water, euen to licke them. And the Pigeons when they happen to find an olde wall whose temper was made of Lime and Sand, and beginneth once to molder away, they will neuer leaue it, nor bee driuen from it.

Now some simple Clowne that neuer knew what learning ment, will perhaps imagine, that they feede vpon the sande, but that is but a blind conceipt, for it is not digestible, whereas this is the verie potable Golde of the Pigeons, and therefore wee are not to thinke that they seeke for ought else then the Lime that is in the morter, and that for the saltnesse thereof. And if they happen to swallow one graine of sand, it is against their willes.

The Oisters for the most part are also nourished by salt, and their shels are compounded of it which they themselues haue wrought vp, and it is very apparant that it is so, for that their shels being cast into the fire, do make a crackling much like to common salt. And if salt bee of that vertue as to woorke an erection of those engendring parts (as I haue said before) it is a thing most certaine and well approoued, that Oisters themselues are of the same operation: which approueth

ueth my former allegation, that those Oysters are for the most part nourished with salt. But for a further confirmation, that salt is not enemie to anie vegetatiue nature, let vs a little beholde the worke of the plaine countrimen of *Ardenna*, in diuers places wherof they cut down woods in great quantitie, and those they couch & range in the earth in such sort, as that there may be drawne vnto them some aire from belowe, then they lay great number of cloddes of earth vpon the same wood, yet such as are full of swarth, and grasse, and afterwardes they kindle the Wood which lyeth thus couered with the turfe, and after they haue burned them all togither sufficiently, they disperse them ouer the face of the whole ground, as wee vse to doe in our dongue, then they plough it, and sowe Rie there, where nothing else but Wood grew before, and the Rie commeth vp aboundantly, and this they do euerie sixteene yeares. And in some partes but sixe yeres, and in some parts but four yeres onely, wherby the ground being spared so long, bringeth foorth afresh as much wood, and as great as at the first. And of this wood they fell so much as is sufficient to enrich the ground for one yeares crop, and burne the same with their turfes together as before: and so consequently euery yeere vntill the number of sixteen yeeres be expired, and then they begin again at the first peece of ground which they had ploughed 16 yeeres before, in the which they find the wood of as great a growth as in the beginning. Hereby it is manifest, that the rusticall opinion of those clownish people of that Countrey is vtterly false, who thinke that the heate of these fires, and the ashes, are the onelie cause which maketh their cold countries fruitfull, whereas in deede it is the salt of these trees, hearbs,

hearbs, and rootes being burnt which they haue left behinde them. And therefore if my wittes were able to search into all the vertues, and properties of salt, I would thinke to doe wonders therby. For euen the *Alcumists* giue a blauncher vnto Venus with the salt of Tartar, or some other kind of salt. And salt is a most necessarie thing for the Diers, because that Alom which is a salt, draweth vnto it the colors of Brasill, and of Galles, and of other matters, and so maketh both cloth, silke and leather, to take their die the better, insomuch as the Diers when they woulde die a white cloath into a redde, are sometimes forced to dippe it first in Alome water. Yea, and some kindes of salt doe so harden yron, and doe giue such temper to the edges of weapons, as that one may cut yron with them as if it were but a peece of wood. What shoulde I say any more of this salt, for it passeth my reach to make anie true description of the excellent vertues thereof? Onely I will conclude with this, that if it were possible to keepe the same from moysture, then diuerse subiectes wherein it is included woulde last for euer, and so the salt that is in Wood, would defende the same from all putrifaction, and if all humiditie might bee defended from entring into a peece of Wood, there would neuer any Wormes breed or engender in the same, for it is impossible that anie putrifaction shoulde beginne, vnlesse some moisture be first kindled by way of putrefaction. Thus much out of the first treatise.

    Nowe I will take out a few of the most principall notes out of his large discourse vppon the title of Marle, and so proceed from these French Theoricks, to some English practises.

    Marle, saith Master Barnard, is commonly a white earth

Art and Nature.

A practicall discourse vpon Marle

earth which men digge out from vnder the ground, and for the most part they are forced to make pits, in such sort, as they doe for wels before they can come at it, and where they find any store thereof, they laie the same vppon their hungrie and barren groundes, first in small heapes, and afterwards they disperse the same vpon the whole fielde, as is accustomed in the common manner of dunging. And this marle will keepe the ground whereon it is laide, some 10. or 12 yeares in hart, and in some countries for 30. yeares. And sometimes the vaine thereof, beginneth at the verie entrance of the pit, and so runneth down many yardes deepe: and sometime we are forced to digge eight or ten yardes before we can come to the vaine thereof. But one thinge amongest the rest seemeth most strange of all other (which I haue heard some men maintaine) that it profiteth the ground very little, the first yeare wherein it is laid abroad, and that by reason of his exceeding heat, whereby it burneth vppe the seede that is then sowne. But this is easilie answered, for that in the groundes bordering vppon the woods of Arden, which are verie colde, they vse lime in stead of dung, and thereby they make ẏ earth most fruitfull which was barren before, Now if lime (which is nothing else but a baked or burnt stone within those fierie furnaces, and whose moisture is altogether exhaled, so as there remaineth therin nothing else, but the terrestriall parts replenished with a fierie vertue) be found so rich a soile, I know not why the heat of marle may not much better be endured. But it is verie requisite to spread the same vppon the earth before the winter beginn, to the ende that the frostie weather may the better dissolue the same.

 There is some Marle that is as white as lime, and

C 3   other

The Jewel-house of

Divers colours of Marle.

other some that is of a gray or russet colour, some of it is blacke, and some is yellowe. The cause of the white marle proceedeth of his long decoction, that which is blacke may haue many causes, whereof the principall is, that there is not any long time past since the matter thereof began to congeale, and this marle is more easie of solution, and peraduenture some putrified wood, or some minerals, haue turned the matter into a blacke colour. And as for the yellow marle, that colour may happen either of some yron mine, or of some mine of Lead, siluer, or Antimonie, and thus you see the reason of the diuersitie of colours that happen to marle.

That Marle is not hote

Marle is no other thing then a kind of clay ground and therefore seeing clay is cold and dry, as it appeareth by the Marcasites, and by wood that is both metalized and petrified in clay groundes, it is manifest that Marle is also cold and drie, and therefore it is not the heat thereof, which bettereth or amendeth barren grounds.

The beginning of Marle with the transmutation thereof

All Marle was earth before it became marle, it is a kinde of clay ground, and chalke it selfe was marle before it became chalke. And that which is more, that which is yet chalke within the Matrix of the earth, wil in time harden into a white stone. And last of all, wheresoeuer there bee any stones that be subiect to calcination, they were firste marle before they were stones, for otherwise by their calcination they could not possibly amend any barren grounds.

Marle to be dissolued by frosts.

When Marle hath once begun to passe his decoction, it becommeth so harde, that the raine cannot dissolue it so soon as wee would haue it, but it remayneth in small peeces vpon the ground vndissolued, & hereby it commeth to passe, that it can impart none

of

Art and Nature.

of his ſtrength vnto the grounde vntill it bee melted and liquified, and for that this cannot be ſuddenly performed as in the firſt yeare, therefore the froſts in ſome reaſonable time after do cauſe a diſſolution thereof, and then it helpeth toward the generation & germination of all ſeeds, that ſhall be preſented vnto it. Alſo chalke and lime, after the froſtes haue taken them, wherby they crumble into powder, do become good marle, and ſerue in ſtead thereof.

Although I would not haue the generatiue vertue of marle attribuzed to his heat, yet my meaning is not thereby to rob Marle of his heat: but *I* labour to confute the fooliſh opinion of thoſe, which attribute the whole vertue thereof to his heate, I ſay the vvhole both inwarde and outwarde. For it is well knowne, that ſalt is inwardlie hot, and therefore it is accounted an helpe to the act of generation, and alwaies in extreame cold weather, a man ſhal finde ſalt to be as cold as water, or any ſtone. Whervpon we may eaſilie gather, that his heat could actuate nothing, vnleſſe it were firſt ſtirred vp by a counter-heate wherin conſiſteth the ſeminall acte, and therefore wee muſt reaſon more deeplie, and looke to the eſſential cauſe that moueth and worketh herein, and then wee ſhall finde out ſome hidden matter that is not ſubiect to euerie meane conceit. *How Marle worketh his effects.*

And this is a fift element (neuer known before to the auncient Philoſophers) which is a generatiue water, cleer, ſubtile, mingled inſeparably with other waters, which water beeing alſo brought among common waters, doth indurate and congeale it ſelf with ſuch thinges as doo happen to bee mixed with it. And although the common Waters doe mount aloft againe by the attraction of the Sunne, whether that the ſame bee in Clowdes, Exhalations, *A fift element and what it is.*

or

or vapors, yet neuerthelesse the second water which I call a fift element is also carried amidst the others, and when those common waters run downewardes, alongst the vallies, whether they be flouds, riuers, or springs, I say that in what sort soeuer they descende, or in what place soeuer they staie, they doo alwaies frame some one thing or other, and most commonly either great stones, rockes and quarries of stone, according to the grosenesse of the matter which is staied with it, and carrieth the forme of his molde wherin it resteth, and this being so congealed, that common water is sometimes drunke vp in the earth, and descendeth lower, or else it is drawne vpwardes, and doth vanish away in vapors and cloudes, leauing his companion behind, which he is not able to carry any longer, And thus is Marle engendred, for before it was marle, it was a certeine earth, into which both these waters had entred, and had reposed themselues for a certeine time: during which rest, the generatiue water became congealed, and the vaporatiue water passed away, and was drawne vp from the other, and so the earth (wherein this congealed water did staie) waxed hard, and became white by the vertue therof, being both wrought vp into one bodie, whereby it commeth to passe, that when this marle is scattered abroad, vpon the arable ground, the seede which is sowen thereon, doth not take of the substance of this marle, to helpe his vegetation, but doth rather glut it selfe with this generatiue, and congelatiue water, which I call the fift element, which generatiue water being once consumed by often sowing of the ground the marle becommeth vnprofitable, as a sign of some decoction finished, the like is to be thought of all other dung and lime.

It

Art and Nature.

It is also to be noted, that the seed which is sowne cannot make any attraction of this generatiue water, if the same were not also moistened with the common water. And that when the ground is moistned either with the raine, or deaw that falleth, the common water that descendeth, together with the generatiue, stayeth the hastie congelation of the other, whereby it commeth to passe, that corne and other seedes doe keepe themselues greene vntill their maturitie, and when they are ripe, and that their roote ceaseth to drawe or drinke vp any more thereof, the exhalatiue water flyeth away, and the generatiue remaineth, and as the decoction in plants beginneth to perfect it selfe, so the colour also chaungeth, as it commeth to passe also in stones and al kinds of mettall. So as this fift element, although it be a water, & mingled with other waters, yet it is the same which doth vpholde both strawe and hey, and al kindes of Trees and plants, yea euen men and beastes likewise, & of this generatiue substance, the verie bones both of man and beast, are hardned & framed in their kind. And euen as we see the pibble or flint stones which are formed and engendred of this congelatiue water, doe endure the strength of fire, and are not consumed therewith, but rather vitrified: so in like manner this fift and generatiue element being within y̆ straw and hey cannot bee wasted away, for if thou dooest burne them, or any other Wood in the fire, all the cōmon water thereof will vanish into smoke, but this generatiue water, which hath sustained, nourished & encreased both the straw and hey remaineth in their ashes, and cannot bee consumed, but turneth it selfe into glasse, being liquified in those hot flaming furnaces, and the same so cleere and transparant, as the

The vse of the exhalatiue water.

D gene-

generatiue water it selfe was before this congelation. But there is nothing that more resisteth fire then the bones of diuers beastes, as I haue often prooued when I haue burned the bones of sheepes feete, and so of egge-shelles, which is a manifest argument, that they haue drawne more abundantlie to themselues, of this generatiue water then any other partes. And there is no doubt but there is great store therof in the apple of the eie, which being continually moistened, and accompanied with the other exhalatiue water, is kept from being hardened into the nature of a stone. Neither is there any kind of stone which in his principall form is not cleere, and white, and those which be clowdie are so by accident, for that in their composition, there happened some earth or sande to bee congealed or hardened with their first matter. Neuertheles, there is no stone so dark & obscure, which by force of fire dooth not become transparent at the last, bicause that principall element whereof I haue spoken so much, maketh al things else become transparent and fyxed, as it is it selfe in his fyrst beeing. This I haue written the rather to encourage thee to seeke out marle within thine owne inheritaunce, to enrich thy barren groundes, that they may yeelde their fruit aboundantlie in their seasons. And in so dooing, thou shalt shewe thy selfe a good husbandman, and become a patterne to all thy slothful neighbours, whereby they shall bee forced to imitate thy good example.

How Marle was first found out. Now concerning the fynding out of this marle, I thinke that those which fyrst happened vppon it, did not obteine this skil by any true theoricall imagination, but that by meere chaunce, they did fynde the same without any seeking, as peraduenture by the

digging

Art and Nature.

igging of some Ditch or other trench, about their ground, and beeing forced to throwe vp that which they had digged vppon the bankes of their arable fyeldes adioyning, and fynding such Corne as happened to be sowne vpon these bankes, to bee more fresh and ranke then in any other part of the fyelde besides, they prosecuted this good happe of theirs further the next yeare, and so spreade the same ouer the whole fyelde: and so by long experience, and in the ende they found the same much more profytable then any other dung, and some others peraduenture might happen vppon the same in seeking for springs, in like manner. Yet it is alwaies to be noted that this marle must fyrst be dissolued throughout the ground before the seed can make any attraction thereof vnto it selfe: euen as flesh cannot purchase a defensatiue againft putrefaction by salt, vntill the salt bee melted and made liquid.

But for the more easie fynding out of this marle, I thinke it necessarie that euerie man shoulde haue a long Auger or Percer, with seuerall large bittes which he may put on and take off at his pleasure, and with these hee may search at what depth hee will, in diuers places of his Lande, alwaies marking what seuerall vaines of earth he fyndeth in the bytte of the Augur, and of euerie seuerall earth which hee draweth vppe, he may make some triall vpon the ground, vnlesse he can be assured by the whitenesse and hardnesse thereof that he hath hit vppon the right Marle: for then he needeth not to proceede to any further Triall. *How men may search for Marle.*

And hauing once found the vaine, hee may lay it open in such sort as may be most conuenient for the euacuating thereof. Nowe if there happen to bee any

any quarrie of soft stone betweene him & the marle: he must firste make his entrance thorough the stone with a piercing worme, and then hauing made waie, he may seeke further with his foresaid Augur.

Colors of Marle. Marle for the most part is white, yet in diuers parts of Fraunce, there is both gray, blacke, and yellowe, and therefore we must not whollie rest vpon the colours thereof, for these other colours may become white by a longer decoction, and as there is a white marle, so likewise there is a white clay, which I think *A white claie.* will serue in steade of marle, especiallie that fulling *Fullers earth* earth, wherewith the fullers vse to scoure oile out of their cloathes.

That Marle is not of a fatty nature It is an erronious opinion, to thinke that Marle may be discerned by the feeling of the hands, as some doe holde, and that it is to bee knowne from other moulds by the fattines, or viscousnes therof, which is false, for if it were fatty, it would be impossible eyther for raine or frost, to dissolue the same, for all oylie thinges do resist and striue against water, yea wee see apparantly, that both clay & marle do help to scoure out all greasie and oylie spots, as Fullers can well testifie, and if marle were of an oylie Nature, it woulde consume in the fire, but if we make any proofe therof, we shall finde the same most violently to resist the fyre.

And in the latter end of his Philosophical abstract, Maister *Barnard* concludeth thus, that marle is a naturall, and yet a diuine soile, beeing an enemie to all weedes that spring vppe of themselues, and giueth a generatiue vertue to all Seedes that are sowne vpon the ground by the labour of man, and heere endeth Maister *Barnard.*

A man would thinke that so learned a Theorick as this

this in a matter so generall, and necessarie for the Realme of Englande, so plawsible to worldly wittes, and set down in so plaine and familiar tearms, could neuer haue beene extant so manie yeares together with so little fruit, and profite vnto all our leane and barren groundes, as (for ought that I can see or heare) it hath beene hitherto, and so is like to continue, vnlesse some studious scholler, or other, will steppe foorth, and take our idle Farmers by the hand, and either leade them ouer shooes into one of Maister *Barnards* Mucke-heapes, or else by violence thrust them into one of his Marle-pittes. For what easier course can possiblie bee directed by the Penne of a-nie Writer, then is heere deliuered for the finding out of Marle? Or what cheaper tooles coulde the witte of man deuise, then an hande, and a piercing Augur to search into the bowels of the earth for all her marrow, and fatnesse? Doe wee thinke that Nature is bounde to cast vp the treasures of her full gorge amongest vs, who will not vouchsafe one pipe of *Tabacco* vpon her? *Effodiuntur opes,* sayeth *Ouid,* vnto all slouthfull husbandmen, and therefore seeing wee may haue such wealth for the digging, let vs not spare the Shouell and Mattocke, till wee haue founde out some Marle-pittes in our owne de-mesnes. For the veynes of Marle are more in number, much longer and broader, and deeper than wee thinke for, and though wee finde them not in one place, yet wee shall happilie finde them in another. It is a small aduenture to hazarde a shilling to gaine a pounde: it is no losse to set poore men on woorke, (which otherwise in conscience wee beeing able, and they beeing honest, we are bounde to relieue) though they gaine vs nothing, our great possibilitie

Howe to find out Marle and the vse thereof.

may

30 *The Jewel-house of*

may easilie counteruaile their small charge. Regarde not the colours of the mould, you see that maister *Barnard* heere telleth you of a white, of a gray, of a blacke, and a yellowe Marle. And whie may there not also bee some other colours of Marle in our Countrey which Maister *Barnard* neuer knew? It is a small matter to trie the seuerall natures of all the veynes which you finde in digging, you may prooue of euerie kinde a little, in diuerse places the first yeare, and so proceede to a greater tryall the next yeare, as your good successe shall encourage you.

<small>Colors of Marle.</small>

And though you finde but small amendment in the first proofe, yet practize againe, for it may bee you layde either too little, or too much thereof vpon your ground: for too little of the best Marle can doe but little good, and too much therof hath beene alreadie founde to bee verie hurtfull to the Corne. And therefore vntill you haue attayned vnto the verie pricke of proportion, learne first all the experience which you can drawe from other men, and then prooue what further perfection you can adde thereto your selfe. Examine the seasons of the yeere, in which it is best to lay abroade euerie kinde of soile, for if the same bee of an harde and binding nature, then Maister *Barnard* telleth you, that it muste bee layde in the begiming of Winter, that first the frosts maie make the same to moulder into small peeces, and so to become apt for solution, and then the raine which commonly dooth fall more aboundantlie in the Winter then in the Sommer time, may perfectlie dissolue the same. If it agree not with one sort of soyle, peraduenture it will agree with another. It

<small>Proportion of Marle.</small>

<small>Season to lay marle abroad.</small>

<small>Vpon seuerall grounds</small>

may

Art and Nature.

may serue an arable grounde, and not a pasture ground, or a fennie, and not an heathie, or a Clay ground, and not a sandie ground. Peraduenture it may proue good for one kinde of graine, and not for another. And therefore you must neuer rest till you haue made a full tryall of all the inward veynes of the earth, in all the seasons of the yeare, in all degrees of proportion, in all kindes of graine, vpon all sortes of grounde, with all such like necessarie circumstaunces, and so in the ende you shall finde out those differences, and make such obseruations to your selfe, as the slugguish and idle loyterers of our time (though they haue the same matter to worke vpon) shall neuer bee able to reach vnto, or imitate. *In seuerall sorts of graine. Circumstances. Fullers earth.*

The Fullers earth which Master *Barnard* heere mentioneth in his title of Marle, and commendeth to the same ende, I haue not knowne at anie time practised in Englande for the bettering of anie ground, but by all presumption the same muste of necessitie bee verie rich, because it is full of that vegetatiue salt, so highlie commended by this French Authour, which appeareth in those scowring effectes, for the which it is diuerse wayes had in vse amongst vs, and if the same bee to bee had in anie plentifull maner, I coulde wish that some exact proofe were made thereof, according to the former circumstaunces. And heere I can not omitte the carefull industrie of that ingenious, though vnlearned olde man. Who hauing long since cutte off that vnprofitable exchaunge of our English siluer, with those French and Leaden trifles: hath also giuen himselfe to diuerse other profitable and ingenious practises,

amongst

amongst the which he hath assured me of this one to be most true, that euen the very clay which he digged vp in Saint Georges fields, beeing laid vppon his pasture grounds which hee there holdeth by lease, did exceedinglie enrich the same, insomuch as hee did neuer regard to seeke after anie other soyle. And this hath also some credite with master *Barnard*, which affirmeth that all Marle is a kinde of Clay grounde, and it should seeme to differ onely in digestion from Marle. And in another place hee setteth downe his opinion of a white Clay, which hee found as hee trauelled in France toward Poicters, and Towers, that he held the same to be equiualent to Marle it self. And it should seeme by all reason, that the like order is to be vsed therein in bestowing it vpon the ground, as is before expressed in Marle.

Clay instead of Marle.

I may not here omit to commend the soyle of the streetes, or residence, and groundes of all Channels, Pondes, Pooles, Riuers, and Ditches, and of all other pannes and bottomes whatsoeuer, where anie store of waters do repose themselues, but especially where any abundaunce of raine water hath a long time setled, for that the congelatiue partes of these waters, bee full of the vegetatiue salt of Nature, as Master *Barnard* noteth, who is verily perswaded that there is no other reason to bee giuen of that heartie fruitfulnesse, which the fallowe groundes doe gather againe in time, but onely the generatiue part of raine water, which dooth fall vpon them so often, whilest they remaine vnsowen with graine. For to imagine that the earth by quietnesse or rest alone, should become fatte againe without the ministring of anie other nourishment or foode vnto it, were as much agaynst all sense and reason, as to thinke that a languishing

The soile of the streats, and the residence of all watrie bottomes.

Art and Nature.

thing patiente shoulde in tyme recouer his former strength by keeping of his bedde only without taking of any cordiall or restoritiue broths for his comfort. Wherefore seeing there be so many pannes, and receptacles for waters in euery shire, in one place, or other, and seeing nature alone ministreth matter enough for vs to worke on, but wanteth handes onely to bring things together, let vs seeke to helpe nature a little with our hands, and she will retourne our labour againe with an excessiue vsurie into our bosomes.

There is also a kind of moorish earth, which being laid after 20. or 30. loades vpon an acre, will amend, and better your pasture grounds a long time after. *Moorish earth.*

I will passe ouer all the triuiall vses of Cow-dung, Horse dung, folding of sheepe, Hogs dung, Pigeons dung, and such like, for that they are already knowne, and common in this land with euery Country *Coridon*, yet I thinke it not amisse to set dowe some necessary obseruations in them, such as I haue partely drawne from conceipted wits, and partely haue imagined my selfe by the contemplation of natures workes. And therfore here I can by no meanes allow of the ordenary manner, in laying abroade of our greate muckheapes, wherein Maister *Barnard* telleth vs that the winter raine which falleth vppon them, carieth also with it a greate parte of their strength, so as the vpper parte of them becommeth very leane, and hungry, and is scarsely worth the carlage, and spreading abroad. But I knowe that the Farmers of our land will aunswere me in this point, that it is too costly to build barnes, or other couerts for dunghills, but my meaning is not to perswade them thereto (although peraduenture if wee did erect a fewe streight trees, or firpoles, and make a loose thatched, or borded *Dung of beastes.* *Muckheaps how to be made.* *A couert for a muckheape.*

E ded

The Jewel-house of

amongst the which he hath assured me of this one to be most true, that euen the very clay which he digged vp in Saint Georges fields, beeing laid vppon his pasture grounds which hee there holdeth by lease, did exceedinglie enrich the same, insomuch as hee did neuer regard to seeke after anie other soyle. And this hath also some credite with master *Barnard*, which affirmeth that all Marle is a kinde of Clay grounde, and it should seeme to differ onely in digestion from Marle. And in another place hee setteth downe his opinion of a white Clay, which hee found as hee trauelled in France toward Poicters, and Towers, that he held the same to be equiualent to Marle it self. And it should seeme by all reason, that the like order is to be vsed therein in bestowing it vpon the ground, as is before expressed in Marle.

Clay instead of Marle.

I may not here omit to commend the soyle of the streetes, or residence, and groundes of all Channels, Pondes, Pooles, Riuers, and Ditches, and of all other pannes and bottomes whatsoeuer, where anie store of waters do repose themselues, but especially where any abundaunce of raine water hath a long time setled, for that the congelatiue partes of these waters, bee full of the vegetatiue salt of Nature, as Master *Barnard* noteth, who is verily perswaded that there is no other reason to bee giuen of that heartie fruitfulnesse, which the fallowe groundes doe gather againe in time, but onely the generatiue part of raine water, which dooth fall vpon them so often, whilest they remaine vnsowen with graine. For to imagine that the earth by quietnesse or rest alone, should become fatte againe without the ministring of anie other nourishment or foode vnto it, were as much agaynst all sense and reason, as to thinke that a languishing

The soile of the streats, and the residence of all watrie bottomes.

Art and Nature.

shing patiente shoulde in tyme recouer his former strength by keeping of his bedde only without taking of any cordiall or restoritiue broths for his comfort. Wherefore seeing there be so many pannes, and receptacles for waters in euery shire, in one place, or other, and seeing nature alone ministreth matter enough for vs to worke on, but wanteth handes onely to bring things together, let vs seeke to helpe nature a little with our hands, and she will retourne our labour againe with an excessiue vsurie into our bosomes.

There is also a kind of moorish earth, which being laid after 20. or 30. loades vpon an acre, will amend, and better your pasture grounds a long time after. *Moorish earth.*

I will passe ouer all the triuiall vses of Cow-dung, Horse dung, folding of sheepe, Hogs dung, Pigeons dung, and such like, for that they are already knowne, and common in this land with euery Countrey *Coridon*, yet I thinke it not amisse to set dowe some necessary obseruations in them, such as I haue partely drawne from conceipted wits, and partely haue imagined my selfe by the contemplation of natures workes. And therfore here I can by no meanes allow of the ordenary manner, in laying abroade of our greate muckheapes, wherein Maister *Barnard* telleth vs that the winter raine which falleth vppon them, carieth also with it a greate parte of their strength, so as the vpper parte of them becommeth very leane, and hungry, and is scarsely worth the cariage, and spreading abroad. But I knowe that the Fariners of our land will aunswere me in this point, that it is too costly to build barnes, or other couerts for dunghills, but my meaning is not to perswade them thereto (although peraduenture if wee did erect a fewe streight trees, or firpoles, and make a loose thatched, or borded *Dung of beastes.* *Muckheapes how to be made.* *A couert for a muckheape.*

E ded

ded cap to couer it, which might slip vp and down at what heigth we thought good, as they vse in the low Countries to make their barnes, (a patterne whereof standeth to be seene nere vnto S. *Albones* not far from Parkmill, in the backeside of one of my tennaunts howses there) that so the goodnes of the soile would in a few yeares counteruaile the charge of our building) but rather that they woulde place the muckheapes vpon the foote of some hill (making a little square receptacle of bricke in the bottome thereof) whereby all such strength, and substance of the dung, as all the showers of raine that fal, shal carry with thē, might with a free discent be conueied into this pit or cesterne, so as the same in conuenient leisure mighte also with scoopes, and other shouels, be continually returned vpon the muckheapes from time to time as it fell, whereby the greatest parte of that vegetatiue salt, which nowe is loste in euery farmors yarde or backside, might be preserued for the better manuring of the ground.

A receptacle of brick.

Some be also of opinion that it helpeth much to the bettering of our dung, if al the brine and powdred beefe broth which is commonly throwne away, were powred vpon the muckheapes, thereby to multiply their salte. And Maister *Barnabe Googe* will haue all the suddes of his landery conueied thereon, and the muckheapes to be couered with bowes, to the ende that the Sunne may not draw away any parte of the strength thereof. And because we are now entred into the most principall, & generall practise of this land whereby the greatest parte both of our pasture, and arrable grounds are vsually bettered; it shall not bee amisse to sette downe some new, though a very easie course, howe wee may the sooner bringe our dung to putri-

How to rot dung speedily.

Art and Nature.

putrifaction, and so thereby not onely obtaine such ranke pasture as now we haue by reason of the same soile, but also that we may purchase a much sweeter grasse, or feeding for our cattell, then hitherto wee haue had, for that (as I conceiue) is the speciall fault of the first crop which our ground bringeth forth after it is newly dunged. And this common errour of ours (if I be not deceiued) is easilie helped, & that onely by making, first a lay of dung of a foot in thicknesse, & then a lay of earth vpon the same, and then another lay of dung vpon that earth, and so proceeding in the maner of *Stratum super stratum*, til your muck heape bee as large and high as you woulde haue it. *To haue sweete gras at the firste yeares dunging.*

But this practise woulde alwaies bee perfourmed, either vpon the ground which wee meane to enrich, or very neere vnto it, least that which we get in the goodnesse of the grasse, we doo happilie loose in the charge of our labour, and cariage. And heere it shall not be altogether vnprofitable, to let all those Gentlemen and Farmors, who are desirous of some speciall good mould, for some small purposes, to vnderstand, that after they haue disburdened ye ground of this great muckheape of theirs, that if they will yet digge a foot and a halfe or two foot vnder the same, that by this meanes they shal obtaine a most fat and rich earth, and very apt for diuers plants, as al our ordinary Gardeners, can sufficiently witnesse. *A rich molde for gardens, & orchards.*

Thus much of the soile or dung it selfe, being dispersed in his grosse body. Now a worde or two of those conceited practises, which I promised before. I haue heard som studious practisers very cõfidently affirm, that if you steep your corn in water ye space of certein houres (but I could neuer yet finde them all agree in on time: for som limit 12. houres, som 18. & som 36. houres, you may proue them all, and keepe the best) *Of steeping corne in dung water*

in water, wherein good store of Cow dung hath lyen in imbibition, for certaine daies (which times you must also serch, if you meane to be an exact maister) euery day stirring the same once, or twise together before you lay in your corne, and after this preperation you sowe the same (though in barren grounds) that so you shall purchase a most rich, and plentifull crop with an easie charge. But this kinde of practise I haue heard both maintained, and impugned aswel by reason as by experience, and that by men of good iudgement on both sides, although if I woulde sette downe mine owne experience herein, I must needes confesse I could neuer yet attaine to any truth in this secret, or to make any apparant difference betweene the corne that was husbanded in this maner, & that which grew of it selfe without any such helpe, yet will I not (for the credit of the Reporters) altogether discredit the Inuention, for that peraduenture I mighte faile in the nature of the graine, or in the time of imbibition. And as it should seem great store of those vsuall receipts, which are common in our ordenary books of secrets, is drawne from this ground, wherby they labour to alter, and change the smells, tastes, colors, and vertues of many fruits and plants, only by steeping the seeds in such Aromatical waters, as they themselues apropriate for such vses, as they entende them, & therfore they tell vs, that steeping of seeds in the infusion of wormewood, centuary, coloquintida, and such like, will defende them from wormeating, which for the present time I do easily beleue, but how then commeth it to passe, that these seeds do not also bring forth bitter fruite, according to their infusion? and yet it is generally thoughte that the clouegilliflower gotte his firste sent from the cloue, which

was

was conueyed into his slip, but this I holde for an erronious opinion, and to bee as false as it is olde, for neither is there any phylosophicall, and inseparable combining of their two natures, perfourmed in this grosse practise; neither can so small a substance (beeing neither truely prepared, nor exalted before) extend it selfe so infinitely from one slip to another, as we see daily perfourmed, in that sweet and beawtiful flower.

I haue here yet one experience more to set down in this kinde, which (because it was the practise of a spiritual Lord, that died of late, and fell out very happilie, as I haue beene credibly enformed by one of his especiall officers, who with diuers others was an eiewitnesse of the same: although it vary not much from the former course,) I wil publish the same vnto al posteritie, vnder such credite, as I my selfe did first receiue it. And therefore, whereas before you steeped your corne in the water, which had sucked out the strength, or salt of the dung, you must nowe mingle your dung, your water, and your corne together, in a great vessell of wood, and you must stirre the same well, with an apte staffe for the purpose, one whole houre at the least: This worke you may begin in the after noone, and toward Euening you must recontinue your first agitation for one halfe houre, or more: then let these substances repose themselues all the night following, and in the morning, or sometime the next day, you must suffer the water to passe away by some tampion, according to the manner of the saltpeter men: & when the liquor is sufficiently dreined, then mingle the corne and dung throughly wel together, and after sow the dung and corne so mixed in a barren and hungry mould, and you shall haue as

rich

rich a crop, as If the groud it selfe had beene dunged before. This experience was made, in an hartlesse peece of ground, which lacked also one tilth, and which no man durst aduenture to sow with any grain and yet my Lord bishop did by this meanes, attaine to a most plentifull wheat haruest.

A practical discours vpon salt. Now let vs proceed to the sweetest, cheapest, and moste philosophicall marle of all other, euen that which both *Valetius* and maister *Barnard* haue so closely, and theoricallie handled, as that (notwithstanding the one telleth vs of the exceeding fertillity, that is found in salt waters, by that infinite generation and multiplication of fishes, yea of Venus her selfe, that *Primum mobile*, in the procreation of children, and the other of those pleasant grapes, growing in the salt Marishes of *Xantoigne*) yet neither of them haue left vs any assured meanes, how wee may purchase any store of this salt, whereby wee may make any great vse thereof. So as notwithstanding we are now brought vnto the riuers of life, and to that goodly tree so laden with golden apples, yet here wee are left with *Tantalus* to starue and perish for want of food. Yea maister *Barnard* himselfe, after that hee had so sweetlie seasoned our eares with his brackishe philosophy, yet in one place (as if hee had repented himselfe of his too much forwardnesse, in these his secret discoueries, nay, as if he had the greatest secret of nature in hand) he telleth vs in plaine termes, that it is not the common salt, but the vegetatiue salt, which he so commendeth. Nay, that which is more, in the examination of the Iudges censure, vpon the groundes of condemned persons, wherin they would haue their landes to be sowed with salt, in token of a prepetual barrennesse, he faltreth and staggereth, and can

can finde no reason to maintaine their iudgementes, vnlesse it were as he saith, in respect of the nature of some countries, where salt was an enemie to al seeds. Why how now maister *Barnard*? Is it possible, that you, which could first find out the meanes, howe to furnish vs in al places, with new springs of sweet and delicate waters, where there was neuer any before, that could first finde a fift element, which nature had hitherto locked vp in her owne cofers, which coulde teach vs the reason of al petrefiyng, vitrifying, & metalizing of earthy bodies, yea which could so learnedlie set downe, the generatiue reason of al vegetables, should now be ignorant howe to reconcile earth and salt togither: or how to turn a common salt into a vegetatiue salt? Yet *Valetius* dealeth more plainely with vs (according to that light which hee had receiued) saying, that if too much or too little, doe in any one thing make an apparãt differẽce in ỹ effects, then surely of al others, the same is most especially to be seene in salt; and so he would haue the cursed effects of that sentence, to proceede from the excessiue proportion & quantity of salt, that is bestowed vpon the malefactors grounds. But suppose that *Valetius* hath not only aimed faire like a gẽtlemã, but also hit the mark, like a a good archer in this point: wher is now this vegetatiue salt become, which M. *Barnard* so highly extolleth? or how shal we obtaine any store thereof, for the enriching of so many thousand acres of barrẽ groũd, as this realm of England doth present vnto vs? Meethinks I am now in the midst of a stop galiard, & were it not, that I should heere offend so great a concourse of people, as I haue nowe gathered together, in mine owne conceit, *I* coulde finde in my hearte to commaunde the Violands to ceafe, and so to breake off

in

in the midst of a rough Cinquepasse. Neuertheles, crauing pardon of all the ancient Philosophers heerin, but especially of M. *Barnard* (who if he had bin disposed, could haue eased me of this labour, & performed it much better) I will onely request with *Sinon*, *Fas mihi Graiorum sacrata resoluere iura*, and so bestow a new taske vpon Nature, who wil be ready to yeeld vs great store of the richest Marle-pittes, and such as haue not hitherto beene discouered, but onelie in phylosophicall tearmes to any Nation, or countrie whatsoeuer: hoping hereby, that as the secret which I haue now in hand, and seemeth almost incredible before it be disclosed, shall procure some further credite & beleefe, vnto the rest of my inuentions, wherof I haue alreadie giuen a taste, by a publique impression, and yet reserue some fewe till I finde a better opinion conceiued of English Artists.

Now then let vs first examine, what essential difference we can finde, in those foure elements, whereof all the inferiour bodies doo consist? or whether they may be all reduced to one, notwithstanding the manifest opposition that seemeth to be in their contrary qualities? And for my part, I must here acknowledge that the best naturall phylosophie that euer I coulde learne in this point, was neither out of Aristotles phisicks, nor Velcuries naturall philosophy, nor *Garsceus* meteors, nor out of any of the olde philosophicall Fathers, that writ so many hundred yeares past; but that little which I haue, I gathered it on the backside of Moore fieldes, where by sundrie vndoubted argumentes, I did heare it maintained, that all those elements, doo onely differ in attenuation, and condensation: so as earth beeing attenuated, becommeth water; and water condensate, becommeth earth;

water

water attenuated beecommeth aier, and aier condenſate beecommeth water; and ſo likewiſe aier attenuated becommeth fire, and fire condenſate becommeth aier, and thus all of them ſpring from one roote, which being admitted is a manifeſte proofe that there is a greate, and neere affinity betweene the lande, and the ſea, wherein we ſhall finde ſalte water enough for our purppoſe. And yet further wee ſee that of the earth, and water together are made one globe, ſo as a ſmale matter will make them frendes being ſo neerely vnited together. And nowe I may well ſay that I am entred into an whole ſea of matter, from whence I muſte fetch the greateſt ſtore of my vegetatiue ſalte, and if this ſtore-houſe faile me, I knowe not whither to repaire for ſuch plenty of ſalte, as I muſt be forced to vſe in this action. And becauſe you ſhall vnderſtand that I am now in a right courſe, let vs conſider of a fewe experiences already performed in the like kinde; which becauſe at the firſte they were found out by meere chaunce, and not by iudgement, the Authors of them could as yet neuer extend them to any generall, or publique vſe: but haue hitherto walked continually like petite conſtables within their own precincts. Amongſt the which, the firſt practiſe that euer I heard of, was of a ſillie ſwaine whoe paſſing ouer an arme of the ſea with his ſeede corne in a ſacke, by miſchaunce at the landing, his ſacke fell into the water, and ſo his corne being lefte there til the next low water, became ſomewhat brackiſh, yet ſuch was the neceſſity of the man, as that he (not whithſtanding hee was out of all hope to haue any good ſucceſſe thereby, yet not being able to buie any other) beſtowed the ſame wheat vpon his plowed groundes, by the aduiſe of a gentle man of good

F   wor-

worship frō whence I receaued the report thereof, & in fine when the harueft time came about, he reaped a rich crop of goodly wheat, such as in that yeare not any of his neighbours had the like, & yet notwithstāding (for ought that euer I could yet learne) neither he nor any other of his countrimē would euer aduenture to make any further vse therof, belike being perswaded, vnles that the corne by chaunce fell into the sea, it would neuer fructifie. What shoulde I speake here of him that of his owne mother witte sowed a bushell of salte long since vpon a smal patche of barren grounde at Clapham which to this daye remayneth more fresh and greene, and full of swarth then all the reste of the fielde about it? But this man had some more reason then the other, not to prosecute so chargeable a practise any further, for that he knew well that one bushell of salte woulde counteruayle two loodes of the beste dunge there, whereas the former practicer, mighte haue had sea water at will for the fetching.

 I mighte here adde the dayly, and vsuall practise in the West partes of this land, where the people to their greate charge in cariage, doe conuaie the saltish sandes, vnto their barren groundes, whereof some of them doe lye fiue miles distant from the Sea. And yet they finde the same exceeding profitable, for that their inheritance is thereby enriched for many years together, and who seeth not that the whole strength, and vertue thereof consisteth in the saltenesse, for otherwise wee mighte happely finde some other sortes of sand that woulde also bee equivalent vnto this. But to sette downe one experience that may serue for a thowsand because it consisteth

marginalia: Salt sowed at Clapham

marginalia: brackish sandes.

Art and Nature. 43

of nothing els but falte. So that here is no partnership at all, no ace of harts nor fiue fingers to bee suspected.

Before you sow your ground, do but only mingle two bushels of bay salte, amongest foure bushels of winter graine, and so disperse them together vppon the ground, and you shall finde a good encrease of corne and the land it selfe muche bettered, and cleered of weedes, as I haue beene very credibly enformed. But of all others I wonder moste of all at the ordinary experience which hath so longe time in the view of so many persons, beene yearely practised in the fieldes, neere adioyning to the salte pits of Nantwitch, where vpon the fall of any greate store of land waters into their pits, being forced to empty, and drawe out all the fresh water which alwaies floteth vppon the brine, and to bestow the same in such places as are neerest, and therewith also emptying some of the brine with the fresh water, they finde in time this earth so strongly seasoned with these brackish waters, that no soile or dunge is comparable vnto it, for the manurance of their groundes. And is it possible, that so many sharpe, and choise wits, shoulde til this day neglect so rare, so rich, yea so inestimable a triall as this, and not one amongest a thousande that hath ridden from thence to Westchester, shuld haue beene able to haue caried the secret so farre, but must so carelesly, and retchleslye drop the same by the way? But to com yet neerer to our purpose, what shall wee saye, or thinke of that surrounded leuell at Erith?

The brine of the Saltpits.

Erith breaches.

I dare not report that exceeding fertilitie which I haue herd commended in those two breaches, euen

F 2 by

worship frō whence I receaued the report thereof, & in fine when the harueſt time came about, he reaped a rich crop of goodly wheat, ſuch as in that yeare not any of his neighbours had the like, & yet notwithſtāding (for ought that euer I could yet learne) neither he nor any other of his countrimē would euer aduenture to make any further vſe therof, belike being perſwaded, vnles that the corne by chaunce fell into the ſea, it would neuer fructifie. What ſhoulde I ſpeake here of him that of his owne mother witte ſowed a buſhell of ſalte long ſince vpon a ſmal patche of barren grounde at Clapham which to this daye remayneth more freſh and greene, and full of ſwarth then all the reſte of the fielde about it? But this man had ſome more reaſon then the other, not to proſecute ſo chargeable a practiſe any further, for that he knew well that one buſhell of ſalte woulde counteruayle two loodes of the beſte dunge there, whereas the former practicer, mighte haue had ſea water at will for the fetching.

Salt ſowed at Clapham

I mighte here adde the dayly, and vſuall practiſe in the Weſt partes of this land, where the people to their greate charge in cariage, doe conuaie the ſaltiſh ſandes, vnto their barren groundes, whereof ſome of them doe lye fiue miles diſtant from the Sea. And yet they finde the ſame exceeding profitable, for that their inheritance is thereby enriched for many years together, and who ſeeth not that the whole ſtrength, and vertue thereof conſiſteth in the ſalteneſſe, for otherwiſe wee mighte happely finde ſome other ſortes of ſand that woulde alſo bee equivalent vnto this. But to ſette downe one experience that may ſerue for a thowſand becauſe it conſiſteth

brackiſh ſandes.

of

Art and Nature.

of nothing els but salte. So that here is no partnership at all, no ace of harts nor fiue fingers to bee suspected.

Before you sow your ground, do but only mingle two bushels of bay salte, amongest foure bushels of winter graine, and so disperse them together vppon the ground, and you shall finde a good encrease of corne and the land it selfe muche bettered, and cleered of weedes, as I haue beene very credibly enformed. But of all others I wonder moste of all at the ordinary experience which hath so longe time in the view of so many persons, beene yearely practised in the fieldes, neere adioyning to the salte pits of Nantwitch, where vpon the fall of any greate store of land waters into their pits, being forced to empty, and drawe out all the fresh water which alwaies floteth vppon the brine, and to bestow the same in such places as are neerest, and therewith also emptying some of the brine with the fresh water, they finde in time this earth so strongly seasoned with these brackish waters, that no soile or dunge is comparable vnto it, for the manurance of their groundes. And is it possible, that so many sharpe, and choise wits, shoulde til this day neglect so rare, so rich, yea so inestimable a triall as this, and not one amongest a thousande that hath ridden from thence to Westchester, shuld haue beene able to haue caried the secret so farre, but must so carelesly, and retchleslye drop the same by the way? But to com yet neerer to our purpose, what shall wee saye, or thinke of that surrounded leuell at Erith? *The brine of the Saltpits.* *Erith breaches.*

I dare not report that exceeding fertilitie which I haue herd commended in those two breaches, euen by the seuerall farmers thereof: and though we may in some measure excuse our grosse capacities for not applying those visible effects of the brackish waters, which had many years togither, reposed themselues in the greater breach, because the same was but lately inned, yet what shall we say for the lesser breach, which hath bin woon so long since? Was it not sufficient, to haue buried so many thousands of our English pounds, in those Dutch and drunken deuises, about the gaining of the grounde (in the time and charge whereof, some English wits that I coulde name, did offer to make a great and gainefull accurtation, and yet could not be heard) but that wheras nature her selfe presented in those breaches, a full recouerie of those expenses, to such as are studious; that yet we should remaine as blinde as beetles, not once examining, from whence this aboundant fruitfulnesse should spring, or growe? Nowe I finde that saying of the Philosopher, as concerning Nature, to be most true: *That she doth offer and discouer her selfe in the most plaine, and vsuall actions*, wherein we doo daily busie our selues, and yet scarcely any man doth apprehend her. The sillie country wench, churneth creame into butter with a simple staffe, and in a plaine vessell, onely by stirring vppe the inwarde fire of nature in his owne center, whereby it maketh a true and philosophical diuision of partes, yet whoe is the wiser for it?

But to returne to our salt againe, and to giue some colour to this weake contemplation of ours, peraduenture some men (and those also not of the meanest conceit) who hauing a continual eie vppon the salt marshes, wher euery acre of ground is so little worth, do therefore vtterly condemne the vse of brackish waters,

waters, as the wastefull destroyers of all generatiue vertue. Indeed I know, and haue found it most true, in mine owne experience, that if any vegetable whatsoeuer, haue by mishap taken any salt water, that the same is most vnapt to bee stirred yppe to any true or kindlie workemanshippe, but the reason heereof, I must conceale for a time, it shall now suffice to aunswer that other obiection, which seemeth like a forceable ramme, to beat down al the foundation & building which we haue hitherto made. But this I may sufficiently refell, by that *Nimium* of *Valetius*, which is daily to be seene in those Marshes, and maketh the grasse thereof euen brackish, to al the cattel that feed thereon, although in the manifestation, and whole discouery of the secret which I haue in hande, the same is else-where, more fullie and plentifully aunswered. What is then remaining, seeing that the salt of Clapham, those Westerne sandes, that brine of the Cheshire saltpittes, the residence of those brackish Waters at Erith, doo offer so liuely demonstration vnto vs of the vndoubted fertilitie, which is ready to ouerflowe our bankes if we wil but onely giue passage vnto it: but that wee doo nowe and than suffer a voluntary inundation and deluge, by those brackish Waters of the Sea, vppon some parcel of land, that is adiacent thereunto? which after they haue sufficiently reposed themselues thereon, we may by conuenient sluces, returne the same againe, and so leaue the earth to her owne workemanshippe, whoe by her inwarde heat and transmuting nature will in some reasonable time, by way of putrifaction conuert that, which was before a common salt, into a vegetatiue salt, so as although wee had iust cause before, to feare the extreame drying, or burning na-

F 3   ture

ture of salt, yet now when the same is made familiar, and as it were of one nature with the earth, it becommeth a most enriching substance: but least (whilst I go about to benefit the poore and honest Farmours of the land) I happen by these newe deuises, to hurt and hinder them against my will, and honest purpose; I woulde wish them firste to consider aduisedlie of the whole discourse, and to read it ouer againe and againe, before they put the same in practise, least peraduenture, they take a sword by the point, and so hurt themselues by that weapon, which was giuen them to defend their persons. And let this be a generall caueat vnto them, that they begin with small practises, and first vppon arable groundes, before they proceed to pasture, or meddowe: and so beeing carefull in those former circumstances, which I haue handled at large in the title of Marle, they shal no way endanger their estates, nor hazzard any great losse, before they attaine their desires. Neither would I haue them perswaded, that my meaning is that they should ouerflow any groundes, which eyther they haue sowed alreadie, or meane to sow presently with their graine, but rather some wast ground or other, which after it hath beene glutted with salt water diuers times, and then reposed it selfe a sufficient time, might serue in stead of marle, or other dung to spread abroad vpon their barren corne groundes; but how often the same should bee ouerflowne, and in what time the earth will sufficiently putrifie and transmute the salt, before it wil bee seruiceable in this kind, I wil not heere determine: yet since the same is so wel performed, neere the salt pits where there is not any artificiall obseruation at al made, I think him to be of a very grosse conceit, who after he hath conferred

ferred with those of Nantwich in this behalfe, should not be able to effect the like, in any parcel of land that bordereth vpon the Sea, or any arme thereof; yet it shal not be amisse for them to know this difference, that the brine of some of those saltpits, dooth holde one third, or one fourth part of salt, whereas the Sea water dooth not for the most part containe aboue one eighteenth or twentith part of salt, which would make a great difference betweene them, but that much land water is also laded out of those pits among the brine.

And now by this time I hope you are well furnished with salt, at an easie price, as also with the meanes howe to make the same of a vegetatiue nature. It were but in vaine here to entreat of the nature of that salt, whereof the Peter men doo gather a bushell or two at the most, from thirtie tunnes of earth, & therfore howe excellent soeuer the same be in his kinde, it wil not profite vs much in this worke, because the store thereof is so little. Now I wil proceede to some other sorts of soile, which be excellent in their kinde, but most of them appropriate only to particular places, and some of them not to be had in any great quātity, and therefore fitter for gardens, or for the trial of maisteries, then for the enriching of arable or pasture grounds, amongst ỹ which, I wil alot the first place to the putrifaction of vegetables, because there may some reasonable store be had of some of them, in certaine places, & then to the calcination of them, wherby they are first reduced to ashes, & after those ashes may be dispersed on such barren grounds, as ỹ proprietors of them shal make best choise of. And for ought that I could yet imagine, I hold ỹ brakes or fern to be both the cheapest, yea most plentiful, and that which

may

The Jewel-house of

may beſt be ſpared of all the vnneceſſary weedes that growe, and that you may ſooner rotte, and putrifie them, you muſt mingle good ſtore of earth amongſt them, or elſe make ſeuerall beds, or layes of earth, & ferne one vppon another; till you haue made as it were a large muckheape of them, and ſo let them reſt till they bee wholly conſumed into a fine earthe, or mold. Although I could name a Yorke-ſhire knight who dooth onely beſtowe the ferne it ſelfe in ſome good thickneſſe, throughout all the allies of his hop-garden, whereby both the rootes of his plants, are keept the moiſter, and alſo hee doth yeerely gather a rich molde out of his allies, to amende, and better his hop-hils withall.

How to putrifie ferne ſpeedily.

And here I haue iuſte cauſe offered me to commend alſo the manner of polling of his hops, which hee placeth in ſuch ſorte, as that one plant may not ſhaddow another: but that his whole garden receaueth the fulnes, & ſtrength of the ſun-beams at once, whereby both his hops are more kindly, and the bels of them much larger then in any other hop grounds, whoſe poles, are erected, and ſtand vpright after our ordenary and groſſe manner. But becauſe my promiſe was not, to deliuer any ſkil at al in hopgardens, I wil reſerue this concluſion, with ſome other ſecrets in hoppe grounds, not yet diſcouered or brought in publike vſe, for ſome apter occaſion, *vt ſemper nouus veniam.*

New māner of poling of hops.

And that *I* may not ſeeme, to haue loſt my ſelfe, in the midſt of theſe brakes, into the which I am now ſo deepely entred, I would haue that, which is heere ſpoken of the Ferne onely, to bee generallie vnderſtood of al ſortes of plantes, or vegetables whatſoeeuer, wherewith the earth dooth ſeemè vnprofitable

char

charged.

Diuers also haue found singular profit in the hayre that is gotten from the hides of beastes being thinly laid vpon the ground, and suffered to putrify. *Haire.*

Now as we may by putrifaction of the ferne, and other plants, in diuerse partes of this realme make the same very profitable vnto vs for such country purposes as are here intended; so likewise by calcination of them, or burning them to ashes, we shall find the like and selfe same effects; as diuerse shires in Englnd can already testifie in their owne experience, who consume their ferne, stubble, strawe, heath, furres, sedge, beane stalkes, and sometimes the very sworde, and swarth of the ground to ashes: and these according to the store of salt, which their ashes containe, do either for a longer, or a shorter time enrich their barren grounds. *Calcination of vegetables.*

And because that nature may be knowne to bee so cunning an artist, as that she hath not made any thing in vaine, the witte of man hath also founde out some good vse this way, euen of the duste and tailes of the malt, which are left in malting, for these being also returned vppon the grounds from whence they came do helpe in some measure to harten them again. The proportion of them is about three quarters to an acre of ground, but this secret extendeth only to malting townes, and there also but to a few acres of ground, yet I thought good to insert the same among the rest, as a member of that body, which giueth vnto each subiect his generatiue, and fructifying vertue. *Malte dust*

I would greatly commende that fine and delicate mold, that is founde in the boddies of olde large and hollow willow tres, that are putrified within, if it were as plentifull to bee had, as it is rich in substance, yet *The earth in willow trees.*

G   hap-

hapily how small ỹ store therof be, it shal not be lost for the gathering, after the best vses thereof be found out, & known among ỹ studious practisers of our age.

And here because of al other places, I woulde bee loth to leaue the most renowmed citty of Englande, wherin I was borne, without some further & sweeter helps for her barren groundes, then shee hath bin hitherto acquainted withal, and for that I daily do see, a most rich commodity trampled vnder foot, and contemned of al men, I hold my selfe euen bound in conscience, for my countries good, not to hide the same any longer, but rather to publish al such profitable vses therof, as I conceiue my self, or haue learned of others, togither with a ful satisfaction of those obiections, which haue bin grounded vpon the long discontinuance therof with the Low country men of Flanders, who are generallie accounted the most skilful & painful husbandmen of al Europe. The matter which I mean, is the wast sope ashes which our sope boilers for the most part, wil giue for the cariage, and som of them also doo pay for the cariage when they are conueyed from their houses: though some fewe of them make a smal benefit of these ashes. And here it shalbe no shame for vs to acknowledg those Flemmings to be our first teachers, in the vse of them: naye, it is rather a great shame, that wee cannot bee prouoked to our owne profit, by the example of others, who haue so many years enriched themselues therby, and haue of late yeares, to their great losse, bin forced to leaue them. As concerning their good opinion, and profitable vse of them, I think wee need no further argument to maintain it, then the price which they gaue for them to the sope-boilers, which I haue credibly heard, was 3. s. or ten grotes a lode, besides ỹ carriage of them into their own countrey. And

Art and Nature.

And yet if the infinite extension of them, the easie charge in bestowing of them together with their especiall nature, in suppressing of weedes, be wel weighed and considered, wee shall finde them to be much cheaper of that price then any common soile, or stable dung whatsoeuer. For howe cheap soeuer our other soile bee, yet the transposing thereof from place to place (if the land lie at any distance) doth make it so chargeable that the poorer sorte of farmors in many places of this realme wil scarcely aford the cariage therof to their grounds, though they might haue the same freely giuen them; whereas two load of these ashes or thereabouts being sufficient for an acre of arable ground is soone bestowed by the labor of one mā without the help either of cart or horse. For their maner about Bridges was after they had sowed the same with greine, to strowe these ashes thereon with their hands till the grounde did seeme to haue gathered a whitish garment vppon it, and that was sufficient for that yeare, and by this practise they might sowe the ground yearely without leauiug it fallow at any time; yea their ground being helped in this manner would yeald them a most rich crop of flax, whose seede of al other doth most burne, & pill the ground for so saith the Poet. *Vrit enim lini semen*. It is also with good probability to bee coniectured, that these sope ashes do not only enrich the ground, but do also help to destroy wormes, weedes, and rushes, that doe spring vp in moist and barren grounds; then let euery wise man imagine what may be saued thereby in that chargeable weeding of woad. *Qre* if brome or ferne may not be destroied by this meanes; and I make no doubt of brome, if the grounde were firste plowed, and after these ashes scattered vpon the same.

And because I would not relie wholie vppon the outlandish experience of those ashes, (least otherwise it might happilie be obiected that they are not agreeable with our soile or climate) I haue thought good to prefix in my demonstratiue table, the portraiture of an eare of Summer barlie, beeing drawne truely and sharpely, according to the breadth and length thereof; which together with sundry others of the same proportion (as by diuers eie witnesses of good credite, I can proue and iustifie) did grow this Summer at *Bishops hall*, where I dwell; to the great admiration of the beholders: the stalke whereof together with the eare was measured to bee an ell, and three inches in length, from the ground to the summitie thereof. And this I did in a barren grounde, by the helpe and meanes of those sope ashes, God blessing my labors therein.

I haue also this yeare, found the like successe thereof in pasture ground, by the meanes aforesaid. *Qre*. If that sope ashes wil not enrich the ground for woad as that thereby wee may continue our yeerely sowing vpon the ground, without any intermission thereof. *Qre*. Also, if the same be not very profitable to be laid amongest the hop hilles, to make the plantes to flourish and prosper the better. For in Lombardie, they like so well the vse of ashes, as that they esteeme it much aboue any dung; thinking dung not meete to be vsed, for the vnholsomnesse thereof. This out of maister *Barnabie Googe*, who dooth also affirme in another place of his booke of Husbandrie, that if we wil haue the Artichoke to prosper well, wee must dung the same continually with ashes, for that kinde of fruit delighteth therein.

And to make the same out of all question, I knowe

a graue and well experienced Cittizen of London, who hath made often triall of them, and hath founde very good successe, by applying them in the Winter time, to the rootes of his owne Artichokes. Now if we will also looke into the reason hereof, we shal find it to be nothing else but the salt of these ashes, which notwithstanding al that sharpe Lee, which the sope-boilers haue drawne from them, do yet remain much stronger, and more saltish then our best ashes, that haue not as yet beene put to any vse; and this wil easilie appeare in some of those other vses, that followe hereafter. All which being well considered, I do hold the same better for winter then summer corne, and very profitable for al colde and moist pasture, & medow grounds, so as they be laide vppon them, about the feast of all Saintes, that the great showers in the Winter time, may make them of an easie solution; whereby the grasse may haue a more speedy attraction of their vegetatiue salt vnto it.

Some be of opinion that these ashes be made for the most part, of that tree which carrieth a small leaf, like vnto our Oke, and whereof the Dansicke Wainscot is made. And some others doo commend another tree, that somewhat resembleth our Witchen Elmes, of whose boughes and branches, beeing burned, they gather these ashes. But it is most certaine that they are not the ashes of any one tree, but of diuers that are consumed together, as they growe in some great wood. Nowe these ashes by a more violent kind of fire, beeing forced to a fusion, whereby they cake and clode together, are then called by the name of sopeashes. But howe then commeth it to passe, if there be such salt and strength, remaining in these waste ashes, that our Fleminges (who wil not

And because I would not relie wholie vppon the outlandish experience of those ashes, (least otherwise it might happilie be obiected that they are not agreeable with our soile or climate) I haue thought good to prefix in my demonstratiue table, the portraiture of an eare of Summer barlie, beeing drawne truely and sharpely, according to the breadth and length thereof; which together with sundry others of the same proportion (as by diuers eie witnesses of good credite, I can proue and iustifie) did grow this Summer at *Bishops hall*, where I dwell; to the great admiration of the beholders: the stalke whereof together with the eare was measured to bee an ell, and three inches in length, from the ground to the summitie thereof. And this I did in a barren grounde, by the helpe and meanes of those sope ashes, God blessing my labors therein.

I haue also this yeare, found the like successe therof in pasture ground, by the meanes aforesaid. *Qre.* If that sope ashes wil not enrich the ground for woad as that thereby wee may continue our yeerely sowing vpon the ground, without any intermission therof. *Qre.* Also, if the same be not very profitable to be laid amongest the hop hilles, to make the plantes to flourish and prosper the better. For in Lombardie, they like so well the vse of ashes, as that they esteeme it much aboue any dung; thinking dung not meete to be vsed, for the vnholsomnesse thereof. This out of maister *Barnabie Googe*, who dooth also affirme in another place of his booke of Husbandrie, that if we wil haue the Artichoke to prosper well, wee must dung the same continually with ashes, for that kinde of fruit delighteth therein.

And to make the same out of all question, I knowe

a graue and well experienced Cittizen of London, who hath made often triall of them, and hath founde very good successe, by applying them in the Winter time, to the rootes of his owne Artichokes. Now if we will also looke into the reason hereof, we shal find it to be nothing else but the salt of these ashes, which notwithstanding al that sharpe Lee, which the sopeboilers haue drawne from them, do yet remain much stronger, and more saltish then our best ashes, that haue not as yet beene put to any vse; and this wil easilie appeare in some of those other vses, that followe hereafter. All which being well considered, I do hold the same better for winter then summer corne, and very profitable for al colde and moist pasture, & medow grounds, so as they be laide vppon them, about the feast of all Saintes, that the great showers in the Winter time, may make them of an easie solution; whereby the grasse may haue a more speedy attraction of their vegetatiue salt vnto it.

Some be of opinion that these ashes be made for the most part, of that tree which carrieth a small leaf, like vnto our Oke, and whereof the Dansicke Wainscot is made. And some others doo commend another tree, that somewhat resembleth our Witchen Elmes, of whose boughes and branches, beeing burned, they gather these ashes. But it is most certaine that they are not the ashes of any one tree, but of diuers that are consumed together, as they growe in some great wood. Nowe these ashes by a more violent kind of fire, beeing forced to a fusion, whereby they ca'e and clode together, are then called by the name of sopeashes. But howe then commeth it to passe, if there be such salt and strength, remaining in these waste ashes, that our Fleminges (who wil not lose so much as the parings of their nayles, much les the vse of so rich a commodity) should wholy abandon them, and for so many yeares togeather discontinew all their traffike and barganing with our sope boilers? It should seeme by al likelyhood that though for a few of the first yeares they found some hartning therby vnto the soile and ground whereon they were bestowed, yet in processe of yeares that these ashes being yearely renewed vpon the same land, did in the ende leaue some hard and barren crust, or *caput mortuum* behinde them, whereby the ground becam either for a long time, or wholy vnprofitale euer after.

These obiections being throughly answered, and confuted, I hope I shall finde an easy sute of it to entreat all our London borderers, who doe occupy themselues in the affaires of husbandry, to step into the dutch mens romes, and to neglecte no longer so rich and so bountifull an offer. Neither yet will I here relie vppon those late troubles, and turmoiles of the low countries, which hath beene a meanes both to cut off a great parte of the entercourse betwene them and vs, and to make them almoste vnwilling to performe any proffitable practise for their owne good least the enemy should like a drone Bee deuoure their hony, nor yet vpon any newe exaction that hath ben demanded of them vppon the transporting thereof, whereas in times past they did cary them freely away for ballist, but I will only at this time vrge that countermanding priuiledge firste granted vpon a color or pretence to haue imploied them very profitablely vpon the making of salte peeter, and brimstone within this realme, whereby al the sope boilers were prohibited from the sale of them to any such as would transport thē, although the patentees could neuer as yet

with

Art and Nature.

with all their chimicall skill, draw out or seperate one pound of peter, or brimstone from them. And for my parte I am vndoubtedly perswaded that their first purpose was no other (howsoeuer the same was masked, or disguised in shew) but only to force the sopeboilers (after they had procured a generall restrainte) to growe to composition with them for setting them at large again, which appeared most manifestly to be so, for that in yend they demanded a certaine rate vpon the tun, which they denied, and therupon the first discontinuance of them grewe betwixt the flemings and the Sopeboilers. And thus I hope I haue remoued this stumbling blocke out of my countrimens way whereby they may beginne a freshe practise of them, and thereby make some vse of that patent, which hath by this time gotten a sownd sleepe, and is now awaked in a good houre.

And as concerning any bad accidente that they should in time leaue behinde them; their melting and soluble nature, whereby in one yeares space they are wholy consumed with those showers, and frosts that ouer take them, is a sufficient argument to conuince all doubtes that can possibly bee obiected this way. But now to some other vses of them: I do find them much better and cheaper then the masons dust for the scowring of our trenchers, and other wodden vessels, and this can our duche liskins, and kitchin maides well approue, whose dressors, shelues, and molding bordes are muche whiter and cleaner keept, then those which are washed, and scalded after the english manner; vppon which reason they must of necessity be very seruiceable for washing of al our wodden floores either of deale, or elme to clense them of all their grease, spots, or soile whatsoeuer

and

and I make no question but that we shall finde them very excellent for the scowring, and clensing of our glasse windowes from all the steines, filth, and clowdinesse, that maketh them in time so darksome vnto vs. I will passe ouer the vse of them in the pauing of the streetes, and laying of bowling allies, wherin also many hundred loades are yearely consumed in London, and the suburbs rounde about it. But I may not omitte that excellent and ingenious practise, of that skilfull and auncient sopeboyler, who looking aduisedly into their binding and knitting nature, hath to his greate credit erected a faire, a strong and costly building of bricke, in the morter whereof, he bestowed good store of his owne sopeashes, which to this day contineweth firme, and solid; and without any shew of ill accident (hapining by these ashes) as any other building, whose stones were laide only with lime, and sand. By whose good example many other also of latter times haue occupied many hudredloads of them for the same purpose, & would hauespent many thousand loades of them ere this day, but that they finde this morter somewhat rough in the laying, and more sharpe and fretfull to their fingers then their vsuall morter which they daily occupy. But if I were able to be a builder my selfe, I woulde soone remedy these two slender falts, whereof the latter I holde rather for an excellent quality, and most appropriate for the nature of morter it selfe, rather then a falte. And yet for the good will which I beare vnto all the excellent vniforme builders of our time, and because thereby I shall giue some encrease of labour to the poore, and painefull people, that may bee employed therin: I will set downe the beste aduise, that I can in this behalfe, the same being such as I dare make warrant warrantise thereof vppon my credit, being carefully handled. As concerning the roughnes of them, who is so blind that seeth not which way to remedy ỹ sam, for it is rather a worke of labor then of skill? For they being either groũd or stamped into a fine powder, before they be mixed with the sand, wil soon be brought into a smooth temper.

And here wee haue no neede to feare the charge that will arise thereby, for I dare vndertake that the profit of one daies labour, will answere the charge of three mens wages, in the difference of price that will be found betweene one loade of these ashes, and one hundred of lime. The sharpnes wherwith they offend the Bricklaiers fingers may in some sort bee auoided by wearing of gloues (without the which, they seldome lay any bricke at all) to auoide the like effects, which they finde in lyme. But for an assured helpe therein (if the same be such as cannot bee endured of workemen) let these wast ashes bee reimbibed with more water for some resonable time, till some farther part or proportion of their salt be deuided from them and then without all question they shall finde them gentle enough, and much of their fretting nature taken from them. See the whole arte of making of the morter set downe in the former book of experiments nu.92. The lalte, though not the least vse of these ashes, which I purpose to discouer at this time, is to make them seruiceable in steade of common ashes, both for the whiting of linnen, as also for the making of buck lee, which are nowe growne to an excessiue price, partly by the greate expence of them in salt peter works: but principally through our late sparing of wood and charcoale, whereby these latter times doe not afford the like store, or plenty of them as we were

For buck cloathes.

H ac-

accustomed to haue in the daies of our predecessors. And I am y rather induced to conceaue well of them in this course, by that auneient, and common experience, which the whitsters, and dutch laundresses haue long since begun, and doe as yet continew amongest vs, for the speedier whiting of yarne with them, which they do most confidently affirme to become more white by this meanes by once bucking of it, then by sundry times with our common and ordinary ashes, and if they shalbe found ouer strong, & sharpe for our linnen (which is the only falte that I could euer here them charged withall) I doubte not but that by the aforesaid manner of imbibition, they may be so weakned, as they shall easily be reduced to the perfect strength of our ordenary ashes, or else for our better satisfaction herein wee may vse such proportion of our ashes amongst them, as may best bring them to bee of one nature, and qualitie with them. Thus much by way of digression of the seuerall vses of these wast ashes, wherein though I haue strayed a little without the bondes, and limits of husbandry yet I hope I shalbe found sufficiently within my text, for that all these particular vses may seeme to maintaine and fortifie their fructifying nature the more, because they are wholly drawn from that vegetatiue salt, wherwith the same aboue all other ordinary dung whatsoeuer is most fruitfull, and abounding.

<small>Salt of Animals</small>

<small>Salt of Minerals.</small>

Thus much of vegetables, nowe a touch of Animals, and so I will knit vp this discourse, leauing those inestimable and hidden treasures of the minerals and their salts, tending also this way vnto the deepe Lullists, and trew english Paracelsians, who no doubt if they liued in thankefull times, woulde begin where I haue left, and not only haue published their philosophical

phicall falt, which nature shoulde haue beene forced to maintaine for euer, but would also haue laide open a verie large veine of golden Marle, whereby they woulde haue so multiplied that radicall moisture of sundry plantes, as that in some good measure they should haue recouered that first perfection, wherein they were created, and which they lost by the fal and disobedience of man. I am crediblie enformed (and the reason thereof is so apparant, as that none but he which will deny the conclusion of a Syllogisme can denie the same) that after such time as the coast-men haue by expression, and other apt meanes, gotten that kind of traine oyle, which they call a pilchard oyle, from the fish of that name, that they doe also bestow that which remaineth of the pilchardes vppon their leane and hungry grounds, the substance wherof, by putrifaction, dooth in time become a most rich and fruitfull molde, and such as giueth hart vnto ỹ earth, for many yeares together. *Pilchards putrified.*

And it is no way to be doubted, but that the carcases and garbage of al other fish, would produce the like effects, for that they must of force resemble the nature of the place wherin they breed and liue: wherof we should haue had a sufficient triall ear this, but that there is no such store of any other fishe so fitlie presented vnto vs for this purpose, as the pilcharde, which serueth to no other vse, after separation made of the oile, but only to engender this fat dung, which we haue in hand. *Garbage of fish.*

Now concerning the bloud, offal, and entrailes of beasts, euery Butcher about London, who for the most part, hath a garden for that purpose, to burie the same in, to auoid offence, can sufficiently testifie. And I haue heard the bloud of beasts commended in *Bloud, offal & entrailes of beastes.*

high

high tearmes, for the forwarding and prospering of all poore and backward vines, so as withall it be tempered with lime, which is vsed to no other ende, but onely to destroy all such wormes, as otherwise the bloud would engender in the earth, which would in time consume all the sap and marrowe, that lyeth in the rootes, and in the end destroy both the root and the vine. Yet this caution I will giue before I conclude: that he which tempereth lime with y̓ bloud, must suffer the first accidentall heate, which happeneth in the slaking thereof, to passe ouer, before hee apply the same to the root, either of the vine, or of any other plant, least that vnkindly and vnnatural heat, (which for the time is stirred vp in the composition) do happen to burne and drie vppe, that radicall moysture, which will hardly be restored againe, by any outwarde Art or meanes whatsoeuer.

Claudite iam riuos pueri, sat prata biberunt.

Here endeth the booke
of Husbandry.

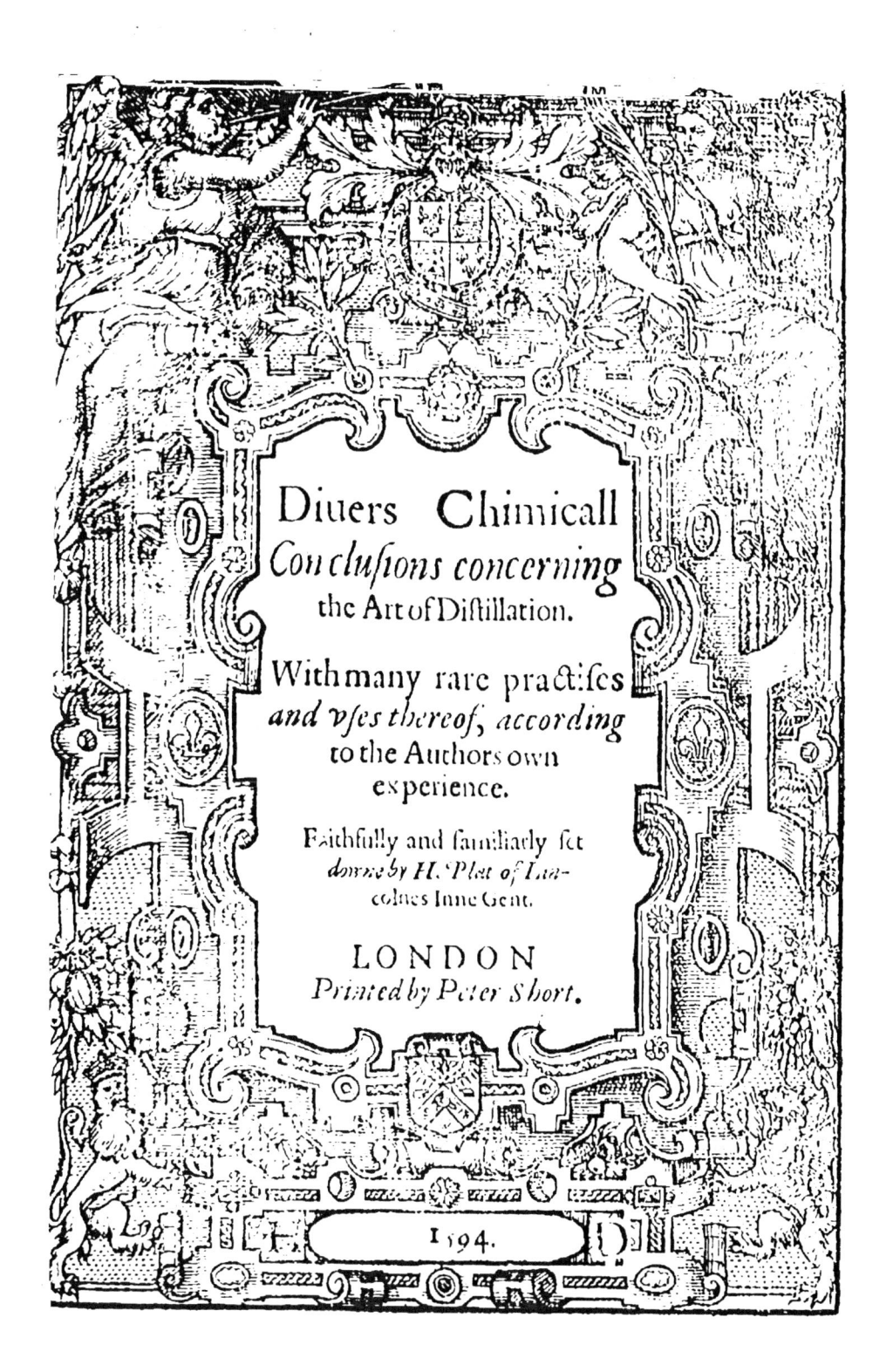

# Diuers Chimicall
Conclusions concerning
the Art of Distillation.

With many rare practises
and vses thereof, according
to the Authors own
experience.

Faithfully and familiarly set
downe by H. Plat of Lin-
colnes Inne Gent.

LONDON
Printed by Peter Short.

1594.

Diuerse chimicall conclusions concerning the Art of Distillation.

The maner of drawing, or extracting of the oiles out of hearbes, or spices with all necessarie circumstances.

1. A Copper body, or brasse pot, with a pewter Limbecke, and a glasse receyuer, are all the necessarie Instruments for the extracting of these oiles, and the greater the potte, or bodie is, and the more you distil at once, you shal make both the lesse waste, and the oyles will be in lesse daunger of adustion.

2. Let the middle pipe of your Limbecke, through which your oyle and water ascendeth, be as large againe as the ordinarie pipes are, and much shorter, and let the bucket, or cooler in the head containe as much more colde water, as our ordinarie Limbecks doe.

3. If you haue cause to draw much oyle at once of one sorte or kinde, then vse the first water againe for the *vehiculum* in your second drawing, because the same hath alreadie receyued his glutte of the oyles, and will not be so hungrie to deuoure your oile as new, and fresh water, that hath not beene vsed to the same purpose before.

4. The water in the cooler may not boile, but you must change the same so often as it groweth scalding hot, and put cold water in the place thereof.

5. You may begin your distillation with a prettie strong fire till the oyle beginneth to ascend, but after-

Diuerse chimicall conclusions concerning the Art of Distillation.

The maner of drawing, or extracting of the oiles out of hearbes, or spices with all necessarie circumstances.

1 A Copper body, or brasse pot, with a pewter Limbecke, and a glasse receyuer, are all the necessarie Instruments for the extracting of these oiles, and the greater the potte, or bodie is, and the more you distil at once, you shal make both the lesse waste, and the oyles will be in lesse daunger of adustion.

2 Let the middle pipe of your Limbecke, through which your oyle and water ascendeth, be as large againe as the ordinarie pipes are, and much shorter, and let the bucket, or cooler in the head containe as much more colde water, as our ordinarie Limbecks doe.

3 If you haue cause to draw much oyle at once of one sorte or kinde, then vse the first water againe for the *vehiculum* in your second drawing, because the same hath alreadie receyued his glutte of the oyles, and will not be so hungrie to deuoure your oile as new, and fresh water, that hath not beene vsed to the same purpose before.

4 The water in the cooler may not boile, but you must change the same so often as it groweth scalding hot, and put cold water in the place thereof.

5 You may begin your distillation with a prettie strong fire till the oyle beginneth to ascend, but afterward

ward let your fire bee so temperate, as that your pipe that runneth into the receauer doe neuer blowe, but only drop apace, or run trickling down the receiuer.

6 Some vse to macerate, or infuse these spices the night before they distill, luting the Limbeck, to their brasse pot, or copper body, the best vse thereof is in my conceipt that the past, or lute wilbe so much the drier befor they begin to worke, but I thinke they gaine not any more oile by that practise. And yet a Neopolitan promiseth to double the oile of Annisseeds, by macerating them ten daies before distillation.

7 The flowers of sage, thime, rosemary, lauender, &c. yeeld more oile then the leaues, and the seedes more then the flowers.

8 To euery pound of seeds, or spice, adde a gallon of faire water at the least.

9 Beate your seedes and spice somewhat grosely before you put them into your pot, or body.

10 All such hearbs whereof you meane to draw any oile, would be laide abroad in the aire to drye, fiue or sixe daies before you draw any oile from them: for so you may distill both more at once, and also you shal haue more store of oile.

11 Those herbs which are hot either in smell or tast, wil giue their oile in this manner in more plenty then those which are of a mild, or gentle smell, or taste: as the sweete marierom, rose, &c.

12 Moste of your oiles will fleete on the top of your water, yet the oile of cinamon and cloues will fall to the bottom, in the manner of a *Balsamum*, and some do hold it for one trew marke of a naturall *Balsamum*, if being powred into another oile, it sincke to the bottome.

13 Your

Art and Nature.

13 Your paste muste consist of beane flower, or other courfe flower, tempered with water only, or some whites of eggs well beaten, and during your distillation you must haue some paste ready to stop all such breathing places in the ioint, whereat any wind shall issue.

14. Let your receiuer being of Hesson glasse containe two gallons, or three pottels, and for your receiuers you may chose those glasses which they call bodies, when they are once cut off with hot irons & fitted to their helmes.

15 For the most parte you shall haue all the oiles of your hearbs, or spices to ascend with the firste pottle of water, neuerthelesse for the more suerty you may draw of a gallon, and proue what you can gather out of the last pottle.

16 You may diuide your oiles from your water, by putting the water, and oiles being temperately warm either into a large head that hath a shorte pipe, or for want thereof, into a greate glasse fonnell, staying your finger at the bottome of the pipe till all the oile do flote aboue the water (except in cloues, and cinamon) and then letting the water to haue a gentle passage by lifting vp your finger a little, vntill you see the oile ready to runne out with the rest, which you shall easily perceaue by the difference of their colors, and then stop the hole with your finger againe, and receaue the oile into a seuerall glasse by it selfe.

17 When you haue diuided the oyles from the waters, then may you rectifie, or purifie them in this manner. Put all your oyle that is of one sorte into a glasse body, and holde the same carefully in some hotte water, mouing the same

vp and down at the firſt, leaſt you breake your glaſſe, vntill all the water be euaporated, and that you perceyue the oyles to become of a cleare and tranſparent colour, and then keepe them in apt Glaſſes. Moſt of all theſe Oyles will laſt exceeding long, and to ſay trulie, I knowe not howe long, for I haue not found anie of them to faile, or looſe their grace, except the Oyle of Annys ſeedes. But ſome in ſteade of clarifying in the manner aforeſayd, doe vſe to rediſtill the ſame againe in ſmall bodies, and heades of Glaſſe with ſome of the firſt water, and ſome drawe them from Roſe water. Note that in this rectifying by aſcenſion you ſhall looſe a great part of their tincture, and if I bee not deceyued, a greate parte alſo of their ſtrength and vertue.

18 If you haue cauſe to drawe manie Oyles one after another, hauing but one Limbecke for them all, let the Oile of Annys ſeedes bee one of the laſt which you drawe, becauſe it will ſeaſon the Limbecke ſo ſtrongly, that you ſhall hardly get out the ſent but with great labour. And for the ſweetning of your Limbecke vppon euerie chaunge of ſtrong Oyle, you maie ſet the Limbecke looſe vppon the pot of water, or Copper bodie, and ſo vrge vp with fire a great quantitie of water out of your pot, till you find the ſent of the laſt oyle to vaniſhe: or elſe put ſome drie Roſe leaues, or ſweete Marierom leaues into your water, and then make fire, as before.

19 Let the paſſage of your water that ſtandeth ſtill in the cooler, bee verie large, whether it bee by cocke, or Tampion. Some doe emptie their cooler with a long crooked pipe, and ſet the ſame on running by drawing the water downe with their

breath

breath a little at the firſt. It is verie requiſite to haue veſſels of colde water readie at hand to poure in preſently vppon the emptying of your cooler, or bucket, and if the ſame veſſels be of equall content with the bucket, you ſhall finde your labour the eaſier. I knowe ſome that to auoide the continuall labour of filling, and emptying of their cooler haue placed a large veſſell full of colde water in ſuch manner as that the ſame by turning of a cocke may runne dropping continuallie into the cooler: and in like manner the cocke that is fixed to the cooler may deliuer as much water into an other veſſell as it receyued from the vppermoſt.

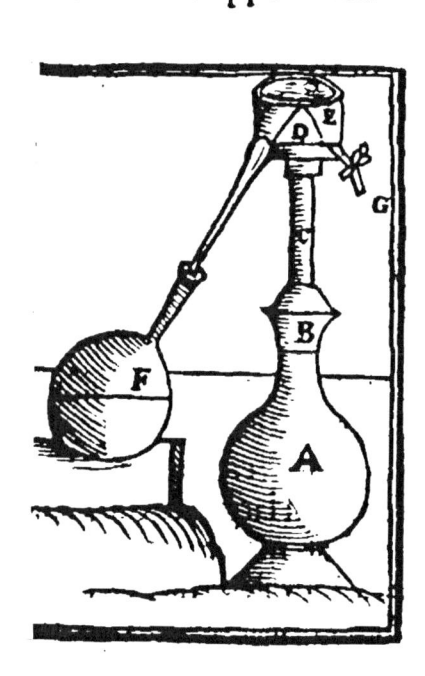

20 Some holde opinion that the beſt drawing of all vegetable Oyles, that will congeale in cold weather, is in the Summer, or Springtime, but a woorkeman will both drawe them, and diuide thē at all times of the yeare.

21 Let there bee alwayes one thirde of your potte, or copper bodie emptie, that there may bee ſufficient roome for the ſpirits to play in.

Howe

How to rectifie the afforesaid oyles.

When you haue gathered some store of oyle together, put the same into a small glasse body, or cucurbite, setting the same in a gentle balneo til al the water bee euaporated from the oile, and that the oile become of a most cleere and bright color. This manner of rectifying is vsed in the extracted oiles of spices, seedes, and flowers. But if you woulde rectifie either oile of amber, iet, waxe, or any of those heauy, and fatty oiles which muste bee vrged vppe with a strong fire, then your beste way is to poure the oile vpon a good quantity of rose water, in a glasse body luting a helme vnto it, and so by rectifying the same often from rose water, a greate parte of that offensiue and aduft smell which they purchase in their distillation, will be taken away.

Diuerse speciall vses of the aforesaid oiles not heretofore published.

To commend them either for their medicinable, and knowne vertues, or for their printed qualities were but loste labor. And therefore I referre all such as be desirous to read them at large, to the plentifull discourse concerning that matter written by doctor *Gesnerus*, in a booke intituled the Iewell of health, and englished by Maister Baker. But of those other more rare, and conceipted vses, which either I haue founde out by mine owne experience, or learned of others; I will here giue some taste vnto all the true louers of learning. And those who

who are desirous to make a triall of these practizes may repaire to Maister Kemish, that auncient and expert Chimist dwelling neere the glashouse, at whose handes they may buy any of the aforesaid oiles in a most reasonable manner.

1. *Diuerse sorts of sweete, or hand waters made sodainely, or extempore with the saide oiles.*

First you shall vnderstande that whensoeuer you draw any of the aforesaid oiles of cinamon, cloues, mace, nutmegs, or such like, that you shall haue also a potrle, or a gallon, more or lesse, according to the quantitie which you drawe, of excellent sweete washing water for your table, yea some do keepe the same for their broths wherein otherwise they should vse some of the same kinde of spice; but if you take three, or foure droppes only of the oile of cloues, mace, or nutmegs; (for cinamon oyle is too costly to spend this way) and mingle the same with a pint of faire water, making agitation of them together a prety while, in a glasse hauing a narrowe mouth, till they haue in some measure incorporated themselues together: you shal finde a very pleasing and delightfull water thereof to washe with, and so you may alwaies furnish your selfe of sweete water of seuerall kindes, before such time as your gests shalbe ready to sit downe. I speake not here of the oile of spike which will extende very farre this way, both because euery man liketh not so strong a sent, and for that the same is elsewhere already commended by an other Author. Yet this I must needs acknowledge to be the cheaper way, for that I assure my selfe there may be fiue, or sixe gallons of sweet water made with

B   one

one ounce of the oile which you may buy ordinarily for a groat at the most.

This way you may also make an excellent sweete water for a casting bottle. Take three drams of oile of spike. 1 dram of oile of Thime. 1 dram of oile of Lemons. 1 dram of oile of Cloues; then take 1 graine of Ciuet, and 3 graines of the afforesaid composition wel wrought togeather, Temper them well in a siluer spoone with your finger, then put the same into a siluer boule, washing it out by little, and little, into the boule with a little rose water at once, till all the oyle be washed out of the spoone into the boule, and then do the like by washing the same out of the boule with a little rose water at once til all the sent be gotten out, putting the rose water still in a glasse when you haue tempered the same in the boule sufficiently. A pint of rose water will be sufficient to mingle with the said proportion, and if you finde the same not strong enough of the ciuet, then you may to euery pint put. 1 grain, and an halfe, or 2 grains of ciuet, to the weight of 3 graines of the aforesaid composition of oiles. If you distil brused cloues with faire water only, in an ordinary leaden still, you shall receiue very good washing water for your table, and the charge thereof will not exceed 3 pence, or 4 pence the pint. All these seueral sweete waters I haue often prooued.

2 *How to make sundry sorts of most dainty butter with the saide oiles.*

IN the moneth of May it is very vsuall with vs to eat some of the smallest, and youngest sage leaues with butter in a morning, and I thinke the common vse thereof doth sufficiently commende the same to be

whol-

Art and Nature.

wholsome, in steade whereof all those which delighte in this hearbe may cause a few droppes of the oile of sage to be well wrought, or tempered with the butter when it is new taken out of the cherne, vntil they find the same strong enough in taste to their owne liking; and this way I accoumpt much more wholsome then the first, wherin you shall finde a far more liuely and penetratiue tast then can be presently had out of the greene herbe.

This laste Sommer I did entertaine diuers of my frends with this kinde of butter amongst other country dishes, as also with cinnamon, mace, and cloue butter (which are all made in one selfe same manner) and I knew not whether I did more please them with this new found dish, or offend them by denying the secret vnto them, who thought it very strange to find the naturall tast of herbs, and spices coucied into butter without any apparant touch of color. But I hope I haue at this time satisfied their longings. *Qre*, if by som meanes or other you may not giue a tincture to your creame before you chearne it, either with roseleaues, cowslep leaues, violet or marigold leaues, &c. and thereby chaunge the color of your butter. And it may be if you wash your butter throughly wel with rose water before you dish it, and worke vp some fine sugar in it, that the Country people will go neere to robbe all Cocknies of their breakfasts, vnlesse the dairie be well looked vnto. If you woulde keepe butter sweete, and fresh a long time to make sops, broth or cawdell, or to butter any kinde of fishe withall in a better sorte then I haue seene in the beste houses where I haue come, then dissolue your butter in a cleane glased, or silver vessell & in a pan, or kettle of water with a slow and gentle fire, and powre the same so diſſolued, into a baſon that hath ſome faire Water therein, and when it is cold, take away the foote, not ſuffering any of the curds, or whey to remaine in the bottome: and if you regard not the charge thereof, you may either the firſt or ſecond time, diſſolue your Butter in Roſewater as before, working them wel together, and ſo Clariſie it, and this butter ſo clarified, wilbe as ſweete in taſt, as the Marrow of any beaſt, by reaſon of the great impuritie that is remooued in this manner of handeling: for I thinke that if you clariſie it thrughly wel, you ſhal find either a fourth, or fift part of droſſe, in the beſt butter that you can buy in the market, which I thinke to be more fit for the dunghill, then for a mans ſtomach, onely it helpeth the butter wiues to make ſom waight: as thogh (ſimple wenches) they knew not which way to helpe themſelues in their ſmall diſhes. *Qre.* What butter the creame of Goates milke would make, becauſe the milke is exceeding ſweet, and nouriſhing. You may eaſily knowe what countrey man I am, by following this London text ſo farre as I doo: neuertheleſſe, let me teach one thing more, to them which knowe it not already, and ſo I will conclude with butter. That in Winter time, it is very requiſit to ſcalde your milk preſently as it commeth from the Cow, before you put it into your pannes, but take heed it ſeeth not; and you ſhall haue very good butter, curdes and cheeſe, when others ſhal want the ſame. And thus I hope, I haue giuen ſome content to thoſe Gentlewomen, which do not thinke themſelues too olde, or too wiſe to learne: and if there be any that can ſay more in the circumſtances of butter, I hope their dairies be greater than mine, that neuer kept but twoe kina, in any one Summer.

3. To.

3. To make any cheese to tast of your aforesaid oiles.

AS before in butter, so likewise if you mingle any of the aforesaid oiles in your curdes, before you presse out the whey, you shall feele the same very sensiblie and pleasantly, in the tast of your cheese, in the which you may easily mingle som rose leaues, or giue them the tast, smell and colour of any flower at your pleasure. There is also a tricke in the making of a cheese, without putting the same into any presse, onlie by giuing the same a gentle peize, whereby ye whey that rundreth from the curdes, will bee as thin as water, and carry no substance with it, and so your cheese wil bee much bigger, and better than otherwise it would be, being made after the common country fashion. I haue beene as bold as I dare, in discouerie hereof, because I would be loath to offend a Gentlewoman that presumeth of a great secree herein, and she is the more daintie of her skil, because shee hath found it out by many labors, and losses of her owne. But I thinke I haue giuen light sufficient to a good dairie Woman to find out al the circumstances therof in time.

4. Wholesome and comfortable Manus Christi, for sick & weake stomaches.

DIssolue some of the whitest Barbary suger you can get, with a little rosewater in a small shallowe pipkin, that cōtaineth 3 or 4 ounces & glased within, and hauing a small lip, boile the same vpon a soft fire, vnto a stifnesse or consistency (as they terme it) till a

B 3   drop

The Jewel-house of

drop thereof being powred out of the lip vpon a cold stone, become hard, and not clammy when it is cold. And when you haue your sugar boiled to this heigth, then hauing a cleane Marble stone, first sprinkeled ouer with fine flower, poure the same out by peecemeale, making each of them of the bignes of a groat or testor, or thereabouts, and when they are thorow cold, hauing a few droppes of the oyle of Cynamon, Cloues, mace, nutmegs, &c. in a siluer spoone, with a small feather, giue each of the *Manus Christi* a tuch onely with a little oyle, on the tippe of the feather, and so you may prepare a great many together of them, with such oyles, as the physician shal giue directions, and in the eating of them, you shall finde them to warme and comfort your stomach exceedingly. Some do put in their oyles in the boyling of the Sirrop, but I holde the first to be the better way, both because you may make of seuerall sorts at once, as also for that these oyles being ouer heated do lose a great part of their grace in tast.

5. *Diuers extellent kindes of bottle Ale to be made with the aforesaid oyles.*

I Cannot remember that euer I did drinke the like sage ale at any time, as that which is made by mingling two or three droppes of good oyle of sage, with a quart of Ale, the same beeing well brewed out of one pot into another. And this waie a whole stande of sage Ale is speedily made. The like is to be done with the oyle of mace, or nutmegs. But if you will make a right Gossips Cuppe that shall farre exceede all the Ale, that euer mother Bunch made in her life time, then in the botteling vppe of your best Ale

tun

vnne halfe a pinte of white ypocrasse, that is newlie made, after the best receipt, and with good spice, with a pottle of ale; stoppe your bottle close, and drinke it when it is stale. I feare some Alewiues, if they had knowne this receipt, priuatly to themselues wold haue hung out holly bushes at their red lettises and so they might haue beene mistaken for Tauerns, of many Ale knights. Some commend the hanging of a rosted Orenge prickt full of Cloues, in the vessell of Ale, till you find the tast thereof sufficiently mended to your owne liking.

6. Wormewood wine made very speedily, and in great quantitie.

Take small Rochell, or Conniacke wine, put a few drops of the extracted oyle of wormewood therein, brew it (as before is set downe in bottle ale) out of one pot into another, and you shall haue a more neat and wholsome wine for your bodie, then that Wine which is sold at the Stillyard for right Wormewood wine. And as for their Rhenish wine, I haue heard them speake it, whom I dare beleeue, that how many fatts soeuer be found at once in some of their cellers, there is none worth the tasting, but that onelie which is abroach, and this is a prettie sleight to deceaue the Purueyor. It may be y̌ the rest of the fats, haue not yet receiued either the brimstone match, or the compound sent which they poure in with it, or the herbe *Galiricum*, which I haue heard greatly commended y̌ way, but how so euer they sophisticate this wine, I am verily perswaded, by that little acquaintāce which I haue had with the grapie God, that for the moste part, these Dutch Brewers, buy no other Wines but
Rochel

Rochel, or Coniack, after 14. or 16. pounds the tun, and with some fiue or six shillings charge vpon a fat, they draw it againe for Rhenish wine, after 32. li. the tunne. I will not touch here the selling of new perry in stead of Rhenish wine in the mustè, wrbooh together in equall proportion, because I feare I haue alreadie vexed the vintners, who find more profit in their secret mixtures, then pleasure in these open discoueries.

7 *How to sweeten the oyle of Almonds with the afore said oiles, so as the same may serue the perfumer in stead of the oile of Benn, which is made of the Italian nuts.*

CHoose the newest, and sweetest Almondes, that you can get (you shal know them by their reddish colours, and I hold the Barbary Almond, far better then the Iordan almond for this purpose) expresse their oyle according to the manner hereafter set down, without warming either the Almondes, or the brasen box, whereinto you put them, least they become ranke in a short time; after you haue drawne some quantitie hereof, let it settle foure or fiue daies, till all the *Fæces* or grounds fall to the bottome, then by declination poure away the cleerest, and take a little thereof, and mingle a few drops of the oyle of cloues therewith, stirring them wel together in an apt glasse, then poure more of the oile of Almonds thereto, working as before, incorporating so much of the oile of cloues therewith, till the sent thereof like you. VVith this oyle thus prepared, the Perfumer may temper his muske, Ciuette, or Ambergreese, as he dooth with his oile of Benn, which serdeth for no other purpose,
but

but onely to conuey such sents, and perfumes into the leather as hee hath wrought together for the selfe same purpose, being it selfe of no sent at all. This I write not vpon bare imagination, but vppon some proofe which I haue seene made with the simple oile of Almonds in gloues of no small price. Although I know this oile to be greatly doubted of by the perfumers, because in a few moneths it will grow somewhat rancke, whereas the salt is in the olde Almonds which the Apothecaries doe chieflie choose because they are more oily then those which are newe, and fresh.

And here if a man were disposed (*Seria miscere iocis*) were a fitte opportunity to discourse of a philosophicall contrition of oiles, thereby to defende them from putrifaction. Also if you labour, and beate well together some fresh oile of Almonds with chaunge of rose water, it wil serue, insteade of a sweet ointment, or *Pomatum*, to annoint your hands with. So likewise of the oyle of cloues, tempered with the oyle of Almonds to rubbe a new gloue in the inside to giue it a sweete sent in the wearing. Here I could commend the oile of beech-mast, if it were in yealde according to the report of a Neopolitane writer: for that which is expressed from the nut I know to be a moste sweete and delicate oile.

8. I could here sette downe an experienced triall for the alteration of tallow candels whereby to make them in a manner as sweete in handling, burning, and putting out as the waxe candle, yet not altogether so hard; the principall parte of which secret consisteth in an artificiall composition of some of the aforesaide oiles. But I muste reserue the same till my second edition which I will hasten according as I finde

C a

Rochel, or Coniack, after 14. or 16. pounds the tun, and with some fiue or six shillings charge vpon a fat, they draw it againe for Rhenish wine, after 32. li. the tunne. I will not touch hole the selling of new perry in stead of Rhenish wine in the bottle, or booth together in equall proportion, because I feare I haue alreadie vexed the vintners, who find more profit in their secret mixtures, then pleasure in these open discoueries.

7 *How to sweeten the oyle of Almonds with the aforesaid oiles, so as the same may serue the perfumer in stead of the oile of Benn, which is made of the Italian nuts.*

CHoose the newest, and sweetest Almondes, that you can get (you shall know them by their reddish colours, and I hold the Barbary Almond, far better then the Iordan almond for this purpose) expresse their oile according to the manner hereafter set down, without warming either the Almondes, or the brasen box wherein you put them, least they become ranke in a short time; after you haue drawne some quantitie hereof, let it settle foure or fiue daies, till all the fæces or grounds fall to the bottome, then by declination poure away the cleerest, and take a little thereof, and mingle a few drops of the oyle of cloues therewith, stirring them wel together in an apt glasse, then poure more of the oile of Almonds thereto, working as before, incorporating so much of the oile of cloues therewith, till the sent thereof like you. With this oyle thus prepared, the Perfumer may temper his muske, Ciuette, or Amber-greese, as he doth with his oile of Benn, which serueth for no other purpose,

but

but onely to conuey such sents, and perfumes into the leather as hee hath wrought together for the selfe same purpose, being it selfe of no sent at all. This I write not vpon bare imagination, but vppon some proofe which I haue seene made with the simple oile of Almonds in gloues of no small price. Although I know this oile to be greatly doubted of by the perfumers, because in a few moneths it will grow somewhat rancke, whereas the falt is in the olde Almonds which the Apothecaries doe chieflie choose because they are more oily then those which are newe, and fresh.

And here if a man were disposed (*Seria miscere iocis*) were a fitte opportunity to discourse of a philosophicall contrition of oiles, thereby to defende them from putrifaction. Also if you labour, and beate well together some fresh oile of Almonds with chaunge of rose water, it wil serue instead of a sweet ointment, or *Pomatum*, to annoint your hands with. So likewise of the oyle of cloues, tempered with the oyle of Almonds to rubbe a new gloue in the inside to giue it a sweete sent in the wearing. Here I could commend the oile of beech-mast, if it were in yealde according to the report of a Neopolitane writer: for that which is expressed from the nut I know to be a moste sweete and delicate oile.

8. I could here sette downe an experienced triall for the alteration of tallow candels whereby to make them in a manner as sweete in handling, burning, and putting out as the waxe candle, yet not altogether so hard; the principall parte of which secret consisteth in an artificiall composition of some of the aforesaide oiles. But I muste reserue the same till my second edition which I will hasten according as I finde

a thankeful acceptance of the first.

How to draw oyle of Waxe, Amber, Iett, Turpentine, &c.

I Haue here aduisedly omitted to set downe at large, the drawing of the oile of Wax, Amber, Iett, Turpentine, &c. because moste of them are offensiue in smell. Yet let this in a word or two suffice, that all of them (except the oile of Turpentine) are to be drawn in sand, and most aptly by waie of retort, which some doo also vse to lute ouer, with lome and flockes well tempered togither: and because those vnctuous and swelling bodies shal not rise vp into the helme, they vse to suppresse them, by the addition of cleane washed sand, powder of glasse, tilestones, and such like. And as for the oile of Turpentine, it wil rise by a gentle Balneo, in a cucurbite of glasse or stone, hauing a helme of glasse luted thereunto. *&c.* If it wil not rise from water out of a brasse pot, according to the maner of the oiles of hearbs and spices, before set down.

Of expressed Oyles.

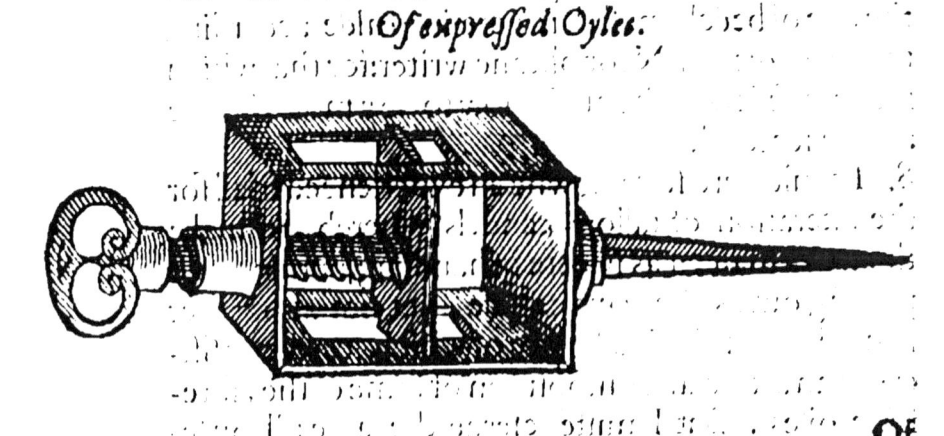

Art and Nature

OF all the aforesaid seedes and spices, as there may be an oyle drawne by ascention, so likewise there may be an oyle had by expression, yea many simples will yeeld their oile by expression, which will yeelde none at al by ascention, but as you shall haue much more quantity of oile this waie, either from the nutmegs, cloue, mace, &c; so the same is much groser then the other, & more fit for outward applications then inwarde medicines, neuerthelesse, they carie a strong & sufsent of the aromaticall body, from whence they are drawn, and haue also their especiall vses. The manner wherof is this. Beat your spice or seeds, throughly well in a stone morter, and thrust them close into a peece of hearecloth, or French boulter, (which before had you must place in your mettaline box, that hath a little lose iron grate in the bottome) then lappe vp the hearecloth, laying the weight vpon it, which presseth downe the spice, and shutteth close into the box. Then put this box with the couer, betweene the sides of your wron presse, which you may laie ouerthwart a ioyned stool, placing y nose of your box, so as it may drop into a pewter peece, which of purpose you must place vnderneath the same, then

C 2 giue

giue a turne now and then with an iron pinne to the screw, til you see no more oile to issue, (some to gain the more oile, infuse the spices in the oile of sweet almonds first.) Note that your seedes and spices, and the box with the other implementes, must bee warmed, before you expresse; and in colde weather, it is best working in a warme place, if you meane to haue store of oile. This waie you may purchace a moste excellent sweet oile of egges, if you doo firste roast them til they bee through harde, and then take the yeolkes onelie, and crumble them verie smal, putting them into a little pewter peece, and set the same in a hot Balneo, til al the watrish humor bee euaporated, and then presse out your oile, according to the aforesaide manner. This oile is of a more beautiful colour, and not so blackish, as that which is made after the grosse manner in a frying panne, which smelleth and tasteth of adustion. It is commended especiallie in a burne, and for taking awaie the inflamation and heat of gunpowder. Thus much I haue thought conuenient to set down for the perfecting of this branch of the Spagirical art. And now I wil proceed to som other necessarie knowledges in the art of distillation, concerning such matters as I am assured that euerie Gentlewoman that delighteth in Chimical practises wil be wiling to learne.

How to make Cynamon water.

THe best way is first in a brasse pot with a pewter Limbeck, to distill from two or three gallons of sacke, or muscadell, so much spirit or *Aqua vitæ*, as will ascend, then poure that spirite vpon as many gallons of faire water, putting to euery gallon of water
and

and spirit, a pound of choice Cynamon first brused, lute the ioynts of your pot and Lymbecke, as before in the extraction of the Aromaticall oyles, keeping the bucket in the head of the Limbecke colde, with change of water, and so draw as long as you finde any reasonable tast of the Cynamon. This of all the ordinarie waies is the best that I know. But if you infuse your brused Cynamon, in spirit of wine onely, or in the spirit drawne from sack lees, or strong ale, vntill you haue gotten out by imbibition, all the tincture, tast, and strength of the Cynamon, which will be in seuen or eight daies, and then if you adde a new proportion of faire water, or rather of damaske rose water vnto it, and so distill in a glasse body and head in Balneo, well luted in the ioynts, I thinke you wil find this the most profitable, and most artificiall way of all others. And least you happen to be deceiued in the strength of your Cynamon water, you must tast euery sticke of Cynamon by it selfe, before you buye it, yea and the same at eyther ende, or else you may happen to be deceiued. If when you haue drawne your Cynamon water, you like not to haue it of a thicke or cloudy colour, as commonly it falleth out in this maner of distillation: some holde opinion, that it wil become cleere, onely by sunning it in an hot sunny day, or two: and some doo vse to circulate the same in Balneo, til it clarifie. But I haue found it an infallible way, to haue the same cleere at the first drawing, by distilling the same in a copper Balneo, with a Lampe onely, or so gentle a heat as may not be idle, and yet procure but a soft and easie distillation: And I thinke this was Doctor *Burcots* waie, who thought himselfe verie cunning in the distilling thereof: because there was not much cleere cinamon water to be had, in his daies,   C 3   How

How to make the extractions of all hearbs.

Some are so curious in this worke, as that no other water, but the distilled water of the herbe only will satisfie their fancie heerein, although I see no great difference betweene the same, and an ordinary water first distilled and diuided from his impurities, but let the Chymist, nowe, hee knoweth them both, take which he list, for I doo rest indifferent, saying that I finde it an infinite matter, to distil so much Water, as wil be requisite, for the gathering of any quantitie of this substance, or tincture as some tearme it. But with whether of them soeuer you begin, you must proceed in this manner. After you haue macerated great store of the Hearbe, in seuerall Waters, vntill such time as you finde each water deepelie died, or tincted with the colour of the hearbe; then hauing a large Balneo, wherein you may place diuers bodies of glasse at once, you must euaporate all the water vntil in the ende you leaue nothing else, but a stiffe & drie substance, which our Chimistes do call the extraction of the hearbe. Some doo choose rather to work vpon the drie hearbe, then the moist *& alij è contra*. But if you worke vpon the distilled water of the herb, as vpon the Rose, Balm, Buglos, *Carduus benedictus*, or any such other Water of good vse or account: then is it not amisse to lute, or set your heades of glasse also vpon the bodies, with receiuers, therby to receiue the Water which ascendeth, so as there may bee no losse of your distilled waters, and yet also you may attaine to that second water which you expect. This extraction, I haue heard highlie commended of many Artistes, and it may be it hath some better vses in

physick

physick, then I know or can imagine. But if I shal deliuer mine opinion thereof, I thinke it to be the fine and subtile earth of the hearbe, or flower, out of the which some curious Limner may draw some excellent colour for this worke, if hee make choice of the flower de Luce, white rose, blew bottle, Marigolde, or some such other Flower, as is of any deepe tincture: but I perswade my selfe, that no philosophicall vulcanist, or perfect paracelsian, will euer finde any true magisterie, tincture, quintessence, or *Arcanum* therein.

How to make the Salt of hearbs.

BVrne whole bundles of dried Rosemary, sage, Isop, &c. in a cleane ouen, and when you haue gathered good store of the ashes of the hearbe, infuse warme water vpon them, and make a strong and sharpe Lee of those ashes: then euaporate that lee, and the residence or setling, which you find in the bottom therof, is the salt you seeke for. This salt, according to the nature of the herbe hath his operation or vse in physicke, and in my conceit, doth worke greater effects in the stomach, than any of the aforesaid extractions. Some vse to filter this Lee diuers times, that their salt may be the cleerer, and more transparent.

How to draw and rectifie a spirit of wine in diuers maners, aswel with fire, as without fire.

IF you would dispatch any great quantitie thereof, you must haue a large Balneo, wherein you may place sixe or eight glasse bodies at once, with their helmes and receiuers, each of them fastened to a leaden triuet, y̌ they may stand steady in the water, wherin in you may put some, haie if you please, poure into each of them a reasonable quantitie of the oldest and mightiest sacke, malmesey, or muscadell, because these wines are strongest, and yeeld most spirit. Your fire must be soft and gentle, so as you may tell eight or ten, betweene euerie drop that falleth. Drawe no longer, then til you may perceiue long veines in the helmes, for if they grow once deawie, or stand full of drops, then you may assure your selfe, that al the spirit is gone, and the flegmatike part of the wine ascendeth: yet there be diuers, and those of good iudgement, who doe most constantly affirme, that before the vaines appeare in the helme, the subtilest spirit of all doth arise in a drie and insensible fume, which condensating by the coldnesse of the ayre, dooth resolue into drops in the receiuer. Some doo vse at the first pinte, alwaies to change the receiuer, and so diuide that, which commeth first by it selfe from the rest, putting all the faint spirit together. And then rectifie them seuerallie in the like bodies and helmes, by a second distillation, in the aforesayd Balneo, & they neuer leaue to reiterate their distillations, vntill by making triall of a little thereof in a spoone, they finde the same being kindeled, to burne all away. Some fasten a spoonge in the mouth of the glasse body, and some couer the mouth of the glasse with an oiled paper, and so perswade themselues, that nothing but perfect spirit will penetrate either the spoonge or paper, and some put the crom of a white loafe in the bottome of the glasse, thinking thereby to sucke and drinke vppe all the faint part of the spirit. But I haue found by mine owne experience, that after there is once drawne a pinte, or a pinte and a halfe of spirit from a gallon of good wine, if the same be put into a

large

Art and Nature.

large bolt receiuer as they terme it (which is a glasse hauing a long straight steale of the bignesse of a musket, or double musket bore, with a great round hollow bal in the bottome conteining some pottle, or gallon, or two or three, if you can get the so large (for the greater in content the better for this purpose) this bolt glasse must be wel fastened to a leaden triuet in Balneo, and then, if the spirit that is so groselie drawne, bee put therein, setting a smal helme of glasse that may fit the steale, with a receiuer at it, then the pure spirit wil onelie ascend, and the flegmatique part not beeing able to mount so high, falleth downe againe to the bottome as fast as it riseth, and so at once rectifieng, you shal haue your spirit perfect enough. Others thinking to attaine to a quintessence, or at least to an oile of wine, that wil fleet and swim vppon anie other wine: they begin with a long circulation of the wine, first either in a Pellicane, or other large circling glasse, placing the same either in horse dung, or in a Balneo, or some other such like digesting heat, by the space either of a moneth or two, or three, euerie one according to his fancie, and then they fal to their diuision or distillatiō by a soft fire, keeping that by it selfe which commeth first, as a most rare and excellent spirit. And al this while, if I be not deceiued, we haue gotten nothing else, but the fierie part of the wine, or rather the burning *Aqua vitæ*, both of the wine and Tartar together, that are vrged vppe by fire, to knit themselues both spirituallie and inseparablie together. Then let vs see, if any truer diuision may be made without this Balneo, or any other outward heat whatsoeuer: naie, let vs consider what may be done in a frosty furnace;

D where

where the Northern windes must stir vppe nature in stead of glowing coales. Here I am affraide either my wit or my will, will soone be frozen vp, neuerthelesse since I am entred so farre, I will either breake the ice, or venture a fall, and if I slip, you shall see how I will frostnayle my selfe the nexte time that I ride abroade in such hard weather. I dare not here commend that newe conceipted way of rowling vppe and downe a large vessell of wine many howers togeather, or after the same hath wrought vppon the seaes, so soone as it commeth to shore, presently to clappe on a glasse helme vppon the bung hole being open, and luting the same close to the caske to receaue that spirite which nature in her heate will sodainely breathe out, and yet I will not altogether condemne the inuention, if such a workeman haue it in hand, as is able to bring the stomacke of wine into a kindly sweate. But suppose this to bee a righte, and naturall distillation, though it be temperatly performed, and without any forren fire, it is not that extreame colde, and congeled worke that was promised. But what if I should send you into Frizeland, or Rushia, or Muscouy, or into some other place neere vnto the Northen pole, and there will you after *Paracelsus* his manner to lay abroad into the open aire, either a but of sacke, or muskadell, vntill the same were congealed into a masse, or lumpe of ice, and then percing the vessell euen to the center, with some apt instrument of iron, to power out that inward life, or spirit which had retired, or withdrawne it selfe from the outward colde, into the warme fort, or castle of nature? I am affraid you would rather forsweare the triall, then take so long a iourny in hande. Then let vs see what may bee donne in this kinde in our owne country, though

not

not in so greate a quantity. I haue founde by those few trialls which I haue made in Lōdon, that if in an extreame, and sharpe weather in the winter time, a glasse of wine containing a pinte, or halfe a pinte in measure, and being well stopte with corcke, and brimstone, or some other strong lute, be exposed to the aier on the toppe of some high leades, that the same will oftentimes congeale, and freeze in one night within the glasse, so as there will not remaine aboue a moitie, yea many times a third parte onely of the wine vnfrozen, which you sha'l finde so deepe of hewe, and color, and so mightie in strength, and taste, as that the beste Gascoigne wine that comes from Burdeaux will seeme but Rochell wine in comparison thereof. Here wee haue an entrance made into nature, and since wee haue gotten such holde, let vs gather in more vppon hir. Peraduenture if the glasses were as thin as any violl, small in contente, rownde, and of an orbicular forme, rising vppe with small long neckes, and the same were placed Northerlie either in snowe, or water, or rather in water wherein some store of salte peter hath beene firste dissolued, to make the water more inwardly colde; or peraduenture if before the stopping of your glasse you did dissolue some reasonable proportion of snow water into your wine, that either some one of these helps, or al together might work a perfect congelatiō of the faint, and phlegmatick part of the wine, and so ye might attain to your desire. But without al peraduēture ther may be (by some means that are known but to a few) such an outward continued cold maintained roūd about ỹ glas, as that in any reasonable cold weather the spirit may be forced to fly inwardly for succor into his own bosome & being once driuen to this

D 2   streight

ſtreight, I account him but a ſimple chimiſt that cannot fetch him out, and diuide him from the reſte of his groſſe body. Proue the freezing of ale, or beere, or of the ſinaleſt kinde of wine, for they are likelyeſt to freeze, becauſe they containe but ſmall ſtore of ſpirite in them. Although I haue ſeene euen ſacke it ſelfe gather a thin icie cruſt in one nights freezing.

To make claret wine to mount vp in a red clowde into a glaſſe of conduit water.

CAuſe a glaſſe to bee made of the faſhion of thoſe which are commonly vſed in hower glaſſes, but of ſome greater content, and with a leſſe lippe, fill the ſame full of faire water, and whelme it vppon the mouth (which becauſe it is ſmall, and wanteth aire, no droppe will iſſue thereat) then put it into a beere glaſſe of the forme here deſcribed, being almoſt ful of claret wine, and if you holde the ſame wiſely, and that the glaſſes fit one another, you ſhall ſee the claret wine aſcende in the forme of a clowd, and that which remaineth in the neather glaſſe to be exceeding feint both in taſt, and color. If either the tincture alone, or the ſpirite of wine did here aſcend, and ſo incorporate it ſelfe with the water, I would hold it for a rare ſecret, and a light into ſome farther matter, but I feare you will finde nothing elſe therein but that when two bodies touch each other, that the wine being the lighter ſeeketh the vpper place

place. And yet I must needes commend the inuention of that honest and learned Gentleman, from whom I had it, and no doubt before the discouerie thereof, it would haue beene thought an admirable conceit, to haue made two seuerall glasses to haue eschanged their liquors, without any farther meanes.

Ad extrahendam vitam è vegetabilibus.

Primum contere herbam, tunc digere Balneo, in vase lapideo benè obturato per octo horas, aut vlterius per noctem: tunc per torcular succum exprime, quem in Balneo moderato non bullienti distilla, et in Alembici fundo gummi quoddam relinquitur: aquam hanc prædictis fæcibus contusis affunde, iterum digere, deprime, & distilla in eodem Alembico, vbi gummi prædictum remanet, hoc opus continuetur donec aqua tincturam prioris, s. herba receperit, aut aliquid gummi post distillationẽ reliquerit: tunc totum illud gummi sic collectum aqua sua digere, qua tum in digestione tincturam, aut puriorem partem eiusdem gummi in se recipiet, et in fundo fæces relinquet, à quibus filtra aquam tuam tinctam quã rursus in Balneo distilla, & sic reperies in vitri fundo herbæ puram essentiam, sicut puluerem, aut gummi speciem præ se ferentem. Aquam serua, & puluerem sicca vsui tuo. This was deliuered me, by the sonne and heire of a Noble man, who receiued it of one of the greatest practisers of my time, and if it aunswere the title, I am glad that it was my good hap to light vpon it.

How to giue a prettie grace both in tast and propertie, vnto the spirit of wine.

IF you infuse the same vppon the rinde of a ciuel sower Orange, or Lymon, you shall finde a pleasaunt and comfortable taste thereby, or if you woulde not haue the same descried by his colour, you may redistill the spirit so tincted in balneo. Some giue a tuch vnto the spirit of wine with rosemary, some with annis seedes, some with sweet fennell seedes: som with one seed, or hearbe, and some with another, by infusing the same a day or two vpon them.

How to draw the spirit of Hony.

After you haue dissolued sufficient store of honie in faire water, to make a good Metheglen, and that the same hath wrought a reasonable time by the addition of yeast, according to the manner of beere, and ale, then when the same is growne vnto a strong and mightie drinke by lying, you may drawe a spirit from it, by distillation, as you doo either from wine, Ale, or beere.

How to distill Rose Water, both good cheape, and at Michelmesse, and to haue as good yeeld, as at any other time of the yeere.

IN the pulling of your Roses, first diuide all the blasted leaues, then take the other fresh leaues, and lay them abroad vpon your table, or Windowes, with some cleane linnen vnder them. Let them lie three or foure houres, or halfe a day, but if they bee gathered in the deaw, then lay them abroad as before, vntill all the deaw be vanished and gone from them, put these rose leaues into great stone pottes that bee leaded within, and well dried (such as the Golde finers call their Hookers, and serue to receiue their *Aqua fortis*, be the best of all others that I know.) And whē
they

they are well filled, ftoppe their mouthes with good corkes all couered ouer with melted brimftone, and then fet your pots in fome coole place, and they will keepe a long time good, and you may diftill them at your beft leyfure, this way you may diftill Rofe-water good cheape, if buying ftore of Rofes when you finde a glut of them in the maket, whereby they are fold for feuen pence or eight pence the bufhel, you put them vp as before. And fome hold opinion, that if in the midft of thefe leaues you put fome leauen, and after fill vp the pot with rofe-leaues to the top, that fo you fhall haue a rofe-vineger from the rofe in your diftillation, without the addition of any vineger at all. You may alfo keepe them in glaffes, and I haue knowne fome kept in little rundlets, that haue bin firft wel feafoned with fome hot licor, & rofeleaues boiled togither, and the fame pitcht all ouer on the outfide, fo as no aire might penetrate the veffell. Qre. If any fpirit will arife, if you make feparation of that which firft arifeth from the rofe-leaues kept as before. Some for the more expedition in rofe-water do firft expres the iuice, and then diftill it, and afterward they do alfo diftill the expreffed leaues, and fo they difpatch more with one ftill then others do with three or four. I haue feene very good rofe-water drawne this way, but yet I take the ordinarie way to be more kindly efpecially if the head of your ftill be made like a Limbecke with a large bucket to hold ftore of rofe water. And fome commend the diftillation of the rofe violet, cowflop, &c. that is performed by a defcenforie, hauing alfo a cooler of cold water about it, which at a certain cock you may emptie as it heateth from time to time, and fill with frefh water againe.

How

and comfortable taste thereby, or if you woulde not haue the same descried by his colour, you may redistill the spirit so tincted in balneo. Some giue a tuch vnto the spirit of wine with rosemary, some with annis seedes, some with sweet fennell seedes: som with one seed, or hearbe, and some with another, by infusing the same a day or two vpon them.

How to draw the spirit of Hony.

After you haue dissolued sufficient store of honie in faire water, to make a good Metheglen, and that the same hath wrought a reasonable time by the addition of yeast, according to the manner of beere, and ale, then when the same is growne vnto a strong and mightie drinke by lying, you may drawe a spirit from it, by distillation, as you doo either from wine, Ale, or beere.

How to distill Rose Water, both good cheape, and at Michelmrsse, and to haue as good yeeld, as at any other time of the yeere.

In the pulling of your Roses, first diuide all the blasted leaues, then take the other fresh leaues, and lay them abroad vpon your table, or Windowes, with some cleane linnen vnder them. Let them lie three or foure houres, or halfe a day, but if they bee gathered in the deaw, then lay them abroad as before, vntill all the deaw be vanished and gone from them, put these rose leaues into great stone pottes that bee leaded within, and well dried (such as the Golde finers call their Hookers, and serue to receiue their *Aqua fortis*, be the best of all others that I know.) And whē they

they are well filled, stoppe their mouthes with good corkes all couered ouer with melted brimstone, and then set your pots in some coole place, and they will keepe a long time good, and you may distill them at your best leysure, this way you may distill Rose-water good cheape, if buying store of Roses when you finde a glut of them in the maket, whereby they are sold for seuen pence or eight pence the bushel, you put them vp as before. And some hold opinion, that if in the midst of these leaues you put some leauen; and after fill vp the pot with rose-leaues to the top, that so you shall haue a rose-vineger from the rose in your distillation, without the addition of any vineger at all. You may also keepe them in glasses, and I haue knowne some kept in little rundlets, that haue bin first wel seasoned with some hot licor, & roseleaues boiled togither, and the same pitcht all ouer on the outside, so as no aire might penetrate the vessell. *Qre.* If any spirit will arise, if you make separation of that which first ariseth from the rose-leaues kept as before. Some for the more expedition in rose-water do first expres the iuice, and then distill it, and afterward they do also distill the expressed leaues, and so they dispatch more with one still then others do with three or four. I haue seene very good rose-water drawne this way, but yet I take the ordinarie way to be more kindly especially if the head of your still be made like a Limbecke with a large bucket to hold store of rose water. And some commend the distillation of the rose violet, cowslop, &c. that is performed by a descensorie, hauing also a cooler of cold water about it, which at a certain cock you may emptie as it heateth from time to time, and fill with fresh water againe.

How

The Jewel-house of

How to dry rose leaues, or any other single flowers in such shape as they growe, and without any wrincles, so as a bushell of moist leaues shal become a bushell in measure when they bee dry; and how to keepe rosecakes, and rose leaues all the yeare without wormes.

YF you woulde performe the same well in rose leaues, you must in rose time make choise of such roses as are neither in the bud, nor full blowne (for these haue the smoothest leaues of all other) which you must especially cull, and choose from the reste. Then take of right callis sand, and washe the same in some change of waters; and dry it throughly well either in an ouen or in the sunne, and hauing shallow square, or long boxes of foure, or fiue, or sixe inches deepe, make first an euen lay of sande in the bottome, vpon the which lay your rose leaues one by one (so as no one of them touche another) till you haue couered all the sand: then with a spoone, or with your hand, strew sand vpon these leaues til you haue thinly couered them all, and then make another lay of rose leaues vpon the sande, and so make *stratum super stratum*, for foure or fiue layes one vppon another. Set this boxe abroade in some warme place in a hot sunny day (and commenly in two hot dayes they will become throughly dry) then with your hande, or a spoone, you muste striue gently to get vnderneath them, and so to lift them vp without breaking. Keepe these leaues in iarre glasses bound about with paper, or parchment in some cupbord that is neere a chimney, or stoue, least otherwise by the damp of the ayer they relent again, and so you loose your labour. I find the red rose leafe beste for this purpose by reason of

his

Art and Nature.

his deepe colour. You may also drie Paunsies, Stock-gilliflowers, and other single flowers, such as will hold their colour best, in this maner, by taking away their stalkes, and pricking them one by one into the sande, and so pressing their leaues smooth with the other sande, which you must lay vpon them. And so you may haue roseleaues, and other flowers to lay about your basons, windowes, and court cupboords, all the winter long. Also this skil is verie requisite for a good simplifier, because he may drie the leafe of any hearb in this maner, and lay it being drie in his herball with the simple which it representeth, whereby hee may easilie learne to know the names of all simples which he desireth. The ordinarie drying of Rose leaues, is to lay them vppon hot leades, in a hot sunnie day, and the sooner you dispatch, the better they will keepe their colour, and sent. And when you haue dryed them throughly, you may fill a Rose-water Glasse therewith, stopping it close, and so they will last good a long time.

The powder of Rose leaues, and so also of all other herbs & flowers, may be kept from all outward accident for one yeares space, if there bee anie reasonable care vsed therein.

If you would keep your rose cakes without worms, you must now and then, when you haue drawne your bread out of the ouen, set them in, in ceenes, or vpon papers, and so of your rose leaues; and if you hang them vp in paper bags, neere some Chimney where fire is somtimes made, you shall be sure to keep them sweete and good, for any vse for which they will serue, although I know diuerse that keepe their rose leaues only according to the maner afore set downe.

Rose water, and rose vineger of the color of the rose, and so of the Cowslip, and violet vineger.

Some infuse rose water vpon moist red rose leaues, and so set it abroad on sunning for a fewe daies, but this color cannot last long, but if you woulde make your rose water and rose vineger of a perfect ruby color, then make choise of the crimsen veluet colored leaues clipping away the whites with a pair of sheres and being through dry put a good large handfull of them into a pint of damaske, or red rose water, stop your glasse well, and set it in the sunne till you see that the leaues haue loste their color, or for more expedition you may performe this worke in balneo in a few houres, and when you take out the olde leaues you may put in fresh, till you finde the color to please you; keepe this rose water in glasses very wel stopt, and the fuller the better. What I haue said of rose water the same may be intended of rose vineger, violet, marigold, and cowslip vineger, but the whiter vineger you choose for this purpose you shall haue it the better colored, and therefore the distilled vineger is the best of all others, so as the same bee warely distilled with a trew diuision of the partes made according as hereafter is set down, but some do highly commend such vineger as is made of elder flowers, choicely pickt, and well dried before imbibition.

How to distill wine vineger or good Aliger, that it may be both cleere, and sharpe for sauce, or other vses.

I knowe it is an vsuall maner amonge the nouices of our time to put a quart, or two of good vineger, into an ordenary leaden still and so to distill it as they do all other waters. But this way I do vtterly dislike both for that here is no seperation made at all, and also because I feare the vineger dooth cary an ill touch with it either from the leaden bottome, or pewter head, or both. And therefore I could wish rather the same were distilled in a large body of glas with a head or receauer, the same being placed in sande or ashes. And note that the best part of the vineger is the middle part that ariseth, for the first is feint, and phlegmatique, & the last wil taste of adustion, because it groweth heauy towards the latter end, and must be vrged vp with a great fire, and therefore you must now and then taste of that which commeth both in the beginning, and towards the latter ende, that you may reserue the best by it selfe. Here I coulde also aduise, or wish al Ladies, and gentlewomen to haue all their vineger serued in at their tables in sawcers of glasse, or purslaine, because if it be strong, and continew longe in a pewter sawcer, it hath an intention towardes ceruse, which I cold neuer heare commended either for wholsome meat, or sawce for a mans stomacke. But it may be this is but one doctors opinion, & that of such a one as neuer deserued his degree in scholes; and therefore I will leaue the same at large vntill som better clarke do hereafter confirme this greene conceipt. Here I cannot omit the profitable obseruation of one of our London Chimists, who after hee had drawn good spirit out of wine from muskadell, did by sunning of the same also make good vineger the fæcicall parte thereof.

Howe to keepe the iuice of Oranges, and Lemons all the yeare, for sauce, Iulepps, and other purposes.

I know no reason why the iuice of the Lymon, or Orange shoulde not keepe as well in small woodden vessels, as either vergis, sider, or perry, and it may bee the want of triall hath only proceeded of the charge that would arise in filling of a small vessell only with such liquor. But how then haue we forgotten to prouide our store in glasses which we may fill with a smal charge when oranges are to bee had for xii pence or xvi pence the hundred? Let vs then expresse their iuice, and passe it through an ypocras bagge to the ende it may bee the better clarified from all his impurities: with this iuice fill vppe a rose water glasse (of what content you please) within an inche of full, couer the same with a lose cap of leather till it haue done his boyling, which I haue seene continew many daies togeather, and when it becommeth stil, and quiet in the top, then fill vp your glasse with good saletoile, and then set it in a coole closet, or buttery where no sun commeth. But the aptest glasses which I can imagine for this purpose were streight vpright ones, like to our long beere glasses, which I woulde haue to be made of purpose at the glasse house with small round holes within two inches of the bottome, in which holes I woulde place fit faucets to draw the iuice thereat, as I should haue cause to spend it. And so the grounds, or lees woulde settle to the bottome, and the oile woulde sincke downe with the Iuice so closely, as that no aier coulde enter to begin any putrefaction therein; or instead of holes if there were glasse pipes, it were the better, and the redier way, be-

cause

cause you shall hardly fasten a fawcet well in the hole. You may also in this manner preserue many iuices of herbs, that cary som store of heat, & fire in them, by couering them a reasonable thicknesse with sallet oile. But there is a better way then this by many degrees (although this bee sufficient for ordinary vse) for the long and true preseruations of all iuices, and liquors, whatsoeuer, that haue had no digestion, or decoction already, wherein neither oile, nor any outward helpe is required, but only a trew, and philosophicall rotation whereby the inwarde fire of nature may be stirred vppe in euery vegetable, to defende it selfe sufficiently againste all putrifying whatsoeuer. And so I haue kept both the iuice of cowslips which (if I be not deceaued) will not last long by any ordinary course of preseruing, and the iuice of oranges simply of themselues without any addition, as sound and perfect at the yeares ende, as they were the first day, or rather (to speake truly) somewhat exalted in kinde. But because such secrets are fitter for a philsophers laboratory, then a gentlewomās closet, I wil not here offer that disgrace vnto nature, to discouer any magistery vppon so base an occasion. And as concerning the keeping of Oranges, and Limons in the same state, bignesse, color, and taste, as they are brought vs out of Spaine, or portingall, it may bee that in my next labours I will write at large thereof, and in plaine tearmes, according to those vndoubted & approued trialls which I haue often made in mine owne house for many yeares together.

Hou

How to purifie and giue an excellent smell and tast vnto sallet oile.

I Haue laboured the more to attaine vnto this secret, because I knowe that oile is a most excellent and wholesome food, and yet my stomach hath alwaies abhorred the same, till of late, that I found the meanes to take away the fulsome taste thereof. But first of all, let vs see, what Maister *Bartholomæus Scappius*, the maister cooke of Pope *Pius Quintus*, his prinie kitchen, hath written in this behalfe. Hee willeth to heate the oyle in a cleane pipkin, and when it is thorough hot, to put therein a peece of bread or of dough, suffring the same to remaine in the oyle, by the space of one fift part of an houre: and this breade or dough will drawe vnto it selfe all the mustie and badde taste or sent of the oyle, and so the oyle wil remaine pure and cleane. And in an other place, hee willeth, to take such oyle as is not ranke, or ouer strong in sent (and if the same oyle bee made of chosen Oliues, it is by so much the better, than the common sort) and to put the same in a vessell of Earth or Copper, that hath a little hole in the bottome thereof, which you may stoppe with wax to open at your pleasure. In this vessel for euery quarte of oyle, adde foure quartes of faire Water, and with a Woodden spatle or spoone, beat them wel together for a quarter of an howers space, and when you haue so doon, open the hole in the bottome, and let out the water, for the oyle doth naturallie fleet aboue, as beeing the lighter bodie: and as soone as the Water is passed awaie, stoppe the hole, and put in other colde water, and begin a newe agitation as before, and worke in

the

the like manner diuers times as you did at the firste, til in the end the oile bee well clensed, and clarified. In the same manner you may also purifie all other sorts of oile; as also capons grease being firste melted, but then it should seem you must vse warm water instead of colde. All this is borrowed of the Popes cooke. *Qre.* If the oile had benne beaten the laste time in rosewater wherein cloues, or nutmegs had benne infused before. And for the speedier clarifying thereof (after your foresaide agitations are paste) you may sette your oyle either in a stoue, or in the sunne till it become cleere. A Grocer of good skill did assure me that by setting of salet oyle in the sunne in the sommer time, hee had seene the same to settle greate store of foule and grose lees, from the which by declination hee powred out the cleere oyle, and kept it till the next winter, and after the same had ben congealed with some frosty weather, hee found it the most sweete, and delectable oile that euer hee tasted in his life. But an oile man of some experience tolde me that if some brused nutmegs were hong in a corse bagge in the midst of the oyle, that in time the same would ouercome any bad and lothsome tast, that by some accident had infected the oyle, and giue it also a pleasant sent withall, or if you sette a iarre in Balneo full of washed oile as before, with some store of brused cloues, and rindes of ciuill Oranges or Lemons, and so continew your fire for two, or three howers, and then lettinge the cloues and riendes remaine in oile, till both the sent, and taste do please you, I thinke that many men which at this day do loth oile (as I my self did with in these few months) wil be drawn to a sufficient liking therof. I do know a means how to make

deiecti-

deiection of the Lee or fæces of y̆ best sallet oyle, that commeth ouer, whereby the same will become most pure and cleere, but I feare that Saturne would frown vpon me (if without his leaue) I should so boldly entermeddle with his charge.

How to dissolue both Corall, and Pearle.

INfuse the iuice of Lymons that is cleere, and hath setled his residence vpon the powder of pearle, and it will dissolue the same, by the experience of a learned physitian who hath made proofe therof, and giuen the same with very good successe in hot burning Feauers. The spirit of Vitrioll also, which riseth presently after the flegme, and before the oyle, will dissolue both corall and pearle, if you set your glasse in warme sande, or Ashes. *Qre.* Whether the same may be safely taken inwardlie, being thus dissolued, or rather fretted insunder, and without any further ablution: but if you take twoe ounces of whole seede pearle, and infuse thereon a quart of distilled vineger in a parting glasse, or in any other strong glasse of an apt forme, you shall in seuen or eight daies, dissolue them into a soft or slimie substance, which you may after cleanse by ablution, if you thinke good. And this is doone without any fire, or outwarde heate, during which worke, you shall see the pearle rising, and falling in the glasse, in the manner of a continuall haile.

How

Art and Nature.

How to clarifie without any distillation, aswel the white Wine as the Claret Wine vineger, wherewith you may make either gellies, or other sawces.

Choose of the strongest Wine vineger that you can get, and to euery six pintes, put the whites of two new laid egges, beate them well togither with a woodden spoone, vntill the whites bee turned into a froath or foame, then put the same into a new leaded or glazed pipkin, and cause the same to boile a little ouer a fire of coales, but not a flaming fire. Then let the same runne through a course white karsey gellie bagge, as they vse to doo gellie: and when it hath runne through the same twise or thrise at the most, it will be verie cleere, and serue for the aforesaide purposes, and it will keepe good one whole yeare. And in the same manner, you may fine or clarifie any maner of wine whatsoeuer. But that which you shall gaine in the cleerenes, you shal lose in the strength of your wine.

How to make any decoction, whether it be of diet drinke or other, in the sommer time to last longer then otherwise it would without any helpe.

I Know this secret will bee verie profitable to all the Apothecaries, who in Summer time sustaine great losse by the sowring, and putrifieng of their decoctions, wherof some be also very chargeable vnto them, and yet I feare, though I know the conclusion to bee true, easie, and not chargable, that it will scarsely satisfie some of them, which are of a curious humour, because it is so plaine and sleight, and therefore derogatorie

The Jewel-house of

gatory to their great skils that they should so lõg time be ignorant in so simple a conclusiõ. Neuerthelese because I know that diuers others (if they should dislik) will make vse thereof, I thinke the same very necessary to be published. One day, or two, before you feare the decay of your decoction, set the same on the fire and giue it a walme, or two, and so nowe and then reboile the same a little, and if you doubt that the same will become either too thicke, or too strong by many newe decoctions, you may alwaies adde so much liquor there vnto made according to the first receipte, as you thinke will wast away at euery boyling, and then keepe the same close, and in a coole place. This may be also performed in another maner without fire, or any other addition, & to last as many months, as it will daies the other way. But here I must keepe *decorum*, and sute grosse matters, with grosse conclusions. It may suffice that I haue sette downe any way for that, which no way was made common before.

How to draw the true spirite of Roses, and so of all other herbs, and flowers whatsoeuer.

MAcerate the rose, either in the water, or in his owne iuice, adding there vnto being temperately warme a conuenient proportion either of yeast, or ferment, leaue them so a few dayes in fermentation till they haue gotten a stronge and heady smell and beginning to encline towards vineger. Then distill them in Balneo in glasse bodies, luted to their helmes, and drawe so long as you finde any sent of the rose to come, then redistill, or rectifie the same so often till you haue purchased a perfect spirite. Also if you ferment the iuice of Roses only without any leaues mixed therein, you may draw an excellent spirit from the same.

same, or if you keepe the iuice of damask roses onely in close vessels well seasoned with the rose, it wil yeald a delicate spirit after it hath wrought it selfe to a sufficient head, by the inward rotation, or circulation of Nature, but this worke asketh a longer time before you can proceede to distillation. The laste way and beste way of all other that I knowe, is by an outwarde fire to stirre vp the moist, and inwarde fire of nature, till the same be growne to the fulnesse of a rose wine. And when you haue once broughte it to a wine then euery Apothecary, and ordinary practicioner in this art will easily diuide his spirit from him, but they will all stagger in the firste digestion, and though they should either reele, or fall, I may not lende them my helping hand, otherwise then I haue donne already, vnlesse I were assured that they were of the nomber of *Hermes* sonnes, and not begotten by some base alchimist.

How to draw the true and simple oile of Roses.

DRy 20. or 40. bushels of damask rosos, according to arte, put them with a sufficient proportion of water (some commende rose water, others rather the iuice of roses) into a large copper body whose heade must haue a cooler of large content; lute the ioyntes well, and after a little maceration giue a proportionall heate vnto the body, and with the water the oile will also ascend and fall into the receiuer. Proue the same manner also with the moiste leafe, and if you see any apparant difference either in colour or thicknes between the oile & the water, then you knowe how to diuide the same easily, but if you can no way difdiscerne the oile, then poure that which you haue in your receiuer, into a bolt glasse, hauing a long steale, or into some other glasse, that riseth vppe in a spiring manner, lesse and lesse toward the toppe: but fill the glasse full, and so peraduenture you shall finde the oile after a little repose, fleeting vpon the toppe like creame, which you must separate with a feather, and keepe by it selfe. This is either a certeine, or a verie probable way of proceeding. But if I coulde sell the secret but for ten yeares purchace, I woulde passe it with a generall warrantize against al obiectios, in the meane time let it suffice thee, that I haue in this little, exceeded my commission.

Ypocras made speedilie.

Take of Cynamon vn.s. white Ginger dr. 3. cloues and nutmegs, of each dr. s. of the greines of paradise, sc. 2. of pepper, sc. 1. let them bee beaten somewhat grosely, and then macerated in halfe a pound, of spirit of Wine, stopping the vessell close with flower and water. Let al these ingredientes remaine six daies in infusion, in a cold wine seller, stirring them togither twise a day at the least: a fewe drops of this composition will transmute a boale of wine into ypocras. This receipt may beseeme the doctor that first deuised it, yet by his fauour, I thinke it requisite, after you haue made the Wine thus Aromaticall, that you also adde a dewe proportion of sugar, without the which in these daies there is nothing accounted either daintie or delicate, and then you must also passe the same through an ypocras bag, till it bee fine, I thinke you may also performe the same with spirite of beere, ale, or wine lees, much cheaper.

A touch at Borax Christalinus.

THere is a certeine proportion of Borax to bee mixed with the *Regulus* of Antimonie, which must be chimically calcined togither, vntill the Borax haue glutted himselfe with the Spirits of Antimonie. And this is thought to be a safer vomit, then either the crude or calcined Antimonie, or the *vitrū Antimonij*, that is broughte to the colour of the Iacinth, because in all these preparations, the body it selfe of Antimony is retained. But in this preparation you take holde of the spirits onely. This may safelie be giuen in powder, in the pappe of an apple, to the quantitie of ten, twelue, or fourteene graines: or else the same may be finelie ground vppon a Marble, and then imbibed with a small proportion of wine, which being dreyned from the powder, must bee taken fasting, in the morning, according to the order of other vomits. I cannot here omit that, which I will neither warrant, nor condemne, (although I knowe to which side I would rather incline before trial) that infinite extention of the glasse of Antimony, vppon which there may be made so many seuerall infusions, and all of them of sufficient efficacie to giue a vomit, as that by some men of note, and good reputation, it hath beene thought to be a necessary part or member of the phylosophers stone.

How to make Camphire remaine liquid in the forme of an oile.

FIrst heate a brasse morter, then beat the Camphir, as thin as you can, put thereto by little and little at once equall proportion of the oyle of Almondes, newly drawne, and incorporate them well together, and it will remaine in the forme of a cleere oyle without any congelation. I thinke the spirit of Wine wil dissolue the same, but when you diuide the spirit by distillation, the oyle is likely to congeale in the bottome of your glasse.

An artificiall extraction, of that sweet sirrop of raisins, currans, and proines.

TO euery Gallon of faire water, put three pound of Malaghie reasons, or reasons of the sunne, either stampt or vnstampt, leaue them seauen or eight daies in infusion, in some little halfe tubbe, hauing a fawcet in the bottome thereof, at the which you may dreine out gently al that sweet sirrop which lyeth in the bottome, drawing so long as you see any deepe colour in the water, then stop the fawcet, and put in some more fruit, and deuide as before, and hauing purchased a sufficient quantitie of this sweet lyquor, boile the same away in an ordinary chafer, or kettle vntill it grow vnto some thicknesse, and then for fear of adustion, you may finish the same in Balneo. Expose this in diuers apt vessels, and in small quantities to the heate of the sunne, against a brickewall, vppon plates of lead, when the sunne is of some reasonable heigth, as in Iune, Iuly, or August. And if you bee carefull in my direction, you shall haue a most rare, and delicate marmelade (if I may so tearme it) and the same also candied and hardened into a very stiffe substance, most naturallie tasting of the fruite from whence it is drawne. You may worke after the same manner, both in figges and currens, which for more

cleanli-

cleanlinesse, I could wish also to be washed in some change of Waters. *Qre.* What an Artist may do in this practise, both in Cherries, Grapes, Damsons, Gooseberies, Barbaries, and generally in all English, and outlandish fruites and flowers. But then it is requisite to dry some of those fruites sufficiently in the sunne, before you make your imbibition, and to roast or partch others with some farther heat, diuiding the skinnes, cores, and other refuse, before you make your extraction.

How to preserue damsons, cherries, peareplums, gooseberies, &c. in their owne iuice or sirrop without the addition of rosewater.

Lay a conuenient number of plums, cherries, gooseberies, &c. in a deepe sallet dish or siluer bason, one by one, couer the same close with some other dish, and set it vpon a chafingdish of coales, beginning with a gentle heat, vntill the fruit haue gathered a great deaw or moysture vnto themselues, then take of the sweetest Barberie suger and strew the same vpon the fruit, beeing first brought into a most fine powder (twelue ounces of suger is a sufficient proportion for one pound of fruit) but if you please you may allow weight for weight) continue your fire vntill such time as you shal find that the sirrup hath piersed the stone euen to the kernel, for then they are boiled sufficiently, but if ý kernel do wrinkle or run together, then they are somewhat ouer boiled. Also you must not forget to turn them now & then, and to obserue al other circumstances, as you vse in the ordinary manner of preseruing.

The end of the booke of Distillation.

The Art of molding and casting.

First you must labor common loame a little moiſtned, to a ſtifnes: working ẏ ſame ſmooth with a rolling pinne, as they vſe to doe paſt, then make thereof a coffen like vnto a pye, ſauing that you ſhall need no other bottome but the bord, or table whereon you worke, and that you muſt faſhion your coffin according to the patterne, which you meane to caſt, for ſparing of your pap hereafter mentioned. Faſten well this coffen, or ſides of lome to your table with your fingers, ſo as the thinne part of your pap may not run out at the bottome, then take a branch of roſemarie, tyme, or Iſope &c. and at the end of the ſteale faſten a little lump of loame made taperwiſe with the ſmall end thereof towards the ſtalke, & the greater end faſten likewiſe to the mideſt of ſome part of the ſides of your coffin in the inſide, ſo as the ſame may ſticke faſt ouerthwartwiſe, and that no part of your braunch either touch your table in the bottom, or reach to the vppermoſt part of the ſides, for which cauſe you muſt alwaies make your coffin deeper thē your braunch, or flower which you meane to caſt, then make your pap in a woden diſh, or ſtone panne, preſently ſtirring the compoſition well togeather,

G   either

either with your finger for a shift, or some other apte brush, or pensill, that there may be a solution, or mixture of the licor, or powders together. Then powre the same speedily about the sides of your branch, hauing care that you doe not losen the same from the coffin, and bee sure that you make pappe enough to couer all your braunche at once, whereat, by often practise you shall easily gesse. Let the same stande a prety while .s. about the fourth part of an houre, and the whole composition will harden into a masse or lump, then take away your lome sides from it which will serue oftentimes, and you haue your branches included therein, then with a little sticke digge out the peece of lome, which you fastened to the stalke of your braunch, but so as you impare not the molde, then lay your branch abroad for a time in som ayrie or windy place, but not in the sun, and after neale it in a little earthen furnace, making first a foundation of Charcoles, and afterward laying your molde vppon them, and then couering your mold with more charcole, and kindling your fire at the vppermost coales, and so continew your fire by adding of freshe charcoles, till you see that the molde be well nealed .s. that it be red hotte, both within, and without, which you shall perceaue by a little hole, which the lome made at the end of the stalke, which they call their gitte: if enclining your body you look therein carefully. Then let the fire goe out of it selfe, and suffer the molde to coole; then hath the branch or flower lefte the impression thereof in the molde into the which when you haue cast your gold, or siluer, you must dipp your mold in cold water, whereby it will fall in pieces, and you shall finde your braunch of gold and siluer, in all points according to the patterne. All other necessary

Art and Nature.

circumstances for this art doth presently ensew.

1 You must first roast or burne the plaister of Paris, before you mixe the same with the reste of the powders, which some men do in this manner. They breake the stones in great gobbets, and then laying some coales in a little stone furnace, such as are solde at more gate; they lay these pieces together vpon the coles, and then couer them ouer with coles, and after kindle the fire at the top, and so let the same burne downewardes, and with one fire so made they will be sufficiently burnt, then beate them into powder, and searce them as before, but if they breake not easily then they doo burne them longer. Others thinke it a better way though more longe and troublesome, to beate the plaster in a great iron morter to a fine powder, and then to sette the same in the fire, in a large strong earthen pot, or pipkin, making a good fire vnder it, and stirring it continually, with a wodden spattle for an houre, or there abouts, and vntill you see the spattle leaue as it were a visible line, or tracte behind it, after you haue stirred the pouder round about there with.

Preparatiõ of the plaister.

2 Let your powder whereof you make your pap consist of burnt aleblaster, and plaster of Paris both of them finely powdred, & searced, & of y̌ like fine powder of newe earthen pots, some vse the powder of bricke in stead thereof. To three parts of the powders of Aleblaster, and plaster first mixed in equall proportion, mingle one parte of the powder of earthen pots or bricke; but many do cast of in wax, only in moldes consisting in aleblaster alone, or plaster alone, or both together without any other composition.

Compositi on of the pap.

There bee some that thinke one shall caste more sharpely if hee doe likewise grinde the aforesaide powders vpon a Marble stone after they bee searsed, but if you searse onely, the searse must bee exceeding fine. *Qre.* If *Gypsum, alumen plumosum,* or spawde bee not good to mingle with the rest of the powders. I haue seene oftentimes many good patternes of mettall, cast off very sharpely in spawde alone, but you must heat the flaskes wel, before you pour in the mettals, and you must sprincle the spawd with some moisture, wherin there is some *sal Armoniack,* before you doo imprint your patternes, some commend ỹ light and downy substance, finely gathered from the vppermost part of the ashes of old coales.

Making of the pappe. 3 Of the aforesaid powders, you must take a reasonable quantitie at once, putting the same into a stone porrenger, or woodden dish, and put thereunto some cleane water, wherein some dissolue an ounce of *Sal Armoniack* to euery pottle of water, and presently stir it wel togither as before, to make a perfect solution and mixture of the matters aforesaide, this pap must not bee made too stiffe, when you cast off braunches of hearbes or flowers, for then it woulde presse the leaues together. Sometimes temper with warme water, and sometimes with colde, to make the pap drie the faster, for some kind of workes.

Preperation of the papp. 4 If you would attaine to a perfection of this pap, you may weigh your powders before you put them into your water, and measure the water, which you mingle with your powders, and trying seuerall proportions of water and powder together, you may obserue which of them proueth best in the moulds, and euer after continue the same.

Waters for the pap. 5 Some doo mingle *Aqua vita,* some vrine, and some put a small quantity of *Sal Armoniack* to a great

Arts and Nature.

great proportion of water, and therwith temper their pap.

6 As you poure in your pap, knock vpon the Table with your fist, hard by the cofin, to make the pap settle the better to the bottome, and more close to the patterne.   *To settle the pap.*

7 If you woulde saue your patternes, as being of plaster, wax, mettall, Aleblaster, &c. Then take some clay that is well tempered, and not ouerstiffe, and make the *basis* thereof in discretion, according to the thicknesse of your patterne, and hollow or dimple the same a little, according as the fashion of your pattern shall require: then presse your patterne gentlye into that hollownesse, and with your fingers and knife together, worke vp your *basis* with more loame, till by as neere a gesse as you may, the iust one halfe of your patterne be euen wrought vp round about, then set vp your lome sides as before in your branches or flowers, and poure in of the pap likewise as before, till you haue couered all the vppermost part of the patterne, that lyeth bare, with some reasonable thickenesse: then let it rest a prettie while, till it bee growne to some stiffenesse; and after take away your sides, & you shal finde the one halfe of the patterne truely imprinted in the dry pap. Then lay that halfe vppon your table, with the hollow part vpwardes, wherein the impression remaineth, and clap on your loame sides againe, leauing your patterne still within the pap, and poure more pap vpon the patterne, till you haue also couered the other part of the pattern with some reasonable thicknesse as before: then let it dry, and take away the sides, and dip the whole moulde a little in water, and you may with your handes verie easilie, deuide the one side from the other. Take out   *Moldes of 2 partes.*

G 3   your

your patterne, and keepe it to cast againe withall, as often as you please. Note here, that you must print some little gutters or hollowes in the lome, whereon your patterne lyeth after you haue fitted it, with the iust halfe of your patterne, and this is because ỹ pap which is powred on the second halfe shal fil vp those gutters or hollowes, wherby you may, after you haue taken out your patterne, knowe howe to shut your mouldes very close together, which otherwise you should neuer be able to doe.

How to neale many moldes at once.
8 You may neale many moldes together, by laying one by one in a chimnie, with a small distance asunder, but first making a good lay of dead charcole vnder them, and after couer them all ouer with charcoles, making sides about the coles of lose brickes, and remember to lay the ends of your moldes where the gitties or entrances into them are made, towards you, that as you shal see cause, you may now & then stoop and look into the moulds, to see when they are throughly nealed, that you may surcease the making of any more fiers.

9 It is also very requisite to haue deep pannes, very full of sand, or ashes that be warme, wherein to set your mouldes, when they are made ready to cast in, and then to fill vp the mouldes euen to the neckes or gitties of them, for by that meanes you shall keepe your gold or siluer, from passing through the molds.

Molding many branches together.
10 Mold many branches of Time, Isop, rosemarie, &c, at once, that if some of them should faile, yet one or other might proue wel, for the charge is not great, neither of your moldes, nor yet in the melting of your mettall.

What heat in the moldes.
11 When you meane to cast any golde or siluer, you must neale the molds red hot againe, & cast presently.

Art and Nature.

sently. But if in pewter or lead, a lesse heat will serue, and some vse no heat at all, but cast the saide mettals in the moulds being cold.

12 You must make a vent with a strawe from the bottome of the mold vnto the top, wherby the mettal (finding aire) may run the better, or rather make a double vent from each side of the mold; this strawe must be laid in the cofin, before you pour in the pap, and when the mold is nealed, the straw consumeth to ashes, and the vent appeareth, yet I haue seene many patternes cast, without giuing any vent at al. *Ventes for the molds.*

13 Before you cast of, cleer your molds from ye ashes which are left behind, vppon the consuming or burning out of the branches, flowers, wax patterns, &c. in this maner, presently after the mold is cold inough to hold in your hand, take it by the great ende, & pat the mouth or gittie which is at the other ende, in the palme of your hand, till you can perceiue no more ashes to issue out of your molds, and after by applieng the nose or pipe of a paire of bellowes against the gittie, and so blowing out the ashes. Som poure in quick siluer at the gittie, mouing the same vp and downe a prettie while, and so cleanse their moulds. *Clensing of the molds.*

14 You may cast off in wax, in the powders aforesayde, but then you must holde your moldes in hot water for a time, and so the work may the easlier bee taken out, and in the said moldes you may cast off in wax diuers times, one after another. Note also, that you must dip the said molds a prettie while in hot water, before you cast off in wax, and presentlie after, you haue taken the molds out of the water, & before you cast; you must drie them with a spunge. *Wetting of the molds.*

15 Some are so precise in this art, as that they will neuer mold any fine patterns but in faire weather, or in summer time, and perswade themselues y^t their *Times to mold in.*

molds

moldes do receiue the impression most liuely, and also do dry most kindly.

Gittee large.
16 Let your gittee where you powre in your mettall be wide and large, according to the greatnesse of your patterne, for that the weight of your mettall being therein, will by the peize thereof thrust downe the rest that runneth firste into the farthest parte, or corners of the moldes.

Hollowing of ye gittee.
17 When your molds consist of two partes, before you neale them, you muste with a knife hollow, or take away some parte of the gittee, in the inside of either parte of your molde, making the same like a gutter thereby to conuey the mettall the better into the whole molde.

Casting in glewe and wax.
18 But if you will caste any imbossed patterns, of waxe, or any other slender or curious paternes, that be vnder cutte as they terme it .s. such as stande antickewise, and whereof you may see some partes behinde, which will not suffer them to come oute of the moldes without breaking either the paternes or the moldes, then must you vse this deuise following. Take one pound of common glew, put thereto one ounce of yellow waxe (some put two or three ounces) but first dissolue the glew by a gentle fire, with a little water into a thicke body, and after this solution, put in your waxe, into which waxe, some doe vse to put a little quantity of the fine powder of charcole searced, and some mingle the blacking only that commeth of the smoke of waxe or rosen therewith. Then laye an euen peece of lome according to the fashion of your patterne, but an inch broder then the paterne and in the midst thereof place your paterne firste oyled, then sette vppe the lome sides of your coffin and powre your glew thereon, being of a temperat heate

and

Art and Nature.

and when it is throughly cold, take away the sides of loame, and take out your patern gently. Note also y̌ whē you haue molded any gentle pattern in glue, you may open the moldes by flitting of them, or bowing them backwards therby the esilyer to get out the patterne without danger of breaking it, and yet the mold will returne to his first shape.

19 Note that you may dissolue your moldes of glew againe, and cast often in them according to the manner before set downe. *Glewe serueth often.*

20 *Qre.* Of hanging patterns by a threed, in the glew aforesaid being first oiled ouer, vntil the glew be colde, and somewhat stiffe, and then carefully cutting out the patternes without impairing the molds. Here a good wit may find greate varietie of matter whereon to meditate, but I holde it not conuenient for the greate hindrance, to all the Iewellers, and workemen in golde and siluer, to discouer all the secrets either of this compositiō, or of the rest that are contained in this discourse, and that for sufficient reasons beste knowne vnto my selfe, and such others as haue spent their time, and thereby attained to any exquisite skill in this art of casting. Although I muste needes confesse that I haue giuen sufficient lighte, euen to the purblinde workeman to performe any excellent conceipts by this discorse. And as I looke for thankes of many that are ignorant herein, so I am sure to receaue blame of those who with long trauaile and expence, haue skarcely attained so muche skill as they may finde in this worke with a fewe houres study. Neither may I safely sette downe the infinite vse of this arte, for feare of the infinite abuse which would follow by the lewde, and sinister practizes of idle, and ill *Whole patternes cast without defacing the patterne or molde.*

H   dis-

The Iewel house of

disposed persons, that are ready with the Spider, to turne euery thing which they touch into poison.

21 Note that your moldes of glewe muste bee throughly colde before you caste your compounded waxe therein, and the waxe must be taken in a temperate heat, least it happen to dissolue the molde.

The trewe heate of your molds and Wax.

22 Note also the moldes of glew, the longer they stand before you cast in them, the lesser they waxe by reason of the water that vanisheth away; and therefore it is an excellent deuise, not only to caste strange and hard patterns in, but also to cast of your patterne into a lesse compas. So that if the grauing of the workmanship of your pattern be grose and wide assunder, by this meanes it will become lesse, and shewe much smaller and finer to the eye. And if at the first casting in glew when your molds haue stoode three or foure daies to dry, your patterne come not little enough to your mind, then caste that little patterne againe in glew, and let that molde lye as longe a drying before you pour in your wax, and so with often casting in this fashion you shall bring your newe paterne to bee of a greate deale lesse compasse, and finer workemanship then the first patern. Note also that it is very requisite to make your moldes of glewe very thicke, for feare of warping, or casting awry. It is also thought very requisite to annoint the moldes within very delicately, with a fine calaber pensill, and with some of the thinnest of the aforesayd oiles, before you put in your waxe.

To lessen your patternes.

23 You may also caste, all your mettaline patterns in brimstone, and from thence in waxe, and after in aleblaster, and so into mettall.

Casting in brimstone.

24 Some will molde greate, and curious patternes in

Art and Nature.

in the crumme of fine manchet wel tempered into a paſt, and preſſed hard vppon the patterne, and ſome commend flower, and the fat of bacon diſſolued, and ſtrayned. *Molding in cromes of breade.*

25 Note alſo that you muſt firſt caſt all your curious patternes in yellow wax tempered with the fine powder of ſmale cole, and wrong through a cloth, and ſome thinke it beſt to put in the ſmale cole powder when the wax beginneth to coole, and then to ſtir it well that they may incorporate together. But if you wil caſt of in red wax, then muſt you put in ſome red ocre inſteade of ſmale cole, to color your wax withall. Some comend this compoſition of wax beſt ſc. 2. parts of old yellow wax one part roſen, & a little blacking diſſolued, and mingled together, and then ſtreyned through a fine cloth: and when you haue once gotten your patternes in wax, then mold thoſe waxen patternes in the afforeſaid plaſters, alleblaſter, and bricke powder, and then burne out the wax as before in flowers, and cleer the moldes, and ſo caſt them into what mettall you pleaſe. Alſo when you haue molded any patterne in glew, you may caſt it of in Alleblaſter if you pleaſe. *Artificiall wax to caſt in.*

26 Some do greatly commende the fine powder of Flaunders melting pots that be new, and bole Armoniack mingled together in equall partes, you muſt put this powder in water, and mak agitation of them together, and then powre away the ſame water ſodainely into ſome cleane veſſell, and put in more water, reiterate your agitation as before, and ſo continew this worke vntill your water which you powre away from the powders becom cleer; then let al this thick water ſo gathered together, ſettle wel, and then dreine away the water by declination, and after drie *Powders to caſt in.*

H 2 this

60 *The Iewel-house of*

this powder, and keep it to make pap thereof at your pleasure. And this was commended to me by excellent men for an excellent receit.

To cast in moldes of wax.

27 In this manner following you may cast of in wax, and also in waxen moldes, which is a delicate, and necessarie secret for them that can tell how to vse the same to the best purpose. You must take three quarters of a pound of rosen (yet some vse no rosen at all) and a pound of yellow wax, and an handfull of sifted ashes, melt them altogether, & put in the ashes when the rest is molten (in steede of ashes some vse spawd, or plaster burnt as before) and presently after the putting in of the ashes you must hold an iron that is red hot, or a great glowing coale in the dissolued substances, chaunging your iron, or coale as often as you se cause, for by this meanes you shall keep your materials from boyling ouer. In this substance you maie mold anie patterne that you please, then take out the patterne, and you may cast therein infinitly with a mixture consisting of two partes wax, & one parte rosen, but let the same bee but of a temperate heat when you pour it in, least you melt your moldes, and after it hath taken the impression, you may forthwith lay your moldes in water to coole your infused substances the more speedily, wet those mouldes onely with a fine cloth, or pensill vsing no oile but in the gittee onely.

Strong moldes for grosse patternes,

28 If you would haue a strong compositiō, or earth wherein to cast great and grosse patternes of copper latten &c. Then take one part clay, tempering the same throughlie well vpon a marble, with flockes, adding therevnto two parts of bricke, and halfe a part of plaister wel burned (as before) work as ẏ said

sub-

Art and Nature.

substances well and painfully together, and cast your mettall therein after you haue molded off your patterns, you must set your moldes in a vessell full of sand and presse the same as harde as you can aboute the molde, euen from the bottome to the toppe thereof. And som vse to cast copper, and latten works in high gate sande, some in lome only, some in cuttle bone, and diuers other substances, which because they are more common then the reste, I passe them ouer in silence.

29 The potters white claie is also very good substance to embosse in, if you drie the same throughly, and after beate into fine powder, and then searce it, and temper it with warme water. In the working, and alwaies when you leaue worke, keep your claie moist in a wet cloath, till you haue cause to vse it againe. *Matters to imbosse in.*

30 Some holde opinion that it is beste to spende your aforesaid powders whilst they are fresh, and before they haue lien longe, for that the plaster of Paris being of an attractiue nature, and desirous to gain the moisture which it hath loste in the burning, will loose his binding force if it bee not quickly spente, but after our molds be once nealed, you may keepe them a long tim so as you stop the gittes of them, that no dust may enter into the moldes. *The lasting of the powders.*

31 Oile al your patterns of mettals, plaster, or wax with a fine pensil, and with the oile of sweet almonds but others esteeme the oile of *Turpentine* or *Spike*, to be the best, by reason of their thinnesse, whereby they will not fill vppe any parte of the worke. Then ou must pat the paterns gētly ouer with a little clean umbast, that you may leaue the oile very thin vpon ỹ patterne, som vse *aqua vitæ* only. And som oile their *Oiling of the patternes.*

H 3 wod-

The Jewell-house of

wodden patternes with oyle of waxe, butter, or larde melted, to keepe them from blistering in the molds.

The heats and toughning of Sol and Luna.

32 Learne of the Goldsmithes howe to take your golde and siluer in their true heates, as also with what additions to make the mettall runne the better and sharper, and how to toughen them both, that your worke proue not brittle. If you finde this work either too troblesom, or too curious, then make your molds ready, and carrie them to some Goldesmithes, which haue their apt furnaces for the purpose, and let them heat, and toughen your mettals, and then cast them in your moldes so made ready as before.

Colloring, & boyling of Sol, and Luna.

33 How to colorish your patternes in golde, and how to boile those that are cast in siluer, I must refer you to the Goldsmithes, although I could easilie set downe both the matter, and the manner thereof, but because therein I should discouer a secret, that concerneth their whole trade, I haue thought good to suppresse it for this time.

Which patterne commeth sharpest.

34 The first time that you cast off your patterne, it will come most sharpely, if the worke be performed as it ought, and euer after more bluntly, but yet the selfesame patterne will serue oftentimes, and deliuer his impression truely, though not so perfectly in the eie of a worke man as at first.

35 Note, that you must haue a little presse of copper or Iron to hold fast your mouldes after they are made ready to cast in: especiallie when your moulds consist of two partes, and the outsides of these pattie moldes you must cramp together, when the molds

are

Art and Nature.

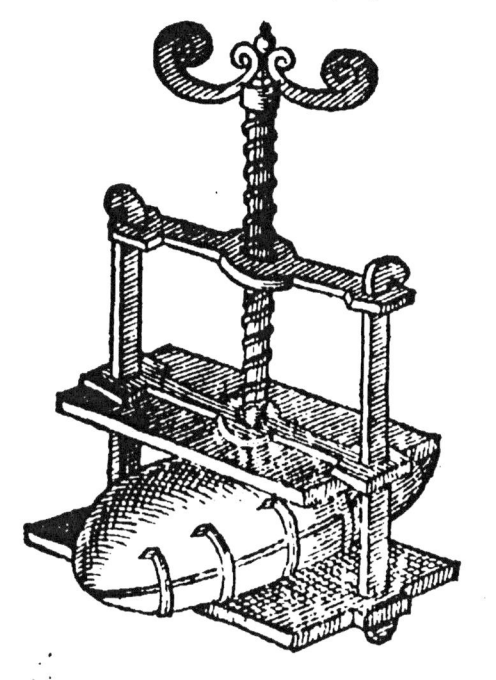

A copper presse.

are cold, with many little Iron VViers made for that purpose; and then with a knife close the ioynts all ouer with some of the said pap, which closing or luting, you must also reiterate if you see cause, after the mouldes be nealed, placed in your presse, and readie to receiue the mettals, at which time it shall not bee amisse in like manner to close vp and stoppe all the crackes, or chinkes of your moulds which you shall finde in them, after they be made ready to cast in, for otherwise, your mettall will oftentimes run through your moldes, and then is all your labour lost. *Cramping wires.*

36 But in the casting of branches, of hearbs or flowers, some commend the sprinkling of the branch, or flower, first ouer with good *Aqua vitæ* well rectified, and some doo wet the branch, first with a little pap that is made very thinne with *Aqua vitæ*, and the afore- *Preparing the herb or flower.*

The Jewell-house of

afforesaid powders. I haue herd that you may stiffen the leaues of your herbs, and flowers with fish glew, finely sliced, and beaten, and after dissolued in a clean leaden pan with som *Aqua vitæ*, or water: the leaues so stifned will drie within one hower after they are dipped therein, and within 2. or 3. howers after at the most you must mold the leaues so stifned, or els they will relent againe. *Qre* if you may not keepe them stiffe as long as you please in a stoue. This I haue not proued but I had the same of an excellent woorkeman, who assured me vpon his credit of the truth thereof, whereof if I cold also assure others (as hitherto I haue not disproued the same, and a small time, or charge would serue to make a proofe thereof) I know not how to commend the same sufficiently for the infinite vses whereto it might be aplied.

A composition of tin. 37 Some do make a composition of 4 parts of new Tyn, to one part of Latten, and cast diuers patternes therein.

Casting hollow. 38 If you would cast an egge, or any other patterne hollow thereby both to haue your worke the lighter, as also to spare gold and siluer, which groweth to be costly in sad workes; then must you line both the insides of the party mold with thin past, made of tough flower, and water onely, and wroughte into an equall thicknes by the meanes of a rowling pin whose portrature you shall finde *Postea* nu. 39. Note also that vpon one of the parts of your mold, there must be made a crosse of wire fastned into the mold by turning of the endes of your wire into the same, then lay both the sides of the mold togither, each of them hauing their thin past fitted within, iust with the circle thereof: then at the gittee of your mold powre in

some

some plaster made into pap, if you cast but in lead or else som of y̌ first composition .s. plaster, Aleblaster, and bricke together, if you cast of in gold and siluer; but first you muste anoynt all your past very nearely with a fine pensill, and with the fat of bacon, melted with a gentle fire, and before it congeleth; for this maketh your worke to come very smoth on the outside. Then take your mold in sunder, and take out the past out of either parte, and hang in the core againe in the first holes, set your mold together againe, cramping, and luting it on the sides, and then neale it, and poure in the mettall, which running round about the core must of necessity be hollow, and of an equal thicknes, then at some hole in the end, or side of your work you may picke out all the plaster, or other composition, and so you may cast any patterne both light and hollow: you must also remember to make your gitty, and to vse the other meanes sette downe *Antea num. 7.* to make the one side of your mold meet with the other.

You may cast hollow, & light either in leade, pewter, or wax, if after you haue cast your work solid, you powre out againe at the bottome thereof so much as will run, but the exact time when to powre out, must be gotten by often practise, and cannot well bee expressed in words.

39 You muste haue a rowling pin of a foot long, made of 6, or 8 inches compasse, and the same taken *The rowling pin.*

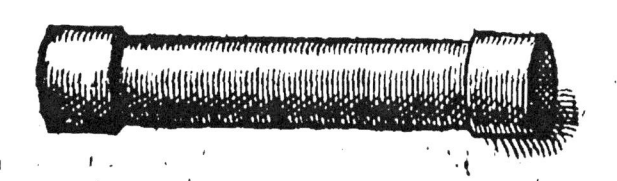

downe the thicknesse of a shilling all the length ther-of, sauing halfe an inch at either ende, whereby you cannot faile to make your past, al of one iust thicknes.

To mold the hand or face of a man.
40 In the foresaide glewe you may molde ones hand, or face if the partie be firste laide on his backe, with his eies plastered ouer, his nose and eares stopt with wooll, and his mouth closed vp, sauing that in the midst he may draw breath by a little hole at a pipe or quil, and then set your sides of lome, as before, a-bout his face, which some annoint ouer with oile (as before) and poure on the aforesaide glue beeing but temperately warme. This is an excellent deuise to haue the liuely counterfeit of the true fauour & coun tenance of euery man.

The placing of your braunches.
41 Some doo hold it best to set your flowers and branches vpright, & not ouerthwart wise, with their tops vpwards, before you moulde them, for so they are perswaded, that the leaues will spread abroad the better, and diuide themselues in sunder, whereby the mettal may run into euery leafe seuerally.

Killing of the beasts.
42 Some doo kill Toades and frogs, which they meane to cast, by leauing them in oyle till they die, and some do put strong water into their mouthes. As for flies, spiders, grashoppers, and such like, you may keepe in close boxes, and let them die for lack of aire, and then mold them whilest they are stiffe.

To print graued pat-ternes vp-on paper.
43 If you would take but the print of any worke, grauen either in brasse, wood, or other bodie. First, with a spoonge lightly wet ouer your paper with fair water (some commend Allome water) then make a sable colour with the fume of searing wax candle, in a spoon, porringer, &c, to the which put a few drops of sallet oyle, or of the extracted oile of cloues, temper

per the same wel together, and put it lightly vppon the ingraued patterne with a quilted leather, such as Printers vse, then clap the print vppon your paper lightly wet as before, and take off the paper, and you shall finde the impression very faire, if you do it carefully. Note, that if your pattern be of wood, you must lay the same first a pretty while to soke in Water, before you lay on your sable vpon it, because the wood wil drie vp the colour exceedingly. Note also, that the smoke of tallow, maketh a good sable, the smoke of rosen a better, but the smoke of wax giueth y̆ best of al other, and thereof is made that excellent veluet blacke, vsed in the art of Lymming.

44 It is a pleasing and commendable practise, by this Art to mold of those excellent counterfeites, of carued or embossed faces, dogges, Lions, Borders, Armes, &c, from toombes, or out of noble mens galleries: as also of pillers, balles, leaues, frutages, &c, therewith to garnish beds, tables, court-cupboords, the lawmes and mantletrees of chimnies, and other stately furnitures of chambers or galleries. But I may not disclose the whole Art with euery circumstance, whereby to make the same contemptible with the vulgar sort: onelie I wil giue a taste thereof vnto the sharper wittes, who with some studie, and practise, may reach vnto the ful perfection thereof. And therefore, whosoeuer can first dissolue Isenglasse or fish g'ew, as it ought to be, and after harden the same by such means, as that no sudden moisture can make it to relent or giue againe, the workeman and Artist whatsoeuer he be (and I am sure there be some such, though but verie few, that I know in England) may cast many rare and excellent patternes, in the fine fi-

Speciall vses of this Arte.

led

led or raped dust of Brasill, box, Ieat, Amber, aleblaster, Ebonie, Elephants tooth, and such like: beeing first well tempered with the glew so dissolued, or with the pap of common paper, beeing wel wrought and laboured with the hande of a workeman. And hee may also make his moldes of the finest and whitest potters Clay, when they haue wrought and tempered it first in their manner. Of els if some excellent Caruer in wood or stone did carue some excellent peece of a border, of halfe a yard long, and a foot in breadth, with antique faces and personages, or other frutages thereon, and with the coatarmors of gentlemen, and other pleasing deuises, to garnish the same; the aforesaid Artist, might thereby easilie and with small cost, cast off whole borders for chambers or galleries, in the aforsaid substances or compositions, which would seeme to be of infinite charge. And for the better encouragement heerein, of those that shal be doubtfull, and suspitious of this skill, let this satisfie them, that I haue seene not farre from London bridge, diuers excellent and carued patternes cast off in sand, and common glew, but they would endure no weather, yet they will serue sufficiently within doores so as they bee kept drie.

Here endeth the art
of Casting.

An offer of certaine new inuentions, which the *Author will bee readie* to disclose vpon reasonable considerations, to such as shall be willing to entertaine them, or to procure some Priuiledge for them.

1 *A new kinde of fire.*

THis fire is of much lesse charge then the ordinarie seacole fire.

2 It is much sweeter in the burning, and more beautifull in shape, beeing made in the form of balles.

3 It is very dureable and lasting.

4 It is not so offensiue either in smoke or cinder, as the seacole fire.

5 It wil employ many thousands of maimed souliers, and other poore and impotent persons, in the making thereof.

6 It

The Jewel-house of

6. It will rather bee a great furtherance than any hinderance vnto Newcastel men.

7. The matter wherewith the Seacole is both multiplied and sweetened is verie plentifull, and cannot faile or grow deare, by the great expence thereof, if such care be had therein as the Author wil discouer.

8. It will be an especiall meanes to preserue Timber for the building of ships, and other necessarie vses.

9. It wil bring charcole and billets to a more reasonable price.

10. And if this secret might, (by anie carefull and prouident meanes) be brought into publike vse, with the good contentment of the Authour: Then the tenth part of the profit that shuld arise therby, might be yearelie distributed amongest sicke persons, and maimed souldiors, or otherwise conferred vpon such other good vses, as should bee thought most conuenient.

2. A vessell of Wood, to brew or boile in.

1. THat the same is truelie and royalie performed, I appeale to the proofes in my Apologie, published An. 1593. And if there be yet anie manner of person, that shall notwithstanding my testimonies therein produced, either peruersly hold the same to bee impossible, or maliciouslie and slanderouslie reprooue the inuention of vntruth; then let him wage such a competent sum of monie, as may counteruail the discouerie of the secret, and the Author wil make a publike shew therof before anie indifferent Iudges. Where, if they shal vpon sufficient trial had, censure against the Author: then he wil forthwith redouble the

the wager vnto such offerer, and for euer heereafter forsweare the publishing of any such woodden conceit againe to the world.

2 But admitting the same to be true (and that my artificiall Salamander will not burne in the fire) then I say that these brewing vessels will be much cheaper then copper kettles: yea almost according to such difference as is betweene copper and clapboord, either in matter or workemanship.

3 These woodden vessels, in respect of the fire, will last twentie yeares at the least, and if the element of water, had not more power ouer them then the element of fire, I thinke we should not need any new vessels, but for new ages.

4 And that which I doo more esteeme and commend in them, then their lasting, is the sauing of fewel; which cannot be lesse then a moity of that which is now vsuallie spent in the houses of all the gentlemen and farmers of this land.

5 These vessels being once prepared by the Author, may afterwardes from time to time, with little labor and lesse cost, be repaired by the owners themselues, with such Art as shall be manifested vnto them vpon their first handsell.

A

A boulting Hutch.

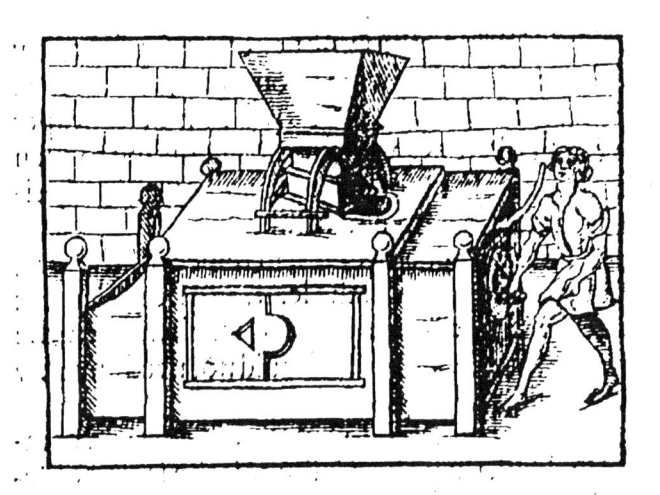

1. THe price heereof is easie in respect of those good vses for which it serueth.

2. This Engine auoideth al wast of meale and flower, and yet it deuideth the bran sufficiently from the flower.

3. It willbee a meanes to saue boulters, which is a matter of great charge vnto the Baker.

4. But the especiall vse thereof, is to auoid all that grose and vncleanlie manner of boulting which the Bakers for want of this engine are forced to vse, the particulers whereof appeere more at large in my Apologie.

5. All obiections that were made against this inuention, by the Bakers of the Citty of London, vpon the view thereof at my house, were sufficiently refelled by the Author, in the presence of diuers Cittizens of good worshippe and account, and therefore

Art and Nature.

what inconueniences foeuer shall hereafter either by them or by any other be pretented against the same, I would haue them holden for false and malicious.

6 This boulting huch is very dureable, neither wil it be chargeable in reparations to the owner.

4 A portable pumpe.

1 IT will be in price one of the cheapest pumps of all that I know or euer heard of, and wil require but small reparations.

2 It is light in cariage and may be transported from place to place, by one single man without any further helpe.

3 With the easie labour of one man, it will deliuer foure, fiue, or six tun of water euery hower, according as it is in bignesse, neither can a man possibly be wearie, though he should worke fiue or sixe houres together, without intermission.

4 Being placed in a fit tub, that is bored ful of holes

or fastened in the water to a peece of Timber, it is a very apt instrument for the dreining of the fen countries, or any other surrounded leauell, or standing water, poole or pond, because it is so portable, and needeth no fastening at all on the grounde, as other pumpes doo.

5 It is also a verie conuenient pumpe, for all such as dwel neere the riuer of Thames, to force vp water for the seruice of their kitchens, which may be performed in a most reasonable manner.

6 It is not amisse, to haue two or three of them in store, for the necessarie seruice of euery shippe in her fight, if any occasion be offred to vse them vpon any great or sudden leak, they are but little, and require small stoage.

5 *A wholesome, lasting, and fresh victuall for the Nauie.*

1 When corne is sold for twenty shillings ỹ quarter, then eight ounces thereof may be affoorded for a pennie, which is a competent meale for any reasonable stomach, and serueth both for breade and meat.

2 It is in shape like wafers, light of carriage, and will last two or three yeares sound and sweet, if it bee kept dry.

3 It may be vsed now & then, for change of diet.

4 Being carefully handled in the dressing (according to the Authors direction) it wil bee pleasing enough to the Marriner, and I haue had the same sundrie times serued in at mine owne table to the good contentment of my friends.

An

Art and Nature. 75

An Engin for the making of this victual.

6 *A speedie way for the inning of any breach.*

1 I Thinke it possible by this deuise (hauing first prepared so many artificial stones as shal bee requisite in this worke) in one monthes space, to shut vp the great breach at Earith, and that in so strong and defensible a manner, as shal be sufficient to withstand all the rage and furie of those surges that shall beate or break vpon it.

2 The charge of euery yard square will bee much about fiue shillings.

3 It

The Jewell-house of

3 It is a very dureable and lasting maner of work, and may be wrought in any time of the yeare.

7. *A light garment and yet sufficient against all rainie weather.*

1 THis garment wil not be much dearer than our ordinarie riding clokes.

2 It may be made as light or lighter, than our vsual garments.

3 A cloke may be prepared in such maner, as that notwithstanding a continual raine, it shall not growe much more ponderous, then it was being drie.

8. *A new conceit in Peter works.*

1 IT is possible, without changing either of the vsuall vessell or furnace, to saue the one moity of the fire which now is spent in al the peter workes of England.

2 The Author of this secret, did of late offer to discouer the same vnto the Peter men, if they woulde haue yeelded vnto him the one thirde of that which they should haue gained or saued by the discouerie thereof.

3 And if the Author might receiue a condigne reward for his profitable trauell, he would peraduenture find out a multiplyeng earth, which would yeeld sufficient store of Peter, for the seruice of this Realme without committing such offenses as are dayly offered, in the breaking vp of stables, barnes, sellers, &c.

Nec omnes nec omnia mihi placuere, cur ego omnibus?
Hugh Platte.

FINIS.

LaVergne, TN USA
04 March 2011
218959LV00003B/45/P